How to Evaluate and Improve Your Grants Effort

Second Edition

David G. Bauer

AMERICAN COUNCIL ON EDUCATION ★
ORYX PRESS ★
Series on Higher Education
2001

*The rare Arabian Oryx is believed to have inspired the myth of the unicorn. This desert
antelope became virtually extinct in the early 1960s. At that time, several groups of
international conservationists arranged to have nine animals sent to the Phoenix Zoo
to be the nucleus of a captive breeding herd. Today, the Oryx population
is over 1,000, and over 500 have been returned to the Middle East.*

© 2001 by The American Council on Education and The Oryx Press
Published by The Oryx Press
An imprint of Greenwood Publishing Group, Inc.
88 Post Road West
Westport, CT 06881-5007
(203) 226-3571
(800) 225-5800
http://www.oryxpress.com

Published simultaneously in Canada
Printed and bound in the United States of America

∞ The paper used in this publication meets the minimum requirements of
American National Standard for Information Science—Permanence
of Paper for Printed Library Materials, ANSI Z39.48, 1984.

Library of Congress Cataloging-in-Publication Data

Bauer, David G.
    How to evaluate and improve your grants effort / by David G. Bauer.
        p. cm.
    Includes bibliographical references and index.
    ISBN 1-57356-363-3 (alk. paper)
    1. Fund raising. 2. Research grants. 3. Grants-in-aid. I. Title
HG177.B377 2001
658.15'224—dc21
                                                                00-010719

CONTENTS

LIST OF EXHIBITS

PREFACE

Over the years, I have been repeatedly asked when a third edition of my book *Administering Grants, Contracts, and Funds* would be available. After many discussions with administrators at colleges and universities throughout the United States, I decided not to write a third edition, but rather to write a new administration book with a different emphasis. The new book's focus is on the subtitle of the second edition of the old book, which is *Evaluating and Improving Your Grants System.*

The purpose of this book is to outline the various functions performed in college and university grants offices, to provide techniques for improving grants systems and the rationale for making the necessary changes, and to examine how the functions of an academic grants office will change in the future. This book contains references to research articles that focus on these issues, and provides surveys and other aids to assist the grants administrator in gathering feedback to evaluate his or her grants system and pre- and post-award services. The contributors have already successfully used some of the aids contained in this book to improve their grants office functions. However, Bauer Associates cannot assume any liability for your use of these materials, such as the survey questions, at your institution. Naturally, we would like to assume responsibility for the improvements and increased efficiency of your grant office that result from the use of these materials, but if we cannot assume responsibility for the negative, it would be wrong to assume responsibility for the positive!

Special thanks go to my partner in Bauer Associates and all that I do, Donna Macrini Bauer, and to the following contributors: Brian Anderson (Eastern Michigan University), Rick Magyar (Eastern Michigan University), Randy Hansen (Oakland University), Pat Beaver (Oakland University), Mary Otto (Oakland University), Eileen Evans (Western Michigan University), and Paula Johnson Roberts (Western Michigan University).

Without the support of Jim Murray, Vice President, Division of External Affairs, American Council on Education, and Susan Slesinger, Senior Vice President, Oryx Press, and the rest of the Oryx staff, this work would still be an item on my to-do list!

INTRODUCTION

When I began to write this book, I asked myself two questions. The first was why I was writing it, or why I cared enough about the subject to invest hundreds of hours creating a manuscript. The second question was why anyone else would invest his or her time to read the book and evaluate and implement its suggestions. I know the answer to the first question goes beyond the fact that the reader purchased the book, because my reasons for writing it and asking the collaborators to share their work have little to do with sales and royalties. I wrote this book to provide a vehicle to explore the evaluation and improvement of a system that is vital to higher education, and our institutions' research and learning environments and missions.

In response to the second question, you should invest your time and resources in implementing the activities you select from this book if you are involved in grants, contracts, sponsored projects, and corporate support and are committed to promoting a dynamic, flexible, and ever-adapting system for the procurement and administration of external funds. In higher education, few areas have greater impact on what our institutions are about than extramural, sponsored projects. Even the all-inclusive goal of teaching and learning is inexorably entwined with grants and sponsored projects. For example, what could have a greater impact on the learning atmosphere than faculty and staff who are actively involved in raising questions in their disciplines and seeking funds to answer those questions? Yet, my 30 years of experience in this field have shown me that at most institutions little time, effort, or money gets invested in making the grants area more efficient and worthwhile.

Offices that handle grants and contracts have had to deal with many dynamic forces in the last two decades. As we enter the twenty-first century, we will be challenged to incorporate even more change. While much of this change is, and will continue to be, a result of advances in information technology, our systems still have to deal with the age-old human problem of how to get potential principal investigators and project directors to become involved in and continue to invest in the grants process. We need to know what they need and want from our grants/contracts system so that we can develop user-friendly systems that encourage involvement in the grants/contracts/research arena. Because attracting and successfully administering extramural funds is critical to achieving our institutions' missions, it is imperative that we continually strive to learn how to better support our faculty's and staff's grant-seeking efforts.

We need to know more about why faculty seek grants and how to enhance those motivators. We should not assume that faculty participate in grant seeking simply because it is a tenure requirement. The gaining of tenure status is only one small reason why faculty seek extramural funding and why this area is so important to colleges and universities. The amount of federal, foundation, and corporate support attained is just one measurable outcome of a grants effort. Of real importance is what sponsored money provides to our institutions in terms of curriculum development, programs, research initiatives, meeting missions, etc. From graduate assistants to work-study grants, and all those areas in between, sponsored funding impacts the university at all levels. In essence, the grants office's influence virtually permeates the campus. Yet when asked how administrators evaluate the functions these offices provide, I am often confronted with long, silent pauses. In reality, there has been little exploration into what grants offices need to improve to promote increases in sponsored activity. When you consider all that is at stake, you would think that a literature search would reveal hundreds of articles on the area of evaluating and improving a grants effort. Yet my research barely came up with a handful!

It is difficult to accurately estimate how many billions of dollars in grants and contracts are put through our nation's colleges and universities. In March 1999 the Association of American Universities reported that there was $221 billion in Research and Development (R&D) spending in the U.S. in 1998.[1] Two-thirds of the $221 billion was carried out by private industry, and most of the remaining one-third by the federal government. What is difficult to determine is how much of the private-sector work was carried out by colleges and universities. To be sure, colleges and universities performed more than half of the nation's basic research ($17 billion of the nation's 1998 basic research total of $34 billion) and worked with private industry on a significant percent of the applied or development portion of the remaining $187 billion in grants, contracts, and subcontracts. Yet research funding is not all, or in some institutions any, of the federal funding handled by the grants office. Grants offices across the nation administer billions more for grants for education, arts and humanities, demonstration projects, etc.

The sheer volume of funding and the impact it has on the ability to meet our colleges' and universities' missions compel me to raise evaluation and management issues. While institutions of higher education are leaders in the teaching of modern management techniques, few of these innovations are applied to the handling of billions of dollars in the grants and contracts process. With all of the vast resources at our institutions, shouldn't we be able to build better systems for handling grants and contracts?

The field of grants and contracts has not typically been thought of as a place of innovative and creative management based upon evaluation and assessment. In my performance of grants/research program process audits over the past 20 years, I have queried administrators about why they have changed their systems. I was hoping to uncover data or some evaluation measures that could be used to demonstrate how effective the changes were. Unfortunately, I did not come up with any. Instead, I found that changes were often made because another college or university had implemented similar changes in their system, and that the so-called improvements created by the changes often went unevaluated.

While many grants and contracts offices have instituted some monumental changes, just how improved the systems are is difficult to discern because there is little reliable data on the problems the changes were to affect. In other words, we have no real way of knowing if the new system is superior to the old. This book provides the rationale for change, the ability to measure what you do, and the tools to analyze the change's cost-benefit return. It provides basic information related to the evaluation, and hence efficiency of grants and contracts systems, and suggests ways in which you can change your system to improve it. It also gives you the software to evaluate your current and future efforts at system improvement. By asking questions and gathering feedback, you will develop more insight into what you do, why you do it, and how you can do it better, and you will become, among other things, more accountable in using your budget expenditures and more accountable, in general, to your institution and your constituents.

The genesis for this book lies in my own desire to define ways, other than the traditional ones, to measure success in grant seeking and grants management, such as

- how much money we have procured,
- has anyone gone to jail, and
- what is our percent success/rejection rate?

The design of this book incorporates the layout of my preceding work, *Administering Grants, Contracts, and Funds*. The subtitle of that book, *Evaluating and Improving Your Grants System*, has become the main focus of this book, which places more emphasis on evaluation and assessment techniques. Each chapter provides

- an explanation of the different functions of a grants office;
- the rationale for including these functions in a grants and contracts system;
- assessment tools to help you evaluate how effectively your office provides each of the functions; and
- strategies for improving, and, where applicable, initiating and implementing the differing functions that help you meet your office's goals and objectives.

Where this book differs substantially from the first is in my attempt to help you develop your ability to assess your system, gather feedback on a routine basis, and accept change as an inevitable part of your evolving system. Keep in mind that your grants and contracts system should never be considered complete or finished. In fact, change and the need to adjust to it should be thought of as integral system components.

This book contains many worksheets and checklists, as well as inventories, at the end of each chapter. Also included are questions for surveying your staff, faculty, and administrators, which are aimed at providing the means to obtain the feedback you need to incorporate change and keep your grants system flexible. By asking the survey questions and completing the inventories that follow each chapter, you will develop a plan for what needs to be done. This book's culminating exercise is to place your plan for change on a project planner (chapter 8) and cost-analyze what it will take to support your dynamic grants office.

Like a dynamic grants office, Bauer Associates is also a learning organization. We are constantly gathering feedback to help us improve. Therefore, please provide us with your comments, criticisms, and suggestions to make the next edition of this book better. Send us your assessment tools and we will include them on our Web site (http://www.dgbauer.com) and in our future efforts to increase the body of knowledge known as grants administration.

REFERENCE

[1]*The Role of University Research in the United States*, Association of American Universities, March 1999.

CHAPTER 1

Developing and Maintaining a Dynamic and Efficient Grants Program

WHY EVALUATE AND IMPROVE YOUR GRANTS SYSTEM?

You may as well deal with this question before you begin any assessment of your office. The "if it ain't broke don't fix it" mentality has many supporters in higher education. Some administrations may fear that once the services and functions of the grants office are evaluated, the office will request more resources. After all, just because an evaluation shows that the grants office staff is wearing down due to excessive workloads and an endless stream of deadlines, that doesn't mean it needs more resources or a better system, right?

As a grants administrator in a large state university system, I became frustrated when a three-time increase in funded projects and grant money was not rewarded with a corresponding increase in staff. Instead of rewarding my office with more staff, the registrar was allotted new staff because registration was a mess. What I learned from the experience was that the squeaky wheel gets the grease, and as long as my system was not malfunctioning it was going to be ignored. It was not until my office was threatened with a federal audit that I was given more staff to "fix" the problem.

In reality, a dynamic grants office does not just work toward improved efficiency when a problem occurs. It works toward improved efficiency at all times. Requests for budget increases and/or changes should be based on

- accountability for expenditures to meet the mission of the institution,
- revisions in staff assignments and job descriptions,
- pay increases based on job performance and evaluation of effectiveness in assisting principal investigators and project directors in pre- and post-award activities,
- the need to respond quickly to changes in the grants and contracts marketplace,

- the importance of the vital function that the grants office plays in ensuring the integrity and image of the institution, and
- opportunities to increase performance through improved technology (computer networks, software, etc.).

The importance of what grants and contracts do for colleges, universities, and society as a whole warrants a closer look. If you need a few compelling statistics to help motivate your administration to support your evaluation and assessment efforts, or if you are interested in adding some poignant statistics to your Web site or newsletter, look to the Internet. By visiting http://www.tulane.edu/~aau/FactSheets.html you can review several articles produced by the Association of American Universities, which are filled with relevant facts and figures, including

- "What People Have Been Saying about Science and University Research,"
- "The Role of University Research in the United States,"
- "How and Why the Federal Government Funds University Research,"
- "Societal Contributions of U.S. University Research," and
- "U.S. University Research: Facts and Figures."

These articles provide great data to bolster your cause. For example, the economic employment impact of scientific research conducted at American universities is outstanding. In 1996 alone, federal Research and Development (R&D) grants to universities and colleges totaled $14.3 billion and accounted for 594,130 jobs; and federal and non-federal R&D expenditures totaled $22.5 billion by doctorate-granting institutions (these institutions account for virtually all academic R&D) and accounted for 946,932 jobs.[1] These figures are quite staggering when you consider that motor vehicles and equipment only accounted for 772,700 jobs and aircraft and related parts, for 376,700. Also keep in mind that the employment figure related to R&D expenditures at doctorate-granting institutions does not take into account the jobs resulting from the billions in federal grants awarded to nondoctorate institutions!

Another consideration is how much money is expended by industry to produce the most effective administration of these resources. Even though in 1996 college and university R&D accounted for 174,232 more jobs than the automobile industry, look at how much more time, effort, evaluation, and feedback is invested in the efficient administration of the auto industry! Billions of dollars have been invested by the auto industry in modernizing management techniques and training and seminars on such topics as time management, quality, on-time delivery, and combined Internet purchasing. In addition to securing assistance from our profit partners, we can follow suit by tapping into the resources of our own business schools, computer and system analysis centers, and nonprofit management programs to apply the latest and most efficient management techniques to the critically important industry of research and grants administration. We must get past the "if it ain't broke don't fix it" mentality and make our institutions' decision-makers aware of how important effective and accountable grants and contract services are to higher education and society.

---

[1]*U.S. University Research: Facts and Figures*, Association of American Universities, January 1999.

Although the evaluation of academic grants and contracts offices has not received nearly the attention it is due, a literature search did uncover a few articles on issues of importance to grants administration. Of particular value is the work of Davis and Lowry, since they asked the question that is the focus of this book[2]: Do institutions of higher education evaluate the functions of their grants offices? Their research focuses on the pre-award area only and documents that there is indeed a lack of current literature addressing the level of evaluation occurring in college and university pre-award research offices. It also shows that:

- of the 133 institutions selected as a representative cross-sampling, 100 responded to the survey;
- 84 percent of the respondents said they have no formal evaluation;
- of the 16 percent that reported an evaluation, the most frequent time frame between evaluations was 5 to 10 years;
- one-half of the respondents have taken part in some form of ad hoc evaluation; and
- evaluation, be it formal or ad hoc, appeared to be increasing—for each of the five-year periods between 1970 and 1989 there had been almost a doubling of the research offices experiencing an evaluation.

Unfortunately, this study did not suggest *how* the results of evaluation were used by the institutions or their grants offices.

It is interesting to note that the area of post-award evaluation yields even less data. One would think that there would be a plentitude of information on the effectiveness of a system that employs 946,932 employees and handles $22.5 billion in expenditures. One explanation may be that the federal Office of Management and Budget circulars, federal assurances, and periodic audits preclude any need for institutional evaluation. However, even though the letter of the law is purported to be followed, how user-friendly the post-award process is has a dramatic effect on the desire of principal investigators and project directors to involve themselves in grant seeking. This alone should be reason enough to evaluate post-award services.

In Jacobsen and O'Brien's study "Satisfying and Stressful Experiences of First-time Federal Grantees," the post-award area provided the most stressful experiences.[3] Managing the budget was listed as the most stressful area. I think the following response of one of the respondents is particularly appropriate in the evaluation of the post-award area.

> I was totally shocked by how my project and I were treated by the school's financial manager. People are always proposing ways in which my funds can be used for some other purpose in the school. Every requisition I send is questioned. I feel like I'm regarded either as a potential embezzler or at best a financial incompetent and that my project is some sort of goose laying golden eggs.

I will relate more of the satisfying experiences in chapter 5, which deals with motivation and grant seeking, but it is noteworthy that the administration of the post-award process was

---

[2] Sharon K. Davis and Peggy S. Lowry, "Survey on the Status of Evaluation Activities in College and University Pre-Award Research Administration Offices: Frequency and Type," *Research Management Review* 7, no. 2 (Spring 1995).

[3] Sharol F. Jacobsen and Mary Elizabeth O'Brien, "Satisfying and Stressful Experiences of First-Time Federal Grantees, " *IMAGE: Journal of Nursing Scholarship* 24, no. 1 (Spring 1992).

the most stressful, especially when you consider that deadlines and other pressures on the pre-award side did not even make the list. Fortunately, the researchers reported that "there was a strong consensus that the satisfying experiences were lasting and the stressful experiences temporary."

Even though this may be the case, you cannot afford to have principal investigators and project directors who feel so negatively about your pre- and/or post-award functions. So the question is, how can you make improvements in your system if you have no reliable feedback on which to base your actions?

Of course, one way to limit any negative feedback about your grants office is never to ask for input! Once while flying, I was seated next to a customer service executive who told me that the reason his airline reports receiving more complaints than any other is because it administers more surveys and makes more requests for customer input than any other. Contrast that to other airlines where customer service telephone lines are answered by a machine and customer phone calls are seldom returned. Naturally, they receive fewer complaints. Because we employ three times as many individuals as the aircraft and related parts industries, the very least we can do is a better job at evaluation and feedback!

If you decide to survey your principal investigators (PIs) and project directors (PDs) to solicit their feedback, remember that they are users of your services. In a sense, you can think of them as clients or customers. They must be convinced of your intention to improve your system or you will not get true and honest feedback. Once a researcher told me she would never make a complaint about the grants office because the people that worked there handled all of her grants and she wasn't about to bite the hand that fed her. Clearly, the quality of your survey vehicle, the promise of anonymity, and convincing the respondent of your intention to use the survey data to improve your system should be paramount.

The use of feedback to improve performance is the basis for many current management theories. By seeking out feedback from those who use your pre- and post-grants systems, you can move toward higher quality and greater satisfaction. The ever-so-popular Total Quality Management theory (TQM) was predicated on voluntary feedback from workers on how to improve products and related systems. In many companies, improvements in worker productivity and profits have been attributed to the implementation of TQM. But even in those cases where greater productivity is attributed to increases in the use of technology, worker feedback on how to improve the utilization of technology plays an important role.

In the case of grants and contracts offices, technology has been incorporated at a staggering rate. But as the studies indicate, we now have a great opportunity to use feedback and evaluation. In order for grants offices to incorporate feedback and to make the changes that will move them to new levels of efficiency, they will need more than the worksheets, inventories, and survey questions contained in this book. They will need to be committed to incorporating, accepting, and promoting change in their systems. To be sure, grants administrators have not been the leaders they could be in supporting systems improvement. However, to be successful at creating a dynamic grants effort, the atmosphere in your grants office and in the administrative unit that you function must be dedicated to the philosophy of evaluation and the constant change that must occur in order to use and respond to feedback.

USING FEEDBACK TO IMPROVE YOUR GRANTS EFFORT

To effectively implement the feedback strategies contained in this book you must do some preliminary work to set up the rationale for the changes you will eventually implement. The preliminary work consists of meeting with key groups, including your institution's administrators, your office personnel, and your immediate staff. The purpose of these initial meetings is to increase the participants' knowledge and sensitivity to the idea of using feedback to make change, encourage them to support seeking the information you require, and accept the changes that will be suggested.

At the administrative level you will need support for possible adjustments in your office's services and functions, changes in job descriptions, purchase of new software and equipment, and reallocation or increases in your budget. You will need to help your office personnel to develop an attitude that is focused on improving how your office functions and making it an even better place to work. Your immediate staff must buy into developing and maintaining an environment that is focused on learning how to do their jobs better, which requires openness to evaluation and change.

Of course, change is not totally new to the grants world. In fact, when you think about it, grants administration has gone from being centralized to decentralized and somewhere in between, and grants office personnel have had to learn how to cope with ever-changing application forms, electronic submittal processes, and new systems for the expenditure of funds. In addition, technology has had a dramatic effect on the grants office in both pre-award and post-award systems.

Ellen Langer in her book *The Power of Mindful Learning* provides some interesting insights about learning and change that can be extrapolated to your efforts to create a dynamic grants office.[4] Langer says that one large barrier to change is the notion that there is always a right way to do something. Many grants offices subscribe to this notion, basing their system on what worked in the past and believing that the future will require more of the same. However, to build a dynamic grants office you need to create a safe environment that allows staff to raise questions instead of feeling they must have the answers. By admitting that you do not have a perfect system and encouraging an environment that welcomes questions, your grants staff will begin to accept feedback and feel comfortable with being asked to provide open-ended, novel solutions for your problem areas or in the areas you need to improve. The result will be more and better solutions and, it is hoped, corresponding changes in worker productivity and output, similar to that which has driven the profit world's economic expansion.

Langer writes of one experiment that demonstrates this point in a dramatic way that can be easily applied to your grants office.

> Participants were required to build a bridge over an imaginary river using small, custom-made wooden blocks. They were told that the height of the bridge would determine the size of the boats that could use the river, so the higher the better. Half the participants were briefly shown examples of how the blocks could be used in a different task (building the longest bridge possible or building a tower). The other half had no prior exposure to the blocks. In the first experiment, 92 percent of the group that saw the examples used

---

[4] Ellen J. Langer, *The Power of Mindful Learning* (Reading, Massachusetts: Addison-Wesley Publishing Company, Inc., 1997).

the blocks in formations identical to the ones they had been shown, whereas only 8 percent of the group that did not see any examples used such formations. The prepared group came up with two solutions. The unprepared group came up with ten. These results were replicated in two other experiments. The hypothesis in these experiments was that the group shown examples would have difficulty forgetting those examples. The hypothesis was confirmed.

The application of this theory to the development of novel solutions to the areas you need to improve in your grants effort is quite simple. First, do not tell your staff about solutions used by other institutions. Copying another institution's solution without knowing why it worked for them and whether the same forces are at work at your institution is dangerous. Instead, have your staff come up with their own ideas by developing workshops, retreats, or brainstorming sessions that focus on creating an atmosphere that fosters communication, the questioning of how to do things better, and the examination of problem areas from several perspectives. (Please note that this concept presented certain challenges to the author. I had to decide whether it was worth including suggestions on how to improve your grants effort in this book at the risk of reducing your likelihood of developing better and more novel solutions. But, rather than provide blank pages for you to fill in, I acquiesced and have attempted to incorporate ideas in this book. However, consider them as food for thought and not as the "right way.")

Langer states that the fear of a system that creates a place for several perspectives is that nothing will remain stable, nothing reliable on which to learn from continuity. Yet, we discover that by viewing the same information through several perspectives we actually become more open to information.

Now that you have some idea of how to create an internal (office) environment accepting of new ideas and change, and an external (administrative) environment accepting of potential resource allocation changes, the next step is to consider how some of the latest management theories can be applied to your office.

In the interest of space and expedience, this book focuses on the management techniques presented by Peter Senge in his books *Fifth Discipline*[5] and *Fifth Discipline Fieldbook*,[6] and how these techniques can provide a theoretical basis for change in your grants effort. Obviously, you can also review the work of other management experts and adapt their techniques to your needs. By talking with professors in your college or university's school of business and/or nonprofit management program, you can get more ideas and take advantage of the best management theories available.

One of the problems with many management theories is that, while they may sound very good, their actual implementation by colleges and universities can be difficult. This is partially because many of their examples and extrapolations are aimed at profit-making companies and marketing, and not nonprofit institutions, such as colleges and universities. However, Senge and his associates at the Center for Organizational Learning at Massachusetts Institute of Technology's Sloan School of Management have developed theories of management that I believe are particularly applicable to academic grants offices. I was

---

[5] Peter Senge, *The Fifth Discipline: The Art and Practice of the Learning Organization* (New York: Doubleday, 1990).

[6] Peter Senge, Art Kleiner, Charlotte Roberts, Richard Ross, and Bryan Smith, *The Fifth Discipline Fieldbook* (New York: Doubleday, 1994).

especially struck by the way their concepts move away from the typical "how do I fix things?" approach, found at most colleges and universities, to one that incorporates feedback to help individuals and systems constantly evolve.

Administrations at colleges and universities are prone to looking at projects or problems in a specific order and completing, finishing, or fixing each one before tackling the next. For example, they will go through accreditation, finish it, look at the grants system, fix it, and then move on to a capital campaign or new graduate program. Instead of addressing each problem or project separately and coming up with one way to "deal" with it, Senge suggests that we create organizations that can learn. By redesigning infrastructures, he proposes creating new types of organizations that deal with the problems and opportunities of today and invest in their capacity to enhance tomorrow by encouraging their members to constantly focus on embellishing and expanding their collective awareness and capabilities. For example, in a learning grants office, staff members are encouraged to speak out without fear of being labeled as troublemakers or individuals with bad attitudes. When confronted with a problem, you, the administrator, could say something like, "I don't know the answer, but I have faith that we'll figure it out. Let's investigate it."

As part of my consulting with colleges and universities I am often asked to perform audits of grants systems. Basically, I am hired to locate problem areas and suggest ways to "fix" them. Often when I am "finished," the static system cannot redirect itself, new problems occur, and I am called back to "fix" them again. If I said, "I don't know the answer but it is probably here. Let's explore the developing of a learning organization so that we will not find ourselves in this situation again," I would probably be fired on the spot.

The truth is, I meet with individuals involved with the problem area, and by establishing a degree of trust (and promising anonymity), they tell me how to solve the problem. When I ask them why they didn't suggest the solution themselves, they often tell me that the administration would not take the solution seriously if it came from the staff, or that they couldn't trust the other staff members enough to brainstorm and share solutions.

Those types of comments always make me think about the grants offices I have worked in and those I have directed. What commonalities did the unpleasant experiences share? What did the good ones have in common? One particular office comes to mind. It was a highly pressured environment like yours—one filled with deadlines, meetings, rules, new administrators and staff, budget cuts, etc. And yet, I liked going to work each day. Why? Because the office environment we created and maintained was terrific. We respected each other and worked as a true team. According to Senge in *The Fifth Discipline Fieldbook*, "Great teams start as individuals who develop knowledge about working as a whole. Over time they enhance their capacity to create what they truly desire to create through their guiding ideas, vision, values, and purpose." Think about your office. Does it seek to maximize a system of resource development that promotes the good of the university and researcher in the most effective manner possible? What are your office's visions, values, and purpose? (More on this in chapter 2.)

DIAGRAMING A PROBLEM, SYSTEM STORY-TELLING, AND FEEDBACK LOOPS

One Senge concept that can be particularly helpful in the grants area is the mapping out or diagraming of problems and the introduction of feedback loops into your system. (Please note that Senge's books provide diagrams specifically for the profit area, not for grants administration, so I have done my best to provide you with adapted scenarios.) The best way to start out your diagram is to focus on a problem and identify the variables or forces that act to create a system that is not performing in a successful manner. You may start by choosing to evaluate a component of your grants system (either pre- or post-award or both) and then using feedback to identify your problem areas. In many cases, your problem area will be identified for you by an administrator.

Begin by stating the problem at a staff meeting. For example, if your supervisor wants more faculty to secure grant funds, you might state the problem in one of the following manners:

- *The problem is* that faculty members are not seeking outside funding opportunities for projects and research.
- *The problem is* that sponsored research rose for 5 years at 10 percent and now it has leveled off.

Try to describe the problem without sanitizing it for political reasons or stating it in a way that shows a bias for a particular solution. In addition, do not suggest solutions in your problem statement (i.e., *the problem is* that we need to subscribe to a grants database).

After identifying and stating the problem it is time to *build a model*. Building a model means developing a theory or hypothesis that could explain why the system is generating the problem. According to Senge's theory, in order to build a model you need to tell a "system story" that has loops and archetypes and is not linear. You should not think of it has having a beginning, a middle, and an end. Instead, you should think of it as viewing a series of events from many vantage points and identifying key themes and recurring patterns. At the heart of a system story-telling is one question: How did we (through our internal thinking, our processes, our practices and our procedures) contribute to or create the circumstances (good and bad) that we face now?

Make a list of the key factors that are critical to telling the story. These are not intended to be right or wrong statements, but are related to understanding and explaining the problem. In actuality these are the factors that may have contributed to creating the problem. For example:

- *One key factor is* that faculty are required to teach more courses and advise more students and thus have less time to work on proposals.
- *One key factor is* that new faculty have greater time-allocation problems because they are setting up new courses, participating on various faculty committees, and teaching more students, and this prevents them from becoming involved in grants.

Depending on your key factors, presenting them in a chart or graph may be helpful. For example, graphing the number of grant office staff for pre-award activity against increases in grant applications might be useful in understanding one part of the problem. By putting key facts and graphs/charts on large self-adhesive "post-it" type notes, you can arrange them on a wall or board so that they can be rearranged as necessary.

You can really uncover the key factors by asking your group to engage in what Senge refers to as the "five whys." Begin by asking "Why is this (the problem) taking place?" Place your group's answers on the wall or board. Follow each answer with a "why" for a total of five whys. For example,

- *Why* are faculty members not seeking outside funding opportunities for projects and research?

  Because they don't have enough time.

- *Why* don't they have enough time?

  Because work loads for new faculty are high.

- *Why* are work loads for new faculty high?

  Because department chairs assign a larger number of students to the basic courses that new faculty are selected to teach, and faculty preparation for these basic courses takes an inordinate amount of time.

- *Why* do new faculty get assigned these courses?

  Because experienced professors normally choose to teach advanced courses with prerequisites.

- *Why?*

Different sets of responses may take you in a totally different directions. For instance,

- *Why* are faculty members not seeking outside funding opportunities for projects and research?

  Because new faculty are not aware of grant opportunities.

- *Why* aren't new faculty aware of grant opportunities?

  Because they do not have their interest profiles in the computer system and therefore do not automatically receive notices of grant programs.

- *Why* aren't their profiles in the computer system?

  Because new faculty have not been made aware of the system.

- *Why* haven't new faculty been made aware of the system?

  Because no one from the grants office participates in new faculty orientation.

- *Why* doesn't anyone from the grants office participate in new faculty orientation?

  Because we have never asked to participate.

- *Why* hasn't the grants office ever asked to participate?

  Because a long time ago someone in the grants office said we did not have enough personnel to send someone to the new faculty orientation.

Other responses may lead in yet another direction.

- *Why* are faculty members not seeking outside funding opportunities for projects and research?

  Because new faculty are not told that grant seeking is important.

- *Why* aren't new faculty told that grant seeking is important?

  Because deans and department chairs do not make grant seeking a priority.

- *Why* don't deans and department chairs make grant seeking a priority?

  Because the provost doesn't make grant seeking a priority with deans.

The purpose of asking why is to illuminate those factors that are influencing the problems on which your grants office is focusing. These factors or variables are *linked* to recurring events or cycles. Senge states, "Links never exist in isolation. They always comprise a circle of causality, a feedback loop in which every element is both cause and effect, influenced by some and influencing others, so that every one of its effects sooner or later comes back to roost." For example, the problem with a leveling in the number of proposals for sponsored research could be diagramed in loops as in exhibit 1.1.

In starting out, select the elements involved without trying to explain why it is happening (yet) and create a visual story of the events involved. Senge suggests you use action words that demonstrate movement. For instance, in the loop diagram you see words such as decrease, fewer, and decline. You could also use positive words such as improve, increase, accelerate.

Your next step in developing your story is to describe the impact that the movement produces on the next element. For example,

- declining awards are met with demands to reduce pre-award staff;
- pre-award staff is oversubscribed time-wise, with fewer staff serving twice as many people;
- new faculty hires are not made aware of the grants office, its Web site, or search functions; and

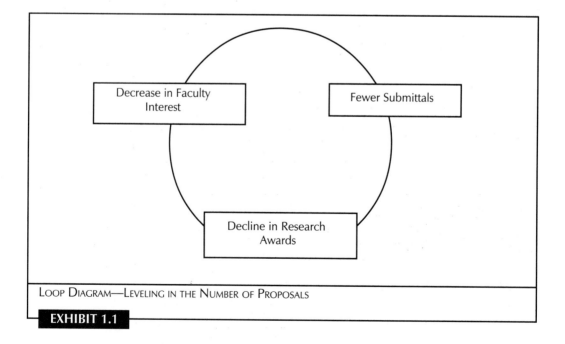

LOOP DIAGRAM—LEVELING IN THE NUMBER OF PROPOSALS

EXHIBIT 1.1

- faculty are not encouraged to become involved in grant seeking as a component of their tenure and performance evaluation.

EXPONENTIAL GROWTH AND COLLAPSE—THE REINFORCING LOOP

Another force that acts upon grants offices (both pre- and post-award) is the concept of exponential growth and collapse. The technical term is a reinforcing loop, and the growth or collapse continue at ever-increasing rates. According to Senge, one can most easily grasp the often surprising ramification of exponential growth by making an analogy to a noninterest-paying piggy bank and an interest-bearing bank account. If you put $100 in a piggy bank each year and $100 in an interest-bearing bank account, the difference between the interest-bearing bank account and the piggy bank would seem small at first because the bank interest would generate only a few dollars per year. But if you left the interest in the bank, the money would grow at any even faster rate. After fifty years (at 7 percent interest) you would have over $40,000, more than eight times as much as the piggy bank would generate.

Another example of exponential growth concerns credit cards and their seemingly small interest percentages. In the end, if you used up your entire line of credit and paid only the monthly minimal amount, you would incur outrageous interest charges and could spend over 30 years paying off your debt! As you can now see, exponential growth takes a large toll in many situations. In the grants office we struggle to get through the day, the week, and the month, and often do not even have enough time to lift up our heads to see the huge changes brought on by exponential growth.

Exponential growth in academic grants efforts is caused in part by assuming two major ideas: *the first, "growth is good"* (after all, we have more money, more indirect costs, more research, more publications, and more prestige for the university. Who would argue with that?); *and the second, "there is no limit to where research funding can take a university."*

However, the reality is that the infrastructure to support exponential growth may not be present. One must look at the impact this growth has on all college/university systems, not just on the grants office system. It is critical to examine and consider all the forces that underlie the growth of research funding. For example, if there is no more space to house grant-supported programs, the grants effort will by necessity level off or decline.

At one institution with which I was affiliated, lack of space was a problem, so we leased and renovated off-campus buildings that surrounded the campus. As the labs and offices moved farther away we encountered problems with crime, transportation, and communication. Although our efforts were Herculean, the problems we encountered ultimately moved us from exponential growth to a vicious cycle of doom. Fewer grants meant fewer dollars, which meant cuts in services. The cuts in services exasperated our principal investigators and project directors as they had more difficulty in hiring students, paying human participants as subjects, etc. The resulting decline was finally felt in cuts to our pre- and post-award staffs. All of this happened while the cry for more proposals fell on increasingly deaf ears.

According to Senge, there can be any number of elements in a reinforcing loop, all in a circle, all propelling each other's growth. Your reinforcing loops should illuminate the overworked and overburdened stressors on the various functions of your grants system and how these forces act out of the exponential growth to create problem areas. Of course, the more overburdened you are, the less time you have to develop feedback, diagram the situation, and implement the prescriptive and preventive processes outlined in this chapter. For some of you, this may be analogous to the person up to his or her neck in alligators while discussions concerning draining the swamp pursue. However, you can take some consolation in knowing that reinforcing loops do not exist in a vacuum and that there are balancing mechanisms that apply limits to the vicious or virtuous cycle. The template in exhibit 1.2 has been developed to help you diagram the reinforcing loops in your grants effort.

For example, on the pre-award side of the grants office, a reinforcing loop might be constructed around problems associated with final proposal sign-off. Your senior administrator may believe the system is in the "virtuous" direction of more proposal submissions yielding more money cycles. However, the "vicious" cycle of sign off and the problems it creates for your office may look more like exhibit 1.3.

A "virtuous" reinforcing loop gone bad can have a lot to do with the pressures put on a grants office for more grant funding, and "the sky is the limit" mentality of administrators who are evaluated (or who evaluate others) on bottom lines such as how much money was brought in, how much was recovered in indirect-cost funds, etc.

The virtuous cycle (and administrator) is focused on other things like those diagramed in exhibit 1.4.

BALANCING LOOPS

Balancing loops represent the forces of nature and the systems that regulate and maintain stability, and work toward some equilibrium. They can, in a sense, put the natural breaks on

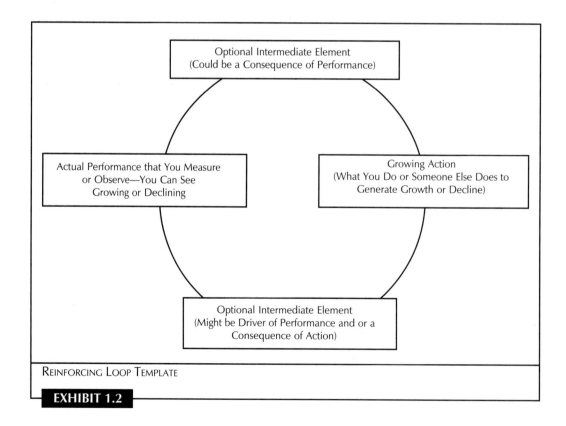

REINFORCING LOOP TEMPLATE

EXHIBIT 1.2

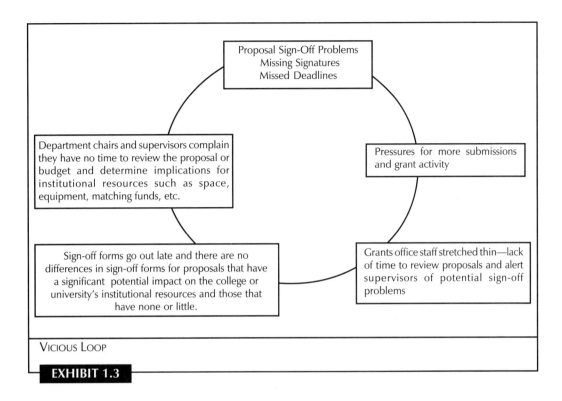

Proposal Sign-Off Problems
Missing Signatures
Missed Deadlines

Department chairs and supervisors complain they have no time to review the proposal or budget and determine implications for institutional resources such as space, equipment, matching funds, etc.

Pressures for more submissions and grant activity

Sign-off forms go out late and there are no differences in sign-off forms for proposals that have a significant potential impact on the college or university's institutional resources and those that have none or little.

Grants office staff stretched thin—lack of time to review proposals and alert supervisors of potential sign-off problems

VICIOUS LOOP

EXHIBIT 1.3

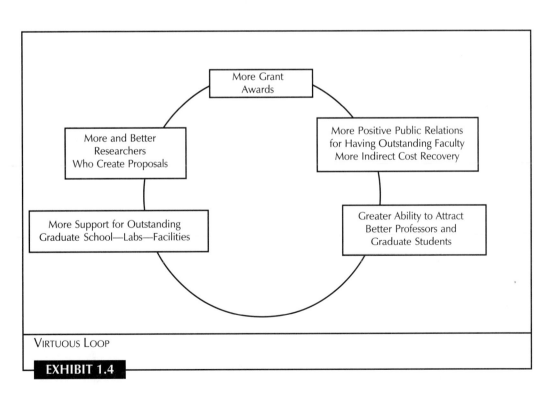

More Grant Awards

More and Better Researchers Who Create Proposals

More Positive Public Relations for Having Outstanding Faculty More Indirect Cost Recovery

More Support for Outstanding Graduate School—Labs—Facilities

Greater Ability to Attract Better Professors and Graduate Students

VIRTUOUS LOOP

EXHIBIT 1.4

both virtuous and vicious cycles. When there is a difference between a balancing loop's target and reality, a gap is created that cannot be ignored. The virtuous cycle diagramed in exhibit 1.4 is not attainable if proposals are not submitted or if the proposals that are submitted are not of high enough quality to keep the cycle going. Poor resource allocation and the inability to provide institutional resources for proposals that require matching/in-kind contributions, space, students, lab support, and/or release time from teaching and advising can also ultimately affect grant funding. By diagraming the reinforcing loop and examining the balancing loops that are causing resistance, you can uncover the forces, subtleties, and relationships that are keeping you from attaining your goals. In the process, remember to ask why. For example,

Why has the demand for sign-off increased? Because there is more pressure by administrators to seek outside funds.

Why? Because outside support is an index of the faculty's involvement in their fields.

Why? Because acceptance of research and model project ideas by peers and foundation and corporate grantors demonstrates acceptance of the questions that the researcher is raising and the need to answer these questions.

Why? Because funding validates the authenticity and compellingness to respond to the gap presented in the researcher's proposal—the gap between what is known and what should be known.

As you can see, the answers begin to point to the real variable that led to the conclusion that submittals yield funding, and that is *quality*. Not the quality of the grants office in searching for grantors, signing off on proposals, and getting them out the door, but the increased acceptance rate of proposals by the grantor because of the high quality of the proposals submitted.

The pressure of the balancing loop to handle more and more proposal sign-offs is now confronted with the reality of how many proposals your grants office staff can conscientiously handle in both the pre-award and post-award stages. And the word "many" is not the operant term; "conscientiously" is. It is quality and acceptance that must be factored in. If the number of proposals submitted is the key indicator of your office's approval rating, then it makes sense to allocate more staff to getting the sign-off signatures and pushing the proposals out the door. However, further analysis usually reveals other controlling variables. For example, the size of the grant and the mix of the grantors may increase or decrease the number of proposals that can be handled, and there are vast differences in the amount of time required to process different grants. For instance, many smaller foundation or corporate grants may take equal or more time to handle than some larger federally sponsored projects.

While proposal quality may not be considered the purview of the grants office, when you raise the issue of more staff and resources to handle more proposal volume (the gap), someone will inevitably ask about acceptance or success rates. This question and the diagramming of accompanying forces will provoke many more insightful questions, such as the following:

- What is the negative positioning value of the rejected proposals?
- Couldn't effort and resources be better invested in developing quality versus quantity?
- How does a conscientious administrator make resource allocation decisions about matching funds, release time, etc.?

Exhibit 1.5 diagrams what the balancing loop may look like.

When the stages on the loops are examined, even more interesting questions may be derived. In fact, at some point, the very discerning administrator may ask a very basic but not often asked question: Why do we have this sign-off procedure anyway? From the grants office perspective, it is good and indeed fruitful to entertain this question. As a learning organization, if a procedure is not meaningful and useful, it should be eliminated. The allocation of scarce resources in pursuit of the idea that a signature means the institution's commitment to the researcher and the grantor should be questioned. If the administrator (department chair, dean, etc.) has had little or no time to read and digest the proposal and to consciously commit resources to the project, then is there really any reason to run all over the institution to acquire the required signatures or to collect them electronically, through e-mail, with an attached file that may seldom be opened and read? By questioning the sign-off process and diagramming the problem, you raise critically important issues concerning your institution's accountability for the allocation of your office's scare resources and its accountability to the grantor.

In the end, the processes of diagramming problems, system story-telling, and feedback loops will ultimately help you define the role of your office and the services you should be providing, and also to improve how you function.

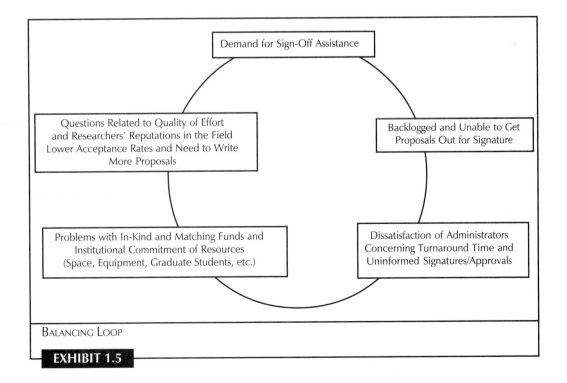

Demand for Sign-Off Assistance

Questions Related to Quality of Effort and Researchers' Reputations in the Field Lower Acceptance Rates and Need to Write More Proposals

Backlogged and Unable to Get Proposals Out for Signature

Problems with In-Kind and Matching Funds and Institutional Commitment of Resources (Space, Equipment, Graduate Students, etc.)

Dissatisfaction of Administrators Concerning Turnaround Time and Uninformed Signatures/Approvals

BALANCING LOOP

EXHIBIT 1.5

CHAPTER

The Purpose of the Grants Office

The office that administers grants and contracts has many names, and the role of this office is far from standard in each of the 3,000-plus colleges and universities in the United States. In some cases, the role of the grants office varies according to the personality and interests of the director or the administrative reporting structure of the institution. Some offices fall under a vice president for academic affairs, others under a provost, and still others under a vice president for research and graduate studies. However, there are certain functions that a majority of grants offices have in common, as well as certain functions that are left unaccounted for or are performed haphazardly and inappropriately by other offices.

The grants office should promote the mission of an institution and provide great returns on the institution's investment irrespective of whether it's identified as the Office of Grants Administration, the Office for Sponsored Projects, or the Office of Research and Development.

MEETING THE MISSION OF THE INSTITUTION THROUGH GRANTS

Without a mission statement or case statement to provide direction, the grants effort cannot play an effective role in helping to achieve the goals of the institution. Yes, that old, dusty document that is used only at five-year planning time—your institution's mission statement or case statement—is critical to the grants effort. This statement of the purpose of your institution will enable you to

- evaluate the extent to which funding sources will be attracted to your established mission and institutional goals,
- set realistic criteria for judging what grant direction to embark upon, and

- determine criteria for the use of matching fund requirements and in-kind contributions.

Without a precise statement of the mission of your college, university, institute, or other large grant producer you will not have a rationale from which to allocate your office's services. Many institutions have entrepreneur types of grant seekers on their faculty and staff. I had one whom I refer to as "Dr. No Problem." Dr. No Problem would announce that he had discovered a "pile of grant money," which he had to apply for immediately, if not sooner. His record of creating pandemonium within our college was overlooked because he brought in lots of money and was a nice person who meant well. Closer examination revealed that his actions had major implications and contributed to harmful, exponential growth. However, without a clear mission or statement of purpose, it was difficult for me to turn down Dr. No Problem and his requests for my office's resources and time.

Money can be the worst element to add to an institution that is already suffering from an ill-defined mission and the changing priorities of new presidents and vice presidents. A desperate need for money may be a warning sign that the institution is no longer focusing clearly on the need it was created to address or that the need has changed and that people no longer view the institution and its programs as viable. Even if the weak financial state of the institution can be attributed to other causes, such as poor fiscal decision making, the temptation to go after any and all money creates a problem when the additional funds move the organization farther from its mission.

Producing a proposal to acquire a "pile of grant money" is advisable only when the project fosters the institutional mission. Any activity that does not foster this purpose, no matter how innocuous it seems, keeps the institution from moving toward its goal and may change or subvert your institution's mission.

While changes in the mission and the pressure of finances may be causative agents of change for an institution, they should be controlled through a conscious decision-making process. Grant funds should be pursued by premeditated measures.

Administrators should not be bullied into sponsoring projects because they do not want to be accused of not seeking all available funds or appear as if they are restraining the entrepreneurial staff member. Remember, a devoted staff member who is well intentioned will not mind relating grant opportunities to the predetermined interests of the institution.

GOALS AND OBJECTIVES OF THE GRANTS OFFICE

Review the goals and objectives of your grants office, and consider adding any of those from the following list. Involvement in such areas will determine the rationale for your institution's grants office. Review statements of purpose from previous annual reports of your office and from accreditation documents or other documents requesting additional staff and resources. All current office functions should be covered under one or more of the following purposes or statements of purposes from your research. The grants/research office supports the following:

- development of opportunities to further the goals of the institution through grants, projects, research, and programs funded by sources outside of the institution;
- promotion of an atmosphere conducive to developing and sustaining interest and involvement in grant-proposal preparation and support activities by staff;

- protection and enhancement of the integrity and image of the institution through management and monitoring of communication with funding sources;
- provision of information on the use of matching funds and in-kind contributions allocated to the grants process;
- ensurance of the integrity of sponsored project funds, and assistance in interpretation and compliance with funders' rules, regulations, and wishes so that both legal and ethical requirements are met;
- analysis of the grants marketplace and the provision, to administration, of funding information needed in fiscal and program decisions affecting the institution;
- provision of leadership in impacting the grants marketplace and increasing funding opportunities for the good of the institution, its project, clients, and benefactors; and
- development of grant strategies on marketplace trends that provide for a mix of grant funds from federal, state, foundation, and corporate sources.

At this point, you may want to review the table of contents of this book to see if other areas that you may want to include in your dynamic grants office are also covered by your statement of purpose. Each chapter is derived from or related to the broad goals that have just been listed.

Many administrators are unsure of the role that they want the grants office to fulfill because they do not know what the office's potential really is. Through completion of the inventories at the conclusion of each chapter, you will develop a description of your grants office. Your office's description should be tailored to the individual needs of your institution. The size and scope of your office and what you want from an organized grants effort will vary and may even change as your institution develops.

List the established goals and objectives of your grants office on the following Grants Office Goals/Objectives Worksheet (exhibit 2.1). To promote feedback upon which to review your system, you may also wish to ask a sample of individuals from your institution the questions listed in exhibit 2.2.

The review of your office's purpose and how it relates to your institution's mission statement should not to be taken lightly because what you are really doing is establishing the rationale for your entire grants office and subsequently, whom you serve and how you serve them.

YOUR CASE STATEMENT: WHO YOU ARE

You may ask, "What has my institution's mission or case statement got to do with getting a grant?" The answer is *everything*. Your case statement consists of how and why your institution's programs were started and how they relate to where the institution is.

1. Why did your institution originally embark on research, sponsored projects, and grants? When were grant proposals first submitted and for what types of projects? How long has your office and institution been accepting funds from public and private sources to conduct sponsored programs? How much money has been accepted?
2. Where is your college's/university's grants and sponsored projects program headed in the future? What is your five-year plan for research and sponsored projects? What new emphasis, changes, and ventures will there be?

Please list the established goals and objectives of your grants office.

1. _____
2. _____
3. _____
4. _____
5. _____
6. _____
7. _____
   _____

Please list any other goals and objectives that you think your grants office *should* have.

1. _____
2. _____
3. _____
   _____

GRANTS OFFICE GOALS/OBJECTIVES WORKSHEET

EXHIBIT 2.1

---

1. Are you aware of your institution's mission statement?   ___ Yes   ___ No

   a.   If yes, have you read it?   ___ Yes   ___ No

   b.   If you are aware of it, but haven't read it, why not?

2. What do you think is the purpose of the grants office?

3. What do you think the purpose of the grants office should be?

SURVEY QUESTIONS—THE PURPOSE OF THE GRANTS OFFICE

EXHIBIT 2.2

---

3. What institutional plans are there for the commitment of new sponsored projects in terms of facilities and equipment? What new staffing plans are there to assure that your grants office will be accountable to funding sources for any increases in sponsored projects administration?

Your case statement also allows you to examine what you are doing today. Have you deviated from the past? Why? What effect has time had on your mission and raison d'être? What are your current priorities, programs, buildings, and unique characteristics? Who are your students?

If your existing case statement is not relevant to today's directions and problems, then update it regardless of your decisions and plans for your grants office. Begin the process of updating your case statement by brainstorming ideas with selected administrators (department chairs, deans, etc.), key researchers, project directors, and grants office personnel. Rules for brainstorming are addressed in the next section.

THE ESSENTIALS OF BRAINSTORMING

One of the best techniques for developing ideas is to brainstorm with your staff, board, volunteers, and advisory committees. In addition to fostering involvement in your institution, this technique has the added benefit of capitalizing on the group's collective genius. Support is built for ideas when others are invited to share in their generation. The project or solution becomes a group project, and everyone is more willing to work to make the idea become a reality.

Brainstorming is a simple technique that quickly generates a long list of creative ideas and solutions to problems. Done properly, your group should follow a strict time limit—usually no more than five to eight minutes.

1. Ask individuals to form groups of five to eight people.
2. Appoint a neutral group leader to facilitate the group process and task. This individual should encourage and prod other members, check the time, and so on.
3. Appoint a recorder. This individual will write down all ideas generated and can be the facilitator.
4. Set a time limit. Ten minutes is more than enough for each area. Five minutes will keep the process going at a fast pace.
5. State one question or problem. What are our current needs (staff, buildings, renovations, improvements, equipment)? What changes will be needed in the future in program areas, clients, and so on? What changes will be necessary in terms of buildings, equipment, and so on, to accommodate future program changes? Changes in facilities include renovations, new buildings, and equipment. Changes in staff include additional staff, training needs, and in-service areas. New areas include service areas, client population, research areas, and program extensions.
6. Ask group members to generate as many answers to the question as they can within the time limit.
7. Encourage group members to piggyback on each other's ideas. (*Piggybacking* is suggesting a new idea that adds to one already given.)
8. Record all answers. Combine those that are similar.
   Two important rules to remember are:
   • avoid any evaluation or discussion of ideas until the process is over, and
   • the recorder can ask to have ideas repeated, but no comments by others are allowed (e.g., "We can't do that," "That's stupid," or "I disagree").

Take time to discuss each idea or suggestion. For example, if you have ten ideas, two minutes per idea, for explanation and questions, will consume twenty minutes of group time.

Because your list can be prioritized later, do not get too concerned with any one idea on which group members may want to focus. When you use a prioritizing or voting system, as suggested in chapter 3 of this book, you will eliminate or weaken any ideas that the group does not hold in high esteem.

DEVELOPING A MISSION STATEMENT FOR THE GRANTS OFFICE

The grants office is directly responsible for assisting the institution in dealing with its current priorities and in preparing for the future. The case statement can be reorganized to provide the grants office with direction and to shape its role in the organization's plan.

The case statement can be developed into the plan for the grants office. Using your answers from question 2 on the Wish List Worksheet (exhibit 2.3) as a guideline, ask yourself what you would do if your institution received a large check (e.g., 10 percent of your

---

Your institution has just received a check for $_____ (10 percent of your institution's total budget). The money was sent by an anonymous benefactor and can be used for anything.

Brainstorm and list ideas for its *present* use.

1. _____

2. _____

3. _____

4. _____

5. _____

Using this money, or part of it, brainstorm and list any changes you would make in the *future* in programs, facilities, staff, etc.

1. _____

2. _____

3. _____

4. _____

5. _____

WISH LIST WORKSHEET

EXHIBIT 2.3

institution's total budget) in the mail. The money was sent by an anonymous benefactor and can be used for anything. Use the Wish List Worksheet to brainstorm a list of present uses with your staff. Also, brainstorm a list of changes you would make in the future in programs, facilities, and staff. Keep a record of the projects and areas for investigation you have developed through your brainstorming.

The role of the grants office is to assist the institution to meet present needs and to prepare for future needs by securing external funds that will move the institution toward its goals. The remainder of this book is designed to provide you with the knowledge of the services that most grants offices provide in seeking to meet the mission of an institution.

The information you gather in performing the suggested activities will provide you with a concise picture of where you are now, and where you want to be in the future. This information will provide a unique description and will make a valuable addition to your grants office Web site.

I recommend that you examine the Web sites of other university/college departmental and sponsored research offices to see how they describe their goals. Start your search by visiting the National Council of University Research Administrators' (NCURA's) list of institutional sponsored research offices at http://www.ncura.edu/resources/sponsored.htm.

The survey questions in exhibit 2.2 come from the Client Satisfaction Survey in chapter 17 and are aimed at helping you promote and develop feedback from your users on the purpose of your office. The Grants Office Inventory (exhibit 2.4) that follows this chapter is designed to help you outline a plan to review the suggestions contained in this chapter. Review the activities/items for their relevance to your office and get your plan down in writing.

For Each Activity/Item listed, Check Status

Activity/Item	Reviewed, Appropriate Part of Grants Office	Reviewed, Appropriate Part of Other Office (List)	Reviewed, Not Applicable	Reviewed, Inappropriate Needs Action	Non-existent, Needs Action
1. Mission statement for institution					
2. Case for grants office					
3. Goals and objectives for grants office					
4. Copies of other institutions' Web sites					

Complete this Section for Each Activity/Item Needing Action

What Needs to be Accomplished?	By Whom? (Office/Person)	By When? (Time Frame)	Resources Required—Personnel, Supplies, Equipment, Programming, etc.	Estimated Costs

GRANTS OFFICE INVENTORY—THE PURPOSE OF THE GRANTS OFFICE

EXHIBIT 2.4

CHAPTER 3

Measuring the Success of Your Grants System

Measuring the success and efficiency of an institution's grants system is dependent upon the criteria used for evaluation. Without understanding the purpose of a grants system, it is impossible to evaluate its success. For example, can you identify which of the following examples describes a successful grants system?

- a grants system that brings in twice the amount of external funds compared with other institutions of similar size and faculty expertise
- a grants system that is so fiscally accountable that every audit substantiates superior grants accounting and generates praise from the funding source
- a grants system that consistently operates within a narrow time frame from the conception of an idea, researching of funding sources, and production of a proposal (This system utilizes computers to provide researchers with funding-source application data instantly and produces budgets, time lines, and proposals with speed and accuracy.)

Each of these examples can be evaluated only on the subjective criteria that are implied or mentioned in each description (e.g., speed, accuracy, etc.). Note that none of the examples have to do with meeting the mission of the institution through the grants system. In fact, many colleges and universities do not evaluate their grants system by its ability to move toward its stated institutional mission or purpose. When meeting the mission is ignored as one of the primary indicators of success, the result is a grants effort evaluated only on the mechanics of the grants process, such as

- how quickly and thoroughly the grants office handles requests for funding-source information; and

- the amount and quality of assistance the grants office provides in writing, editing, developing the budget, reproducing, and delivering the proposal.

Lacking criteria on which to evaluate the functions of a grants office leads to the superficial evaluation of the observable, technical assistance that most grants offices provide or the more common measure of success of the grants system: *money*, or how much grants and contracts funding the office handles.

Asked to describe the grants effort at their institution, most administrators will be quick to relay the total amount of support in dollars, or they might make a reference to the success rate or number of proposals funded as compared with the number submitted. These two commonly used "indicators of a successful grants effort" may have little to do with moving the institution toward its predetermined mission or goal. When the institution does not have definite expectations on which to measure the grants office's course of action, it is not surprising that 84 percent of respondents in the Davis and Lowry study said they had no formal evaluation (see chapter 1).

Preparing proposals *solely* aimed at meeting the funding sources' or grantors' needs may be counterproductive to the goals of the institution. In fact, it may be wise to eliminate a grants office if the institution's resources are being used to seek funding for *only* those projects that have the least risk of rejection and the greatest promise of money. If a grants office's only goal is to amass a great amount of money and develop a high success rate that looks good on its annual report, it may be

- subverting the original mission of the institution, or
- using space and other resources for nonmission-related projects at the expense of projects that are priorities.

In the hustle and bustle of the grants world, the tendency to "follow the money" is an ever-present danger. Predetermining why your institution is supporting each particular project is an important component of a truly successful grants system that works for the advancement of the institution.

However, on occasion, an institution of higher education may have to take a less-than-optimum path to move toward accomplishing its mission. When the available funds to move in the predetermined direction are limited, nonexistent, or highly competitive, proposals may be written and grants accepted to help with overhead and to stay in business while a more appropriate mission-related granting program is sought.

The purpose of this chapter is to assist you in assessing the grants potential of your institution and developing a plan for grants success.

PRIORITIZING THE GOALS/OBJECTIVES OF YOUR GRANTS OFFICE

The key to evaluating the success of your grants office lies in your efficiency in identifying and securing the best funding sources and grant programs for your institution. The "best" sources and programs are those that provide your institution with a bright future, ensure your institution's credibility as a grantee, and move your institution toward meeting its mission.

To measure the success of your grants office it must have priorities. Locate the Grants Office Goals/Objectives Worksheet in chapter 2 (exhibit 2.1) and put the items in order of priority. Also give your list to selected individuals and ask them to prioritize it. Rank-ordering the list will help focus your effort.

Remember that the grants effort may be used to attract some or all of the components of a priority. For example, a list of priorities for the grants office of the Department of Pediatrics at the University of Rochester School of Medicine and Dentistry included

- improving the department's capacity for accomplishing more bone-marrow transplants and research,
- developing a focus on research in children, and
- providing a means for parents in an eleven-county region to remain close to their hospitalized children.

A ranking process revealed that providing a means for parents to remain close to their hospitalized children was the number-one priority because it was a component of several other priorities. The result was a concentrated effort to provide support to construct a Ronald McDonald House.

If the priority of the grants office had been to accumulate as much money as possible, and money had been the sole criterion for evaluating the efforts of the grants office, it might have been wiser to invest staff time and effort into securing bone-marrow and/or other research grants. However, reaching our institutional mission and the priorities of our projects, not the total amount of grant dollars secured, were the measurement criteria.

PRIORITIZING YOUR INSTITUTION'S NEEDS

To determine which grant-related projects should take precedence over others and how your grants effort can help achieve your institution's priorities, you need to identify your institution's priorities. Ask your institutional leaders and administrators to identify the institution's areas of priority. Once they have been identified, list them on the Priorities Worksheet (exhibit 3.1) and send or e-mail them to the participants who are selected to be involved in the prioritization process. Request that they rank the areas listed numerically with "1" as their highest priority (first choice), "2" as their second priority (second choice), and so on.

Rank-ordering can be done in a group setting or individually, and even in a decision lab with computers at individual stations. In many cases, the individual rank-ordering process is preferred so that anonymity can be maintained and group pressure controlled. Provide direction and focus by reminding participants that they need to review the list from the institution's perspective, and not just their own, and that they should keep in mind special considerations, such as space and equipment needs, which may be necessary to accomplish the priorities.

Through the rank-ordering process you will arrive at a "weighted" list of priority areas. Ask the evaluation experts at your institution to design a computer program that summarizes and tallies all the responses. The resulting file will essentially be a database of your rank-ordered institutional needs—the needs from which you will focus your grants effort.

ANALYZING AND DETERMINING YOUR INSTITUTION'S GRANTS/ CONTRACTS POTENTIAL

Now that you have developed a prioritized list of your institution's areas of need, your next step is to determine the likelihood of being successful in attracting external resources to

---

The following areas have been identified as priorities for this institution. Please assist the grants effort by rank-ordering the listed areas. The area you assign number 1 will be your first choice. Your number one choice should be the area you feel is most important for receiving grant funds. The area you assign 2 will be your second choice, and so on.

Area	Rank Order
_____	_____
_____	_____
_____	_____
_____	_____
_____	_____
_____	_____
_____	_____
_____	_____
_____	_____

PRIORITIES WORKSHEET

EXHIBIT 3.1

---

these areas. Many colleges and universities act as though they have limitless potential to increase external funding through grants and contracts (i.e., the virtuous cycle discussed in chapter 1). This is unrealistic. Your goal is to develop a realistic estimate of your institution's likelihood of being successful in attracting grant funding to your identified priorities and to provide this information to your administration. By providing your administrators with a realistic base from which to proceed, you can keep them from wasting their valuable time dreaming up initiatives and priorities that simply are not marketable in the grants arena. Once one of my superiors decided that a new international program would be the hallmark of his leadership, and he asked me to look for funds to support his initiative. Needless to say, he was disappointed when I reported to him that there was not much available in the way of grant funds to support this particular type of project—especially because he had already announced the high-profile program to the faculty and staff!

The assessment of your institution's ability to attract grant funds cannot consist solely of comparing your college or university to others with a similar mission, student body size, and/or programs. Just because a similar institution attracted $10 million in grant funds, that does not mean you will or can. In addition, simply knowing how many awards and how much money the various funding sources distribute annually is also not enough. You must dig deeper to discover the variables that will truly help you assess your potential to attract external funding and to realistically evaluate your office's functional level.

KEY VARIABLES TO ASSESSING YOUR INSTITUTION'S GRANTS/CONTRACTS POTENTIAL

By researching the following three areas you will be able to develop a more valid assessment of your grants potential.

1. The Grants/Contracts Marketplace

- How many grants and contracts programs fund the areas of priority you have identified?
- How many grants and contracts have they funded?
- Is the trend in appropriations going up or down?

2. Your Competition

- Which institutions are getting the money now?
- Who are the principal investigators (PIs) and project directors (PDs) and what are their records like (education level, publications, etc.)?

3. Your Institution

- How does your profile match that of the current players in terms of resources, faculty, staff, etc.?

As you investigate these three areas in more detail, you will begin to be able to provide your administrators with

- estimated amounts of grant and contract funds that are likely
- ideas of what additional commitments they may be required to make to support the infrastructure necessary to compete effectively for funding.

1. The Grants/Contracts Marketplace—Your faculty may have brilliant project ideas or hypotheses, but how much money is there to explore their priority areas? To answer this question, start by conducting a database search using the keywords that describe the field of interest and/or the benefits of the research or model project. This will result in a list of potential funding sources, both public and private.

A. Public Funding Sources

- Federal Government Grant Funding—There are approximately 1,300 government granting programs that award $80 to $90 billion annually. How many programs were uncovered in your search? How many grants do each of the programs award? What is the number of awards versus the number of applications? Who were the successful institutions? By contacting program officers, you can request a list of successful grantees or recipients that you can then use to help you analyze the competition.

  Contacting program officers can provide you with a plentitude of information. For example, a researcher of yours may have heard that NIH received an increase in its appropriation and therefore, assumed that there would be more awards in his or her program area. In reality, the proposed 2001 federal budget did set NIH's budget at a new record high of $18.8 billion, and Congress could add more. But because the average size of grants has risen, NIH's number of competitive grants will fall from 2000's 8,950 to 7,641—a decrease of 1,309. By contacting program officers you can gather information on an agency's specific programs and develop a much better idea of your true potential.

- Federal Government Contracts—There are no accurate or verifiable estimates of the number of federal government contracts. One reason for the confusion is the fact that each of the agencies that offer contracts have different computer and accounting systems. If your search reveals potential interest from the Department of Defense, you can get an estimate of your potential by contacting the program's contracts officer. Ask this person how many contracts have been awarded in your priority area, and if the budget for this area is going up or down. Because successful contractors are published in the *Commerce Business Daily*, you can also ask if the contracts officer will provide you with a list of their current contract holders (to be used in your analysis of the competition).

- State Government Grants and Contracts—States distribute funds through both the grants and contracts mechanisms. It is more difficult to develop an estimate of your institution's potential in this arena. However, as with federal government grants and contracts, a few phone calls and/or e-mails will provide you with valuable data from which to develop a more accurate picture.

B. Private Funding Sources—This sector of the marketplace can be divided into two main components—foundations and corporations.

- Foundations—At some institutions grants offices are not allowed to tap into the foundation sector because it is reserved for the development office. This is unfortunate, because development offices are usually looking for funding for capital support (i.e., capital campaigns, endowments, building, and renovation), which accounts for 24.2 percent of foundation dollars; while over 50 percent of foundation grant dollars goes to support programs (projects) and research. If your grants office is currently unable to go after private foundations for funding, use these statistics to help you develop the rationale for opening the foundation marketplace to faculty-initiated grants projects. You can refine your foundation research by using the Foundation Center's database of grant makers—FC Search. For more information on how to access this database and the Foundation Center's other valuable resources, visit their Web site at http://www.fdncenter.org. In addition, your development office may already belong to the Foundation's Center's Associate Program, which provides an array of services including discounted custom computer searches for potential funders.

- Corporations—Corporate support for your priority areas can be approached through the following four main avenues:
  - Corporate Foundation—If the corporation utilizes a corporate foundation, there are Foundation Center resources that can enable you to review the grants awarded by the foundation and compare them to your priorities. Some corporations also have Web sites that list their foundations' grants.
  - Corporate Contributions Program—You can also find out about corporate contributions programs through Foundation Center Resources and at corporate Web sites.
  - Marketing—Corporate marketing departments are a growing source of support for grants and gifts. You may find support here if your research or model project can be used to position corporate products.
  - Research and Development (R&D)—Corporate R&D may be a valuable resource to you if your institution's project places it on the cutting edge of the field.

2. **Your Competition**—By thoroughly researching a particular funding source or program you will obtain a list of current grantees or successful contractors. Review this list to compare your institution, faculty, PIs, and PDs to the winners. To determine how well your faculty and proposed project directors (PDs) and principal investigators (PIs), compare to the awarded grantees, examine the following areas:
   - Advanced degrees—Where did the winners get their degrees?

- Publishing records—How often have they published? What have they published (i.e., texts, books, articles, etc.)? In what journals have they published?
- Position in the field—Are they icons in the field? Are they speakers at conferences, conventions, meetings, etc.?
- Whom they know—Do the successful grantees have linkages to the prime movers in the field and/or the funding agency? Whom did they study under in graduate school?
- With whom did they do their post-graduate work?
- Reviewers—Have the successful grantees also been reviewers or panel members for funding agencies?
- Frequency of funding and amounts—Does the PI/PD have a consistent funding record?

You may choose to have your grant seekers complete the following Principal Investigator/ Project Director—Fundability Analysis Worksheet (exhibit 3.2) to help them compare themselves to those who have been awarded funds. The worksheet can be used to compare chances of success for several professors in an institute or consortium, or for one or two researchers who are seeking to analyze their individual likelihood of attracting funds.

3. **Your Institution**—How does your institution compare to the current, successful grantee's institution?
   - Rank in the Field—While it is possible to "break into" a successful group of grantees, it is still important to analyze the list of successful institutions to determine if there is a discernible profile. For instance, are the grant winners consistently the leaders in

---

Please provide the names of the degree-granting institutions, journals in which articles are published, linkages, etc. where appropriate.   Comparison ratings can be designated with an "x".

	Profile Successful PI/PD	Profile Your Proposed PI/PD	No Match	Comparison Some Match	Excellent Match
Advanced degrees					
Ph.D. granting institution	___	___	___	___	___
Publishing record					
· no publications	___	___	___	___	___
· published article	___	___	___	___	___
· published text, book	___	___	___	___	___
Position in the field					
· icon	___	___	___		___
· guest speaker	___	___	___	___	___
Linkages					
· whom they know	___	___	___	___	___
Review experience					
· reviewer/panel member	___	___	___	___	___
Previous grant funding					
· frequency of funding	___	___	___	___	___
· amount of funding	___	___	___	___	___

PRINCIPAL INVESTIGATOR/PROJECT DIRECTOR—FUNDABILITY ANALYSIS WORKSHEET

EXHIBIT 3.2

their field? The information you gather could be useful in helping you select grant-winning partners for a consortium, and in discussing why and how their collaboration is necessary to become a successful grantee. Exhibit 3.3 provides a list of the top 46 institutions by amount of federal research and development expenditures in fiscal

Institution	Amount
Johns Hopkins University	$724,526,000
Stanford University	$332,272,000
University of Washington	$320,784,000
Massachusetts Institute of Technology	$311,396,000
University of Michigan	$296,028,000
University of California at San Diego	$274,860,000
University of California at Los Angeles	$238,919,000
University of Wisconsin at Madison	$233,760,000
University of California at San Francisco	$229,323,000
Harvard University	$222,612,000
University of Pennsylvania	$217,125,000
Columbia University	$212,180,000
Cornell University	$205,521,000
University of Minnesota	$200,149,000
University of Colorado	$192,201,000
University of Southern Colorado	$191,809,000
Yale University	$189,124,000
Washington University (Mo.)	$186,993,000
University of California at Berkeley	$186,349,000
Pennsyslvania State University	$185,206,000
California Institute of Technology	$164,225,000
University of Pittsburgh	$160,833,000
University of Illinois at Urbana-Champaign	$156,366,000
Duke University	$155,894,000
University of North Carolina at Chapel Hill	$153,985,000
University of Arizona	$152,221,000
University of Texas at Austin	$151,954,000
University of Alabama at Birmingham	$150,501,000
Texas A&M University	$145,066,000
University of California at Davis	$123,673,000
Ohio State University	$122,582,000
University of Chicago	$121,683,000
Case Western Reserve University	$120,992,000
University of Rochester	$118,477,000
Georgia Institute of Technology	$112,544,000

TOP INSTITUTIONS IN FEDERAL RESEARCH AND DEVELOPMENT EXPENDITURES, FISCAL 1997

EXHIBIT 3.3

year 1997 (*Chronicle of Higher Education*, August 27, 1999). By comparing your institution to the leaders, you can develop an estimate of your institution's chances of making this list. (The entire list can be found on the Internet at http://chronicle.com/weekly/almanac/1999/facts/13money.htm.) Just remember that the list is dynamic and ever-changing, and institutions that are developing their competitive edge are constantly moving up. Just when you reach a level where you are satisfied and believe your grants effort is reaching maximum efficiency, wham, you can be knocked down and overtaken by another institution. (Please note that similar lists of amounts of federal funding by institution can be obtained from individual funding agencies such as NSF, NIH, etc.)

The Institutional Fundability Analysis Worksheet (exhibit 3.4) will further help you determine your potential.

You can better determine your chances of attracting a grant from a particular agency by knowing how many proposals the agency funds. Exhibit 3.5 provides an example of the projections of competing grants at the National Institutes of Health (NIH) at the time of publication of this book (*Health Grants and Contracts Weekly*, February 17, 2000). Many researchers read of increases in appropriations at federal institutes and *assume* that increases in appropriations will translate into more awards and higher success rates, which will equate to improved grants success for them. A closer analysis of exhibit 3.5 reveals that noncompeting grants will take $6.6 billion in 2000 (up from $1 billion in 1999) and grow to $7.7 billion in 2001. This will

---

Comparison ratings can be designated with an "x."

	Profile Successful Institution	Profile Your Institution	No Match	Comparison Some Match	Excellent Match
Institutional Ranking					
Total Money Awarded	_____	_____	_____	_____	_____
Money Awarded in Field	_____	_____	_____	_____	_____
Special Facilities/Equipment					
	_____	_____	_____	_____	_____
	_____	_____	_____	_____	_____
	_____	_____	_____	_____	_____
Institutional Support for Research Projects					
Release Time	_____	_____	_____	_____	_____
Graduate Students	_____	_____	_____	_____	_____
Other Assistance (e.g., lab personnel, etc.)	_____	_____	_____	_____	_____

INSTITUTIONAL FUNDABILITY ANALYSIS WORKSHEET

EXHIBIT 3.4

Institute/ Center	Actual N/C Grants 1999	Estimated N/C Grants 2000	Estimated N/C Grants 2001	Actual Success Rate 1999	Estimated Success Rate 2000	Estimated Success Rate 2001
Cancer	1,157	1,200	1,188	32%	32%	30%
Heart	917	1,066	804	36%	39%	29%
Dental	113	133	116	24%	24%	19%
Diabetes	712	694	712	33%	32%	34%
Neurology	657	687	476	35%	36%	25%
Allergy	544	522	510	34%	32%	31%
General Medicine	1,036	1,001	862	39%	32%	26%
Child Health	412	406	300	30%	27%	20%
Eye	264	291	233	40%	42%	34%
Environment	133	170	180	27%	25%	23%
Aging	396	383	314	28%	22%	17%
Arthritis	193	215	214	24%	25%	24%
Deafness	168	191	139	34%	30%	21%
Mental Health	442	541	461	27%	31%	23%
Drug Abuse	253	254	176	34%	31%	21%
Alcohol	170	162	115	30%	32%	23%
Nursing	39	78	46	14%	24%	14%
Genome	47	42	42	38%	28%	32%
Research Resources	104	49	49	34%	15%	13%
Alternative Medicine	12	31	18	52%	31%	26%
International	40	42	48	39%	26%	27%
Library	59	71	91	N/A	N/A	N/A
AIDS	756	792	643	N/A	N/A	N/A

COMPETING GRANTS AT NIH

EXHIBIT 3.5

impact the unfunded researcher by actually reducing his or her chances of winning a competing award from NIH. Under the current 2001 budget, proposed funds for competing grants would also decline from $2.9 billion to $2.5 billion. In addition, there is pressure in all federal agencies, including NIH, to increase the average size of grant awards, which could also negatively impact the unfunded researcher's chance for funding. For example, the National Science Foundation's (NSF's) average grant size will go from $80,000 to $100,000, but success rates are expected to stay at 31 percent. NIH's average award size is expected to raise to $329,000 in 2000 from $294,000 in 1999, while the 2001 budget calls for a decrease to $321,500. When reviewing exhibit 3.5 again, you will understand why some programs actually show a decrease in success rates, even though appropriations are up.

By looking at your priority areas and checking the projections from those agencies expected to support your institution's increases in grants activity, you can provide your grant seekers with insight into their likely success rates. This information can also be obtained and updated by visiting the agency's Web site and/or contacting its public information officer.

The more detailed information you can gather about the funding source, the better you can assist your prospective grant seekers in estimating their potential. The better able your grant seekers are at estimating their grants potential, the easier your job becomes.

Consider putting an excerpt from this chapter and/or the worksheets on your office's Web site (see Chapter 15) and invite your grant seekers to assess their potential and the institution's. They may want to discuss the results with a representative from your grants office, their department chair, or colleagues.

Assisting your faculty and staff in assessing the competition and developing a profile of the grant winners in their field of interest will affect the position that your grants office holds. Your office can fulfill the role as the grants strategist on campus. If your desire is to make your grants office a more vital, proactive, and an integral part of the institution, assistance in analyzing potential may be a function you and your staff want to place more emphasis on. Developing a short workshop on this topic and using an example of an assessment that you have performed for a faculty member or group would underscore the concept with your potential grant seekers. As part of the workshop you could even provide a demonstration of how to use the Internet to collect the data necessary to analyze potential.

ANALYZING YOUR GRANTS POTENTIAL WITH GOVERNMENT CONTRACTS

There are several additional variables to consider when assessing your researchers' and institution's ability to successfully attract government contracts.

1. The amount of money available for contracts is more difficult to determine than for grants. Contracts from federal agencies are estimated at two to three times the potential of grants. Contract funds from Congress are allowed to be accounted for differently. For example, rolling over federal agency funds allocated for contracts is considerably easier than rolling over federal agency funds allocated for grants. As a case in point, contracts funds from the Department of Defense may be rolled over for several years while the agency decides exactly what it wants. Because any one contract may seek to utilize the most current state of the art technology, the scope of work may keep shifting.

2. The contracts mechanism is inherently different from the grants mechanism, and most faculty have not had this difference explained to them in a way that can be incorporated into their research strategy. Remind the faculty and staff in a newsletter or on your Web site (see chapter 15) that, in general,

   • government grants are federal and state mechanisms wherein the area the grantor seeks to impact is defined, but the strategy, project, or plan is left to the grant seeker to design and convince the reviewers and federal staff that their plan will bring about the desired change; and that

   • government contracts are federal and state mechanisms that allow researchers to submit a bid to develop what the government agency has already decided that it wants—creativity may be limited because the Request for Proposals (RFP) or the Request for Quotes (RFQ) may be very specific.

To assess your faculty and institution's potential to be successful in attracting government contract funds, apply the same general techniques as in a grants potential assessment. Assess both your faculty and your institution and ask questions such as the following:

- Who are the successful contractors?
- What are their credentials?
- What types of consortia, partnerships, and subcontracts exist?
- Who are the sponsoring institutions?
- Where are they located?
- Are they in close proximity to government facilities?
- What is their position in the field?
- What resources did the sponsoring institutions include in their successful attempts to secure funding?
- How do our facilities and equipment compare to theirs?
- What type of infrastructure do they have compared to ours?

You can uncover the answers to these questions by researching those agencies that your database suggests may be a good match to you researcher's interests and by talking with the program and project officers from those agencies.

As with grants, the data on contracts are always based on last year's and yesterday's projects. However, your research will reveal a track record of contract winners. It is possible to become a member of this meritorious group, but it is hard work. The secret is to host a discussion between your researcher and the contractor to talk about the benefits of your person's research. If the government agency wants your potential product, they may overlook any researcher or institution shortcomings.

A SPIN search once suggested that one of my researchers should consider talking to the Department of Defense's (DOD's) contracts officer about his (my researcher's) work on mathematical decision-making models. My grants office helped the researcher by getting an appointment for him with DOD in Washington, D.C. and underwriting his travel. As it turned out, the contracts officer was so excited about my researcher's project that he (the contracts officer) wrote an entire new RFP, and based it on the experience of the researcher and the facilities at our institution. This made perfectly good sense; how can a contracts officer really request a proposal until he or she knows what may be possible for tomorrow's research project?

To really understand and benefit from the assessment of potential strategy, your researchers must know who is doing what in his or her field of interest. It takes more than desire and a great idea to get funded. By teaching your faculty and staff to research their contracts potential, you are also setting them up for the successful utilization of your grant office's resources, and saving yourself from handling proposals that are destined to be rejected. My rule of thumb has always been the following: If your researcher has not seen the contracts officer, obtained the criteria that successful contractors should meet, and received feedback on how his or her approach meets or exceeds the agency's needs, then he or she, and you, should save yourselves the effort.

ANALYZING YOUR GRANTS POTENTIAL WITH FOUNDATIONS

Private foundations may provide a degree of hope for the smaller or less well-known institution and PI or PD. This may be the avenue to take if you are looking for a small grant to develop preliminary data or to fund a small model project. An analysis of 990-ARs (Internal Revenue Service forms) shows that many foundations fund colleges and universities with appealing projects or unique solutions with little regard for institutional image and/ or stature. A sincere commitment to solving a problem and a record of integrity can carry an institution a long way.

However, do not be too idealistic or confident. A recent survey of foundations revealed that a relatively large share of grants (29.2 percent) are awarded on a continuing basis. While this number demonstrates willingness among foundations to assist recipients in assuring longevity for their programs and services, it may also indicate that funders feel more comfortable giving more of their money to known entities and past grantees, making it difficult for the new grantee to enter the marketplace.

Use the computer-based research services available at your institution or the Foundation Center Library's regional collection to identify several sources that have funded projects in your faculty members' fields of interest. (To locate your closest regional collection, visit http://fdncenter.org/collections/index.html.)

Review the list of past grantees carefully. Who were the chosen institutions? Will you look good to the funding source? A recent survey of grants made by foundations demonstrated the importance of performing a survey of funded projects by geographic location of the grantee. Organizations located in five states (California, the District of Columbia, New York, Pennsylvania, and Texas) received 46.5 percent of the total funds awarded to U.S. recipients.

It is important to discuss your grants potential with your administration to determine how to handle your faculty's access to the foundation and corporate marketplace. Review the data on foundation grants for more than $10,000 in the Foundation Center's *Foundation Grants Index*. Use your grant seekers' keywords to compare their interests with the funding interests of foundations. This information will be very valuable when you discuss your faculty's potential in this marketplace with your administration and especially your institution's development office.

The following materials are recommended to assist your faculty and staff in objectively analyzing their grants readiness: the Winning Grants Self-Assessment Worksheet (exhibit 3.6), the Grant Winner Worksheet (exhibit 3.7), the Winning Grants Time Line (exhibit 3.8), the Winning Grants Systematic Approach Worksheet (exhibit 3.9), and the Winning Grants Plan for Improvement (exhibit 3.10).

The Self-Assessment and Grant Winner Worksheets (exhibits 3.6 and 3.7) are designed to provide faculty and staff with a method to assess their position in the field and to allow them to develop insight into their productivity in terms of those indexes of involvement most frequently used in the grants/research field. By using these materials, individuals can analyze their own fundability.

You can use the results of this analysis in a variety of ways. One way is to compare your project personnel with those who worked on a previously funded grant. If your grants office has obtained a copy of a funded proposal, your prospective grant seeker may compare his or her fundability with that of the successful project director or principal investigator through

1. Area(s) of thesis and dissertation:

2. People I studied under (advisers, professors, thesis/dissertation committee members, etc.) in graduate school:

3. Areas of interest other than thesis and/or dissertation areas (i.e., new areas of interest):

4. Key factors that will assist me in developing a plan to become more involved in the grants area and research (e.g., changes in lifestyle, changes in work style, shifting of time commitments, reallocation of priorities):

5. Major factors that will keep me from becoming more involved in the grants area and research:

WINNING GRANTS SELF-ASSESSMENT WORKSHEET (MY UNIQUENESSES, STRENGTHS, AND AREAS TO IMPROVE)

EXHIBIT 3.6

an analysis of the biographical sketch or curriculum vita in the funded proposal. This process will reveal your prospective grant winner's strengths and weaknesses. The comparison of key project personnel may lead the project director to secure letters of endorsement or develop arrangements with other investigators to build staff fundability.

The two self-assessment worksheets—Winning Grants Self-Assessment Worksheet (exhibit 3.6) and the Grant Winner Worksheet (exhibit 3.7)—can also be used to begin the process of setting personal goals. As mentioned before, a good idea is not enough to get a grant. Researchers must also publish, present papers, attend meetings, and so on. These exercises help develop an awareness of the competitive grants game.

The Winning Grants Self-Assessment Worksheet (exhibit 3.6) helps users develop insight into their areas of past research, new areas of interest, and lifestyle and to determine how these

1. Number of research articles I have read within the last two years

_____0 _____1-5 _____6-10 _____11-15 _____16-20 _____21 plus

estimate _____

2. Number of conferences and/or major meetings I have attended within the last two years

_____local _____state _____ regional _____national

3. Number of articles I have submitted for publication within the last two years

_____0 _____ 1-5 _____ 6-10 _____ 11 plus estimate _____

4. Number of articles I have had published within the last two years

_____0 _____1-5 _____ 6-10 _____11 plus estimate _____

5. Number of books I have had published within the last five years _____

6. Number of chapters I have contributed to textbooks within the last five years

_____

7. Number of presentations I have made within the last two years

_____ local _____ state _____ regional _____ national

8. Postdoctoral work I have completed within the last five years

_____

9. Number of fellowships, stipends, and sabbaticals I applied for/received within the last five years

fellowships: applied _____   received _____
stipends: applied _____   received _____
sabbaticals: applied _____   received _____

10. Number of grants I obtained funding for within the last two years

_____ 0 _____1-5 _____ 6-10 _____11-15 _____ 16-20 _____ 21 plus

estimate _____

11. Number of consortium arrangements (grant related) I have been involved in within the last two years

_____ 0 _____1-5 _____ 6-10 _____11 plus estimate _____

GRANT WINNER WORKSHEET

EXHIBIT 3.7

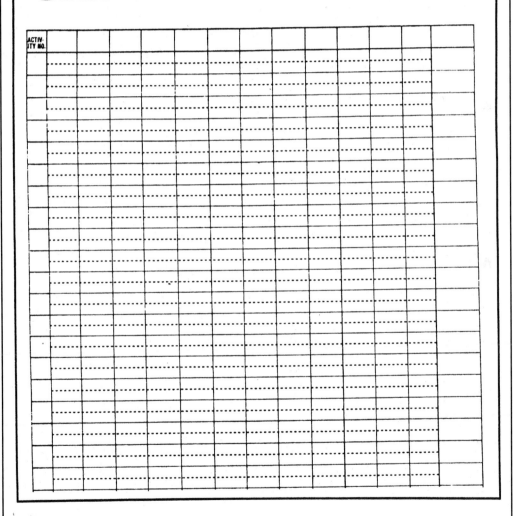

WINNING GRANTS:

David G. Bauer Associates, Inc.

TIME LINE

WINNING GRANTS TIME LINE

EXHIBIT 3.8

Systematic Approach Worksheet
David G. Bauer Associates, Inc.

Objectives/Activities	Action Steps	Resources Needed	Key Personnel Needed

WINNING GRANTS SYSTEMATIC APPROACH WORKSHEET

EXHIBIT 3.9

1. Review the Winning Grants Self-Assessment Worksheet. If you are still interested in your dissertation area or other areas of past work, how can you update your knowledge of the field(s)? For example, what can you read to bring you up-to-date?

2. Make a list of past advisers, dissertation committee members, mentors, and professors who worked with you or who continued research or interest in your area of study. Contact them through your former department, alumni office, or colleagues. Review databases to uncover research articles and research in progress by these individuals. List any current interest areas of yours that relate to those uncovered in your search.

3. If you are no longer interested in the specific area of your past work, what are your new areas of interest? If you are unsure, what can you do to determine areas of interest? For example, brainstorm possible fields to study, list potential research ideas and questions of interest, etc.

4. Develop a plan to address each of the items on the Grant Winner Worksheet. How will you increase your participation in each of the activities? Put your grant winner's action plan on a self-learning contract.

WINNING GRANTS PLAN FOR IMPROVEMENT

EXHIBIT 3.10

factors are related to grants competitiveness. Questions one through three are designed to identify those individuals with whom the proposed grant seeker studied. This review can also include fellow students and others who have since become involved in research.

Questions 4 and 5 deal with the proposed researcher's professional and personal lifestyle. Research requires time, including time to read the relevant literature and time for the other factors noted on the worksheet. Because the would-be grant seeker typically has not developed the lifestyle and time-management skills of a successful grant seeker, he or she must determine what personal decisions and forces in his or her life impede progress.

The Winning Grants Plan for Improvement (exhibit 3.10) ties the previous two assessment tools together by asking the participants to list the "action steps" they will take as a result of their self-analysis. In some of my seminars, I copy the Winning Grants Systematic Approach Worksheet (exhibit 3.9) on two-part carbonless paper. I carefully review questions 1 through 3 and encourage workshop participants to review the other self-analysis tools. In this way they can determine the personal objectives and the action steps that they need to take to increase their chances of being funded.

By analyzing the resources needed, participants can also calculate the cost of their personal development. Those who have made it their objective to receive funding or a certain score by reviewers can develop actions steps such as

- getting to the office one hour earlier for one year and using the extra time to read X number of research articles in their grants field,
- joining the appropriate professional organizations and attending regional and national meetings,
- developing a grants-review committee to examine past proposals in an area and brainstorming funding strategies, and
- searching through the literature to determine the status of those individuals they studied with in terms of their publications and grants they've received.

The Winning Grants Time Line (exhibit 3.8) encourages individuals to list their activities or action steps and draw them on a time line that represents when the activity will begin and end. Calendar months are listed in the top of the twelve columns; the first column represents the month that the individual is performing this exercise.

If the Winning Grants Systematic Approach Worksheet (exhibit 3.9) has been completed on carbonless paper, you can encourage the participants to place one copy in an envelope, seal it, and address it to themselves. Your grants office will then mail a copy to each participant after an agreed-upon period. I return self-made agreements after sixty or ninety days. This concept, known as a *self-learning contract*, is designed to encourage the self-change and self-direction that your staff must undergo to be successful researchers.

Review the survey questions (exhibit 3.11) to determine which questions will best uncover feedback on the success of your grants system. Complete the Grants Office Inventory (exhibit 3.12) to move you one step closer to developing your plan.

1. Are your institution's priorities in seeking external funding (grants and contracts) articulated clearly?

_____ Yes   _____ No

2. Are your priorities and interests in seeking external funding clearly defined?

_____ Yes   _____ No

3. Have you researched, identified, and analyzed your competition in attracting external funding in your area of interest?

_____ Yes   _____ No

4. Has the grants office provided you with activities and/or materials to help you analyze your fundability?

_____ Yes   _____ No

a. If yes, how helpful have these activities and/or materials been?

___ Of Little Value   ___ Somewhat Helpful   ___ Very Helpful

b. If no, do you think such activities and/or materials would be of value to you?

___ Yes   ___ No   ___ Don't Know

5. How would you rate your institution's support for your research/project in comparison to the support given to your competition?

___ Inadequate ___ Adequate   ___ More Than Adequate ___ Don't Know

SURVEY QUESTIONS—MEASURING THE SUCCESS OF YOUR GRANTS SYSTEM

EXHIBIT 3.11

For Each Activity/Item listed, Check Status

Activity/Item	Reviewed, Appropriate Part of Grants Office	Reviewed, Appropriate Part of Other Office (List)	Reviewed, Not Applicable	Reviewed, Inappropriate Needs Action	Non-existent, Needs Action
1. List of institutional priorities					
2. List of priorities of the grants office					
3. Criteria to evaluate the functions of the grants office					
4. Activities/materials to assist staff in analyzing "fundability"					

Complete this Section for Each Activity/Item Needing Action

What Needs to be Accomplished?	By Whom? (Office/Person)	By When? (Time Frame)	Resources Required—Personnel, Supplies, Equipment, Programming, etc.	Estimated Costs

GRANTS OFFICE INVENTORY—MEASURING THE SUCCESS OF YOUR GRANTS SYSTEM

EXHIBIT 3.12

CHAPTER 4

Developing and Evaluating a Preproposal Review System

Most proposal-generating nonprofit organizations have a proposal sign-off procedure (see chapter 10) to ensure that all responsible administrators are aware of the commitments and obligations that they will have to take on if the proposal is accepted and the funds are granted. Therefore, it is quite surprising to find that many of these same organizations either do not have or do not effectively use a preproposal sign-on system that requires the administration to approve all proposal concepts in advance and indicate, in writing, any special conditions that must be met for final approval.

The theoretical basis for providing faculty and staff with a system that provides feedback on administrative concerns relative to investment in a proposed project is as simple to understand as it is difficult to implement. This book's previous analogy to the corporate world of automobile production can be applied here. Would an automobile manufacturer allow an engineer to talk to customers about designing and producing a new car before having some idea of the company's support for the venture? Absolutely not. In fact, in the corporate world such an idea would be ludicrous. It would not be tolerated on an occasional basis, let alone as a standard operating procedure. Corporate decisions to proceed on new ventures are made only after serious evaluation and planning. For example, the manufacturing of the Saturn car was meticulously planned by corporate people for years before the first Saturn actually came off the production line.

The bottom line is that the 5 million-plus profit-making corporations in the United States would never allow individuals representing them to interest a potential buyer in a product that may not even be produced by the corporation. Yet, in the not-for-profit grants field, individuals contact funders without the knowledge of the organization and attempt to interest them in supporting (buying) a project that has not been approved by the organization.

In the academic world, a principal investigator or project director often contacts potential grantors, discusses approaches, and develops proposals for hundreds of thousands of
dollars with little or no input from his or her department chair, dean, provost, etc. Typically,
university administrators are asked to sign proposal sign-on sheets on the spot while the
clock ticks down to the electronic submittal deadline or the Federal Express person paces in
the doorway. Often, the administrator does not have time to read the sign-off sheet or to
discuss

- the matching or in-kind contributions required in the proposal,
- release time for the faculty involved in the project,
- office space for added personnel,
- required lab space,
- existing equipment use, or
- new equipment and maintenance agreements.

This is not surprising considering the many responsibilities of the university administrator. The traditional role of the department chair is a far cry from that of a front line
corporate administrator. The chair's job is to keep the wheels of higher education rolling no
matter what, and in so doing, he or she has many issues to deal with, including new courses,
programs, and degrees; staffing concerns; and the procurement of new equipment and
resources, etc. With all of this on his or her plate, it is understandable why the chair would
sign on to a proposal with little review or anticipation of consequences. Looking at it from
the chair's point of view, the proposal might not be funded anyway, and if it is, he or she
could always object later on before the grant is finalized!

Irrespective of whether the system places unfair and unrealistic expectations on department chairs, having a proposal sign-off procedure with no sign-on component or an
ineffective sign-on component is analogous to having an airport with strict landing requirements and rules but no take-off regulations. The organization is letting anyone represent it
in grant seeking while having little or no control or knowledge of the grant-seeking
overtures.

If you already have a preproposal review system in place or if you would like to initiate
one, take the time to identify the forces involved in the sign-on dilemma. Consider the
following loops and how they could be adapted to your system, and then solicit feedback
from your faculty members and administrators.

PREPROPOSAL REVIEW SYSTEM FEEDBACK SURVEY

In order to determine the readiness of your grant seekers and administrators to endorse,
accept, and utilize your preproposal review or sign-on system, it will be necessary to educate
the users regarding the benefits of the system. The survey questions at the end of this
chapter (exhibit 4.2) will give you an idea of perceptions and levels of readiness, and they
will help you uncover areas that may need more explanation to ensure acceptance and
efficient use of your preproposal system.

Use some or all of the questions to develop your surveys and add your own questions as
needed. Different surveys should be developed for each of the audiences—one for faculty
members (researchers and other proposal writers) and one for administrators (especially

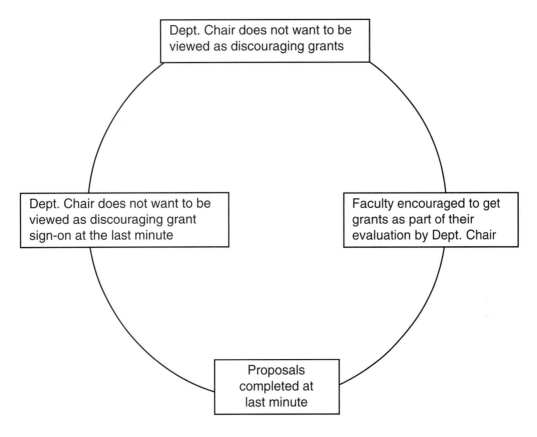

Dept. Chair does not want to be viewed as discouraging grants

Dept. Chair does not want to be viewed as discouraging grant sign-on at the last minute

Faculty encouraged to get grants as part of their evaluation by Dept. Chair

Proposals completed at last minute

department chairs). You can survey entire distinct populations or randomly choose survey respondents from each group. In addition, the survey instruments can be used in a variety of ways. You may try them in both pre- and postproposal settings so that you can develop insight into whether the factors that underlie the need for this system are perceived to be problems at your institution as a whole or only in certain departments, colleges or programs. You may find that a preproposal review system is relevant only to those who are experiencing problems that such a system could correct, and that the implementation of a college- or university-wide system may not be appropriate. You be the judge. But remember, if you do not periodically request feedback, you will not know if a problem exists or when it becomes an issue.

If you do not have a preproposal review system in place, you may be reluctant to initiate one after discovering the problems such a system can pose. In addition, you may feel that asking grant seekers to participate in another procedure would be a waste of time; because many cannot even get their completed proposals signed off in a timely fashion. Or you may be hesitant to ask grant seekers who are investing their "spare" time in the grants pursuit to complete another form. However, before you make your decision, remember that a successfully operating preproposal (sign-on) review system has several advantages.

1. It coordinates the grant seeker's initial interest in seeking funds with that of the grants office and fosters a proactive grants system that reinforces forethought and an organized grants effort. This organized effort contrasts with the last-minute proposal-development efforts produced when reacting to deadlines only.

2. It reduces the chances that several grant seekers from your organization will contact a funder with no knowledge of the others' efforts. An organization's image as a well-managed and responsible prospective grantee is damaged when the funding source is subject to several unorganized and haphazard contacts from the organization that indicate that the "grants homework" on the funding source has not been done. Although entrepreneurial grant seekers may be well intentioned, they can make serious mistakes that can result in a poor image of your institution and lessen your future credibility with funders.

In a case in point, a college president and his grants person were caught off guard when visiting a foundation to explain a major college grants initiative. The foundation director remarked that he was very interested in an idea proposed by Professor Goodwriter from their college. When the president looked surprised and confused, the foundation director explained that Professor Goodwriter had just left his office one hour ago. The director was quite surprised that the professor, the president, and the grants person had not traveled the 250 miles to his office together. The president, demonstrating superior presidential qualities, remarked, "You mean Professor Goodwriter, who *used* to be at my institution?" But in spite of the humor, the damage had already been done. Most likely, the foundation director had already begun to question the institution's fiscal controls and the integrity of its grant-seeking system.

A preproposal review system will provide "traffic control," so that funding sources receive a clear, organized image of your organization's management system and grant-seeking priorities.

3. Preproposal review will ensure the efficient use of your staff's time. The requirement that a grant seeker must seek approval before approaching prospective funding sources guarantees that he or she will not waste time pursuing a funding source or a proposal idea that would not receive your institution's final approval. In one instance, I worked extensively with three professors on a health-related training grant. I checked with administrative officials verbally over one part of the project that might evoke controversy and received a tentative approval. When the proposal was circulated for final approval and signature (sign-off), it was decided that it might encourage other proposal writers to use a similar approach, and while the proposal was not necessarily improper, it could not be submitted. The proposal was already at the print shop. Fifteen copies had partially been produced, and the four of us had spent many hours working on it. It would be a long time before I would see another proposal from those professors.

The fact that I did not have anything in writing and that the administrative officials developed selective amnesia and did not recall my original conversation persuaded me to develop a preproposal review system.

4. A preproposal review system allows the institution to evaluate the relationship between its mission and the proposed grant. Because every grant requires the allocation of space and a commitment by the staff, it is imperative to address how the institution's mission will be met by the proposed activity. Even if the proposed project is *totally* supported by the funder, the question of whether it is appropriate in meeting the mission must still be addressed. The process of preproposal review is even more crucial if the proposal calls for matching funds or in-kind contributions.

Grants can actually subvert the mission and move an institution away from its goals and objectives. The temptation of grant seekers to "go for the gold" at the expense of an organization's mission has steered many not-for-profit organizations away from their purpose and caused confusion in the board and staff.

Ideally, preproposal review is insurance that final sign-off, allocation of grants-office support, and approval for matching funds will be forthcoming.

5. Preproposal review may also include an assessment of the quality of the proposed project. A committee may be formed to review the idea that the proposal is based upon and offer suggestions for improvement and alternatives for locating and securing funds. This preliminary review can then be followed by a more extensive review when the proposal is fully developed and the funding source identified.

You may use the following Preproposal Review Form (exhibit 4.1), or a variation of it, to implement a preproposal review procedure or to help you improve an existing one. The form should be tailored to meet your institution's needs. For example, more space could be added for outlining the solution, protocol, or approach to the problem. You can even use the form as a cover sheet, briefly explaining the project, and attach another page describing the protocol.

The purpose of the form is to obtain a "license" to "hunt" for funding sources. It is your administration's responsibility to make comments in the left-hand margin of the form. This is the administration's opportunity to outline concerns or conditions that the grant seeker must address or be aware of to be eligible for final review and sign-off.

This form should be circulated to the administrators who may have valuable advice or who must sign off before submittal. The section at the bottom of the form designates those projects that will not be endorsed under any circumstances (rejected) and those that must meet certain conditions before they will receive endorsement (e.g., space is a problem, so the project must be done out of the facility).

This sheet should then be returned to the prospective grant seeker so that he or she will be aware of any and all limiting conditions that must be dealt with in the grant-seeking process.

The reviewing administrator in your institution should receive a copy of this form with the final sign-off sheet so that he or she can see the original comments. Although meeting the considerations that were originally identified should result in official sign-off and endorsements, it is important to remind grant seekers that special circumstances may cause a proposal that was originally approved to not receive final sign-off.

Completing exhibit 4.3 will help you determine what you need to accomplish to initiate or improve your preproposal review system.

This form is designed to give the potential proposal writer insight into the administration's feelings concerning the appropriateness of this project, the amount and type of resources that will be committed to it, and an indication of any areas that will need to be addressed to secure final signature at the time of submittal.

Comments

Problem Area:

Solution:

Relationship of Proposal to Mission/Purpose

Project Director(s):
Duration of Project:
Funding Sources to be Approached:

Non-personnel Resources Needed:
  Equipment:
  Supplies:
  Facilities/Space:
  Other:

Personnel Resources Needed:
Position   % of Time   Salary/Wages/Fringes

Matching Requirements/In-Kind Contributions
  Money:
  Staff:
  Space:
  Equipment:

TOTAL MATCHING/IN-KIND CONTRIBUTION:
TOTAL AMOUNT REQUESTED FROM FUNDING SOURCE:

( )   ACCEPT proposal as outlined.
( )   ACCEPT WITH RESERVATIONS. Conditions must be met as listed in
       Comments section.
( )   REJECT. Idea is unacceptable and will not be supported under any
       circumstances.

Name of Reviewing Official:
Signature of Reviewing Official:
Date:

PREPROPOSAL REVIEW FORM

EXHIBIT 4.1

Faculty/Staff Survey Questions

1. Please indicate which of the following areas, if any, you believe you can obtain committment for from your supervisor/department chair:

_____   release time for you to carry out your proposed project/research
_____   matching funds for in-kind contributions to support your project
_____   access to special equipment, computers, and/or software required by your project
_____   staff required by your project (graduate students, lab assistants, secretarial support, etc.)

Department Chair/Supervisor Survey Questions

1. Please rate the following as they relate to your allocation of resources to grant proposals:

• Releasing faculty from other responsibilities (such as teaching and advising) to work on funded grants
   ____no problem ____little problem ____medium problem ____big problem

• Being able to calculate and commit to providing matching funds and in-kind contributions to support grant-related projects
   ____no problem ____little problem ____medium problem ____big problem

• Providing access to special equipment, computers, and/or software for funded projects
   ____no problem ____little problem ____medium problem ____big problem

• Providing staff for funded projects (graduate students, lab assistants, secretarial support, etc.)
   ____no problem ____little problem ____medium problem ____big problem

• Providing space for grant-related staff, lab facilities, etc.
   ____no problem ____little problem ____medium problem ____big problem

2. In the space provided, please list the most important factors related to problems in the allocation of the resources outlined above.

_____
_____
_____
_____

SURVEY QUESTIONS—DEVELOPING AND EVALUATING A PREPROPOSAL REVIEW SYSTEM

EXHIBIT 4.2

For Each Activity/Item listed, Check Status:

Activity/Item	Reviewed, Appropriate Part of Grants Office	Reviewed, Appropriate Part of Other Office (List)	Reviewed, Not Applicable	Reviewed, Inappropriate Needs Action	Non-existent, Needs Action
1. Preproposal review system • "sign-on" sheet or preproposal review • preproposal review committee					

Complete this Section for Each Activity/Item Needing Action:

What Needs to be Accomplished?	By Whom? (Office/Person)	By When? (Time Frame)	Resources Required—Personnel, Supplies, Equipment, Programming, etc.	Estimated Costs

GRANTS OFFICE INVENTORY—DEVELOPING AND EVALUATING A PREPROPOSAL REVIEW SYSTEM

EXHIBIT 4.3

CHAPTER 5

Increasing Faculty and Staff Interest in Proposal Development and Grant Involvement

Why do individuals write grants? What motivates your institution's faculty and staff to get involved in the hassle of proposal preparation? When asked how I have kept my interest in grants and contract procurement over the past thirty years, I have to stop and think. I have always been motivated by the grants opportunity. The prospect of using someone else's money to do what I've always wanted to do, or to meet my organization's needs, was real enough for me to pursue grants. However, not everyone views the opportunity to become involved in grant seeking with the same enthusiasm, and even I realize that my grants record's highs and lows have not always been related to changes in the marketplace. On some occasions, my particular situation or grants environment affected my productivity.

I asked the participants in one of my Winning Grants seminars to complete the following sentence: "When I hear the word *grants* I think of _." The words used to complete the sentence included *rushing, deadlines, panic, chaos, burning the midnight oil, heart attacks, audits,* and *rules*. With this negative image of the grants process, it is a wonder that individuals become involved in this area.

When grant involvement is included in part of an individual's job description or is required for tenure, grant-seeking activities can be understood. But what about the thousands of individuals who get involved in grant seeking without being "forced" to? What motivates these people?

Grants administrators often tell me that they are not concerned with what motivates the grant seeker, because their job is to administer grant funds, not procure them. However, I point out that there would be no funds to administer if proposal initiators decided not to get involved in the highly competitive grants system. The grants system is dependent upon individuals who get involved, and everyone involved in the support of this system should be sensitive to the reasons why their grant seekers perform as they do. By examining the psychological theories of Abraham Maslow and Frederick Herzberg and applying these theories to grant involvement, you may be able to assist your grants office in developing a better understanding of your institution's faculty and staff.

Maslow, in his hierarchy of needs theory, might say that individuals become involved in grants because

- their security is threatened;
- they have a need for social approval, to belong to a group, and to feel they are a part of a greater good;
- they desire esteem, self-respect, and the respect of others; and
- they desire the maximum development of self and to achieve their highest potential (self-actualization).

Grant writing may result when an individual's security is threatened. In this instance, possible deprivation may move the individual to action. For example, when grants success is an employment requirement, faculty and staff members may pursue grant opportunities to keep their jobs, and/or to increase their chances of tenure.

Our need for social approval, to belong to a group, and to feel that we are part of a greater good may also spur some of us to become involved in the extra work of proposal preparation. The growth in the number of nonprofit groups, and the hours that are volunteered to their causes attest to the fact that most individuals in the United States reach this level. This would explain some of the so-called selfless work done for the good of others. The desire to belong to a cause or group is also a strong motivator, and not-for-profit organizations build upon this desire by providing a focus to help the less fortunate and/or joining together to expand understanding and knowledge in a particular field. Both the motivation for social approval and the desire to serve others lead to a greater good while satisfying the need to belong.

The desire for esteem, self-respect, and the respect of others may also motivate people to produce proposals. This desire for self-esteem may explain why advocates and volunteers become involved in the grant-seeking process and invest large amounts of time with no remuneration. It may also be why faculty and staff who have positions that do not require involvement in grant seeking will invest their time and effort in the process and why the dissemination components of a grant are so important (publishing, speaking engagements at conferences, etc.).

The highest level in Maslow's theory is self-actualization—achieving potential within self, creativity, and the desire for maximum development of self. Few of us reach this level and because life is in a constant state of flux, this level is reached and then lost when an individual has a problem with one of the previously mentioned supporting levels. As much as we might like to think that self-actualization is the level of achievement and the ultimate motivation of most grant writers, the other levels probably have a greater influence on proposal development.

Note that money is not viewed as a motivator in Maslow's theory. Although remuneration can help to fulfill a person's security level, pay is not the reason that most individuals write proposals. More likely, the desire for respect, esteem, and self-actualization may be the key to why people put in the effort.

According to Herzberg's theory of motivation, the extra effort required to produce proposals may be derived from "motivators" or "satisfiers." Based on this explanation of human motivation, five environmental or "hygiene" factors must be provided for in the work setting. They include the following: policies and procedures, supervision, salary, interpersonal relations, and hygiene and pleasant working conditions. Individuals must know what is required of them. They must understand the role of supervision and the remuneration policies associated with the different standards of work. In addition, the work setting must allow for interpersonal relations with co-workers and other facilities for bodily needs and functions.

Herzberg explains, however, that meeting these five needs *alone* does not necessarily result in superior performance. These factors act primarily as preventive maintenance. They must be provided for but do not necessarily provide the motivation or the satisfaction that is required to encourage superior performance. The motivators are

- *achievement*—the opportunity to satisfy the need to achieve;
- *recognition*—fulfilling the need to be rewarded through recognition for work;
- *the actual work itself*—the opportunity to be involved in the field or area of work and the addressing or solving of the problem;
- *responsibility*—the opportunity to be responsible for and in control of additional resources; and
- *advancement*—fulfilling the need to move up the organizational ladder.

Examine the willingness of your faculty and staff to become involved in grants based on the motivational factors identified by Maslow and Herzberg. Examine their willingness to perform superlatively.

Please note that neither of these theories pinpoints money as a significant motivator. Furthermore, individuals do the extra work involved in grant seeking even though federal and most state-funded grants do not allow project directors or principal investigators to be paid additional salaries or wages. If the grant requires the time of this key individual, he or she must be released from his or her normal responsibilities. For example, a full-time faculty member who allocates 50 percent of his or her time to a grant must be released of 50 percent of his or her former full-time job responsibilities. In addition, individuals prepare proposals in their spare time because most institutions do not give them release time or free time to do so. Proposal development and the reasons to seek grants clearly lie in areas other than monetary remuneration.

When veteran grant seekers were asked why they seek grants, the responses included the following:

- Grants allow me to explore my areas of interest.
- Grant proposals help to move my institution/department toward its goals.
- Students/clients/the field of knowledge needs the results grants generate, such as equipment, therapies, research findings, etc.
- A funded grant makes me feel important, needed, and powerful.
- I can get things that my institution cannot afford to give me and my colleagues (e.g., equipment, secretarial assistance).
- Grants can lead to publishing, the deliverance of papers at professional meetings, and travel.

What techniques has your institution developed to provide your grant seekers with the components related to superior performance? Review the factors identified with high levels of motivation. Compare your present techniques and those suggested on the following Motivational Assessment Worksheet (exhibit 5.1). Use this worksheet to help you assess and improve your grants environment.

It is important that you validate what you and your staff believe motivates others in your institution to get involved in grants by obtaining your faculty's ideas on the subject. Survey your faculty and staff to get a better picture of their perceptions and to develop feedback concerning the motivational environment of your grants program. Select from questions at the end of this chapter (exhibit 5.2), or use them as a starting point to develop your own survey questions. Complete the Grants Office Inventory (exhibit 5.3) to assist you in developing the portion of your plan related to increasing faculty and staff interest in proposal development and grant involvement.

List the factors that motivate your institution's faculty and staff (social approval, esteem, recognition, achievement, etc.). List the techniques or activities currently used to increase/maintain faculty/staff motivation.

Motivators	**Activities**
_____	_____
_____	_____
_____	_____
_____	_____
_____	_____

Review the following list of techniques and activities useful in increasing faculty/staff motivation. Of these, are there any you are not currently using? If so, place a check mark next to those you will initiate.

_____ Awards Program—grants person of the month, year, etc.

_____ Recognition Program—plaques, stipends, etc.

_____ Public Relations—external recognition through newspaper releases, pictures, publications, conference presentations, etc.

_____ Professional Recognition—recommendation for membership in prestigious professional groups, honorary societies, etc.

_____ Achievement Recognition—increase in status in institution, special parking area, flexible time, special purchasing power, increased budget, acquisition of new or limited-quantity equipment, etc.

MOTIVATIONAL ASSESSMENT WORKSHEET

EXHIBIT 5.1

1. What are the most important factors that predispose you to pursue grant/ contract funding?

2. Rank order the following motivational strategies in terms of how much they appeal to you and how likely they are to increase your grant/contract involvement. (4 being the most appealing, 1 being the least)

_____ Awards Program—grants person of the month, year, etc.
_____ Recognition Program—plaques, stipends, etc.
_____ Public Relations—external recognition through newspaper releases, photos, publications, conference presentations, etc.
_____ Achievement Recognition—increase in status in institution, special parking area, flexible time, special purchasing power, increased budget, acquisition of new or limited-quantity equipment, etc.

3. Does your unit head (department chair) support your grant activity?
___ Not At All   ___ Somewhat   ___ Completely

4. Do your colleagues support your grant activity?
___ Not At All   ___ Somewhat   ___ Completely

5. In your opinion, what factors would need to be present to help those faculty and staff who are not involved in grant seeking get involved? Please check those that apply and add your own ideas to the list.

_____ Department chair's/unit head's emphasis and support of grant seeking
_____ Vision, leadership, and support from dean on grant seeking
_____ Greater support of grant activity from colleagues

_____ _____
_____ _____

6. How would you rate the overall grant-seeking atmosphere in your institution?

___ Excellent   ___ Good   ___ Fair   ___ Poor

7. What additional services could the grants office provide to promote sponsored projects activity?

SURVEY QUESTIONS—INCREASING FACULTY AND STAFF INTEREST IN PROPOSAL DEVELOPMENT AND GRANT INVOLVEMENT

EXHIBIT 5.2

For Each Activity/Item listed, Check Status:

Activity/Item	Reviewed, Appropriate Part of Grants Office	Reviewed, Appropriate Part of Other Office (List)	Reviewed, Not Applicable	Reviewed, Inappropriate Needs Action	Non-existent, Needs Action
1. Techniques/activities designed to increase faculty/staff motivation • award program • recognition program • public relations—external recognition • professional recognition • achievement recognition					

Complete this Section for Each Activity/Item Needing Action:

What Needs to be Accomplished?	By Whom? (Office/Person)	By When? (Time Frame)	Resources Required—Personnel, Supplies, Equipment, Programming, etc.	Estimated Costs

GRANTS OFFICE INVENTORY—INCREASING FACULTY AND STAFF INTEREST IN PROPOSAL DEVELOPMENT AND GRANT INVOLVEMENT

EXHIBIT 5.3

CHAPTER 6

Evaluating and Improving Your Grant Opportunity Research System

The opportunities that your grants office provides to prospective grant seekers are a function of how broadly your grants system defines its role in fostering grant-seeking. Many college and university opportunity systems are confined to narrow definitions based primarily on providing access to potential grantor databases. The more aggressive grants officer not only provides his or her potential proposal developers with the opportunity to locate grantors on a computer-based search system, but also seeks out innovative strategies, partnerships, and consortia to create opportunities for faculty and staff to produce high quality, winning proposals.

As in the other chapters of this book, this chapter will not suggest any one perfect or correct way to operate a grant opportunity research system. Instead, the ideas and activities presented here are aimed at helping you assess your current system and focus on the activities that will further your institution's mission. When you share these ideas and activities with your faculty members, be prepared for comments like, "That's not the way it was at the last college or university where I was," or "We can't do that here." But just remember the quotation by English author Joyce Cary (1888–1957): "It is the tragedy of the world that no one knows what he doesn't know—and the less a man knows, the more sure he is that he knows everything." The fact that your grants office has not already tried the activities explored in this chapter does not mean they should not be considered now and reconsidered as you re-evaluate your system throughout the future.

How do you define "grants opportunity?" More importantly, how does your supervisor and your institution's faculty define it? Ideally, your definition should provide the basis or rationale for the activities your office provides. I suggest a definition that includes creating an environment in which your grant seekers identify potential grantors, are provided opportunities to position themselves with potential grantors, and are able to develop the most fundable ideas and best consortia partners possible to attract grant funding.

For purposes of discussion, my ideas on ways to foster grants opportunities fall into six major categories:

1. computer software programs and Internet-based grantor research systems;
2. other grants and contracts research tools;
3. grants newsletters;
4. strategies for involving grant seekers with funding sources;
5. supporting consortia and subcontract efforts with other colleges, universities, and profit and nonprofit partners; and
6. programs to support grant-seeking opportunities.

(Please note that many of the suggested ideas within each of these categories can be incorporated into your grants office Web site. While the grants office Web site is referred to in this chapter, the development of an effective Web site is covered in detail in chapter 15.)

1. COMPUTER SOFTWARE PROGRAMS AND INTERNET-BASED GRANTOR RESEARCH SYSTEMS

The two most popular grants research systems at colleges and universities are the Sponsored Projects Information System (SPIN) and the Illinois Research Information System (IRIS). Both of these systems provide information on thousands of public and private funding opportunities and offer valuable searching functions using keywords. Another popular research system is GrantSelect, which allows purchasers to subscribe to its entire research grants database or to any of its five special segments including arts and humanities, children and youth, community development, biomedical and health care, and K-12 schools.

In a recent test of these three major databases (SPIN, IRIS, GrantSelect), all three identified the same *major* grantors in the specific fields examined. However, differences between the three were seen in the lists of the other suggested grantors—those that were not considered major, but still significant funders in the specified fields. In order to test the comprehensiveness of your system, request a trial search from the other purveyors.

A small survey conducted with a few colleges and universities revealed that SPIN and IRIS were the general favorites. However, the specific functions of all three of these databases that were judged most useful included the availability of a daily e-mail alert service that notifies grant seekers of any new funding opportunities within their area of interest.

While the searching components of all three of these databases were generally rated as very good by most faculty, a closer examination revealed a few shortcomings related to the use of these and other computer-based search systems. When incorporating computer software and Internet-based research systems, be aware that when left to their own devices, faculty have a tendency to develop and submit one list of key words and never take the time to change their key search terms as their projects and interests change. In addition, many faculty may fail to investigate the suggested funding sources beyond the abbreviated information provided in the database search or e-mail response system. In other words, they will not look at the complete source of information that can be found in publications such as the Catalog of Federal Domestic Assistance (CFDA) and/or agency publications like the NSF Bulletin and the NIH Guide, and end up reducing their ability to uncover hidden agendas and/or develop insightful questions to ask in preproposal contact (see chapter 7). Be sure to build checks and balances into your system to combat such shortcomings.

The following provides more information on the databases already discussed and lists other databases you may wish to investigate based on the results of your evaluation of this area and the feedback you gather. Complete ordering information for each entry can be found in the bibliography. While a few of these resources are free, many of them are quite costly. Therefore, it is imperative that you check with your development or advancement office regarding issues of access to private sources and the databases and research services they subscribe to before purchasing any new databases or research services.

- *The Sponsored Programs Information Network (SPIN)*

  This database of federal and private funding sources for sponsored research and creative activities contains over 11,000 records.

- *Illinois Researcher Information Service (IRIS)*

  The IRIS database of funding opportunities contains records on over 7,700 federal and nonfederal funding opportunities in the sciences, social sciences, arts, and humanities.

- *GrantSelect*

  This database is updated daily and provides information on more than 10,000 funding opportunities in the United States.

- *GrantScape CFDA*

  This is an electronic edition of the Catalog of Federal Domestic Assistance, including the full text of all federal grant programs included in the CFDA.

- *American Association of State Colleges and Universities (AASCU): Office of Federal Programs*

  AASCU is composed of more than 430 public colleges and universities. Their interests are wide-ranged and include listing grant opportunities for members institutions. Their database "GrantSearch" provides a wealth of information on federal sources. However, your institution must be a member of AASCU to access it.

- *Community of Science (COS) Funding Opportunities*

  This database allows the researcher to place his or her keyword profile in an e-mail response system for reviewing updates and new matches. In addition, it allows the researcher to go beyond general program information and develop insight into the program by providing lists of successful grantees and abstracts of successful grants.

- *Computer Retrieval of Information on Scientific Projects (CRISP)*

  Maintained by the Office of Extramural Research at the National Institutes of Health, CRISP is a searchable database of federally funded biomedical research projects conducted at universities, hospitals, and other research institutions. The database provides valuable information on National Institute of Health (NIH) current and past grantees supported by the Department of Health and Human Services. For more information visit http://crisp.cit.nih.gov/.

- *FC Search*

  This is the Foundation Center's database on CD-ROM. It covers over 52,000 foundations and corporate givers and hundreds of grant-making public charities, and includes information on 200,000 grants linked to the largest U.S. funders and an index of more than 200,000 trustees, officers, and donors. It also provides links to over 1,000 grant-maker Web sites.

- *Dialog OnDisc Grants Database*

  This database lists approximately 10,000 grants offered by federal, state, and local governments; corporations; professional associations; and private and community foundations.

- *Federal Assistance Program Retrieval System (FAPRS)*

  The FAPRS provides access to federal domestic assistance program information. All states have FAPRS services available through state, county, and local agencies as well as through federal extension services.

- *Federal Information Exchange (FEDIX)*

  FEDIX is a free online database of federal grant and research opportunities for the education and research communities. Participating federal agencies use FEDIX as an outreach tool to enhance communication with colleges, universities, and other educational and research organizations. FEDIX also offers US Opportunities, a fee-based subscription service of foundation and corporation funding announcements.

- *Congressional Information Service Index (CIS Index)*

  CIS covers congressional publications and legislation from 1970 to date. Hearings, committee prints, House and Senate reports and documents, special publications, Senate executive reports and documents, and public laws are indexed.

- *Agency Web Sites*
  Consider placing links on your Web site (see chapter 15) to the agencies that are the most likely sources of grants for your faculty's projects. For example:
  Department of Education—http://www.ed.gov
  National Science Foundation—http://www.nsf.gov
  National Institutes of Health—http://www.nih.gov
  National Endowment for the Humanities—http://www.neh.fed.us

2. OTHER GRANTS AND CONTRACTS RESEARCH TOOLS

The following is a list and description of common research tools used by many grants offices to provide information on federal, foundation, and corporate grant opportunities. Complete ordering information for each entry can be found in the bibliography.

Please note that, although various agency newsletters, requests for proposals (RFPs), guidelines, and annual reports are not individually listed, many federal agencies and foundations publish such items to inform individuals about the availability of funds, program accomplishments, and so on. These materials are available to the public upon request, and quite often, on the Internet. The Grants Research Tools Worksheet (exhibit 6.1) will help you build a library of research material.

FEDERAL

- *Commerce Business Daily (CBD)*

  This is a government contracts publication that is published five times per week and announces every government Request for Proposal (RFP) that exceeds $25,000, as well as upcoming sales of government surplus. It is available in hard copy or online at http://cbdnet.access.gpo.gov. Most grants offices have a link to the CBD on their Web sites for those researchers who are capable of competing for and attracting federal contracts. Assessing the CBD is particularly useful for researchers who are trying to build their competitive capabilities and want to learn not just about about potential contract opportunities, but also who the contractees are, because one way to break into this marketplace is to subcontract with successful bidders.

- *Catalog of Federal Domestic Assistance (CFDA)*

  The CFDA is an instrumental federal grant-seeking tool. It is the government's most complete listing of federal assistance programs with details on eligibility, application procedures, and deadlines. It is available in hard copy form or online at http://www.gsa.gov/fdac/default.htm. By placing this link to the CFDA on your office's Web site (see chapter 15), you can provide your grant seekers who receive abbreviated announcements of federal grant programs with the ability to go to the primary source to further their research. This database provides the same information as *GrantScape* CFDA but is less user-friendly. However, it is free.

- *Federal Register*

  This is the official news publication for the federal government. It makes public all meetings, announcements of granting programs, regulations, and deadlines. It is available in hard copy or online at http://www.nara.gov/fedreg/.

- *U.S. Government Manual*

  This is the handbook of the government. It describes all federal agencies and provides names of officials. You may access it online at www.access.gop.gov/ or order it in hard copy.

- *Federal Directory*

  Includes names, addresses, and phone numbers of federal government agencies and key personnel.

- *Congressional Record*

  Provides the day-to-day proceedings of the Senate and House of Representatives; includes all written information for the record (all grant program money appropri-

The following materials are basic to a grants office. Check off those items that you have currently available and those that you need to order. For those items that are currently available, list the location, edition, and date of publication. For those items that are also available online, list the appropriate Web site address.

Available	Order	Material/Title	Location	Date/Edition	Online Address
_____	_____	Catalog of Federal Domestic Assistance	_____	_____	www.gsa.gov/ fdac.default.htm
_____	_____	Commerce Business Daily	_____	_____	cbdnet.access. gpo.gov
_____	_____	Federal Register	_____	_____	www.nara.gov/ fedreg/
_____	_____	U.S. Government Manual	_____	_____	www.access.gop. gov/
_____	_____	Federal Directory	_____	_____	
_____	_____	Congressional Record	_____	_____	www.access. gpo.gov/su_docs /aces150.html
_____	_____	Listing of Gov't Depository Libraries	_____ _____	_____ _____	www.access.gpo/ su_docs/ libpro.html
_____	_____	The Foundation Directory	_____	_____	
_____	_____	The Foundation Grants Index	_____	_____	
_____	_____	National Guide to Funding in Higher Education	_____	_____	
_____	_____	Corporate Foundation Profiles			
_____	_____	National Directory of Corporate Giving	_____	_____	
_____	_____	Annual Survey of Corporate Contributions	_____	_____	
_____	_____	Dun and Bradstreet's Million Dollar Directory	_____	_____	
_____	_____	Standard and Poor's Register of Corpora- tions, Directors and Executives	_____	_____	
_____	_____	Taft Corporate Giving Directory	_____	_____	

GRANTS RESEARCH TOOLS WORKSHEET

EXHIBIT 6.1

ated by Congress). You may access it online at http://www.access.gpo.gov/su_docs/aces/aces150.html.

- *Listing of Government Depository Libraries*

  This lists locations of public and university libraries that allow free access to government publications. Locate a library in your area by visiting http://www.access.gpo/su_docs/libpro.html on the Internet.

Foundation

All of the foundation resources and many of the corporate resources listed are available from the Foundation Center. Visit their web site at http://www.fdncenter.org or call (800)424-9836 or (212)807-3690 for more in-depth information and current pricing.

- *The Foundation Directory*—Now available in print version, on CD-ROM and online, the 2000 edition provides information on more than 10,000 foundations that hold assets of $3,000,000-plus or distribute $200,000 or more in grants each year. The CD-ROM and online versions also provide links to nearly to 600 foundation Web sites.
- *The Foundation Grants Index*—Provides information on recent grant-maker awards. The 2000 edition covers the grant-making programs of over 1,000 of the largest independent, corporate, and community foundations in the U.S. and features over 97,000 grant descriptions in all. By reviewing the Index, you can locate grant makers that have funded projects within your researchers' specific fields, discover foundations that favor your geographic area, and target foundations that made grants to institutions similar to your own.
- *National Guide to Funding in Higher Education*—The fifth edition provides facts on over 5,200 foundations, corporate direct giving, and public charities, each with a history of awarding grant dollars to higher education projects and institutions. It also provides over 15,000 descriptions of recently awarded grants to demonstrate the foundations' proven giving interests and has a range of indexes to help you target funders by specific program areas favored and geographical preferences.

Corporate

- *Corporate Foundation Profiles*—Published by the Foundation Center, the 11th edition provides detailed information on 195 of the largest corporate foundations in the U.S.
- *National Directory of Corporate Giving*—The sixth edition of this Foundation Center publication provides information on 1,900 corporate foundations and an additional 1,000-plus direct giving programs.
- *Annual Survey of Corporate Contributions*—This annual survey includes an analysis of beneficiaries of corporate support but does not list individual firms and specific recipients.
- *Dun and Bradstreet's Million Dollar Directory*—This five-volume directory lists divisions, subsidiaries, and affiliates of thousands of companies with addresses, telephone numbers, key persons, employees, etc.

- *Standard and Poor's Register of Corporations, Directors and Executives*—Available in both print and electronic versions, this three-volume annual register provides up-to-date rosters of over 500,000 executives from 75,000 nationally known corporations and includes names, titles, and business affiliations.
- *Taft Corporate Giving Directory*—This directory provides detailed entries on 1,000 company-sponsored foundations and includes nine indexes.

3. GRANTS NEWSLETTERS

A grants newsletter should serve many purposes on a college/university campuses. Besides providing a visible testimony that the grants office is alive and well, it should also keep the faculty and staff aware of the institution's progress toward meeting its mission while also serving to

- increase awareness and interest in grants;
- reinforce successful grant-seeking techniques (e.g., comment on how a preproposal contact was made);
- promote projects that have multiple area or division interests (e.g., announce that Sarah Jones is interested in a project and is looking for a co-investigator from the area);
- increase knowledge of the general grants marketplace (e.g., publish a brief summary of articles or research on corporate philanthropy in the local area);
- develop sensitivity concerning the success rate of awarded versus rejected proposals (advertise the monthly percentage of success);
- promote grants tips and successful techniques; and
- encourage staff to become peer reviewers.

Updating and improving your newsletter entails more than putting it on your Web site for easy access (see chapter 15). For instance, when your faculty has multiple areas of interest, your objectives may be better achieved by producing several shorter, tailored newsletters than one generic newsletter. A generic newsletter that goes to the entire institution forces grant seekers to read about many funding sources before finding something that suits them. Even if the newsletter is online, having to look through the whole thing can result in a waning of interest and an increase in the likelihood that the newsletter will be ignored. With electronic and technological advances, each of your institution's areas of interest, programs, departments, or divisions could receive their own special online newsletter. However, you may use the same cover page on each newsletter to develop the overall grants "spirit" of the institution. This cover page should be used for brief updates on new awards, and pictures of projects and staffs can also be used to highlight accomplishments, presentations, new equipment, and other improvements made possible by the institution's grants efforts.

Ideally, grants newsletters should meet a range of needs including increased grants activity. While the visibility and public relations value of a grants newsletter is of some value, the expenses associated with it must be examined in relationship to the results it brings about. Set up a feedback loop to determine who your newsletter assists, how it assists them, and how it assists your office to reach its objectives.

4. STRATEGIES FOR INVOLVING GRANT SEEKERS WITH FUNDING SOURCES

Early in my career as a grants administrator, I tried to involve my grant seekers with potential funding sources. The grantors themselves suggested ways to get the faculty involved at the grass roots level and many program officers welcomed the opportunity to interact with potential grantees early on in the proposal-preparation process.

While making preproposal contact with a federal program officer for a team of researchers, I once remarked that I wished she could meet with my team to discuss their ideas in person. She responded by suggesting that I invite her to my college to make a presentation on her program's grant opportunities. She informed me that I would have to invite other institutions to her presentation but then suggested that my team of researchers meet her at the airport and transport her to the presentation site. As it turned out, not only did they bring her to the presentation site, but they also had lunch with her and transported her back to the airport, giving them ample time to discuss their proposed project with her. While the other participating institution had the opportunity to hear the program officer's presentation, my researchers' personal contact with her resulted in a funded project, and I was left thinking of other ways to promote grant opportunities through contact with funding sources!

What can you do to promote contact with potential funding sources that will benefit your faculty and their consortia partners? Could you invite a foundation or corporate grantor to participate in a forum, round table, or panel? Remember they (the grantors) want to promote the best grants they can, and you can help them!

You can expand on this theme in a variety of ways. For example, volunteer your university as a site to review proposals for a federal program. Dr. Eileen Evans of Western Michigan University volunteered her institution as a site to evaluate proposals submitted to the Department of Education's Fund for the Improvement of Post Secondary Education (FIPSE). This provided an opportunity for her faculty to become familiar not only with agency personnel but also with the review process and scoring system used by the Department of Education.

If your geographic area has a group of foundation and/or corporate officials that have developed a consortium group of grant makers, you can also invite this group of grant makers to your college/university to discuss its grants agenda or to explore solutions to problems in your mutual fields of interest. Don't be afraid to initiate the first move. Your institution has many resources that can be used to focus on problems that grantors want to impact. For instance, your faculty's expertise and your institution's evaluation and statistical design teams, training and curriculum development efforts, and computers and facilities are all community assets that can be brought to bear on the problems. Do not feel as if you are prevailing on the good intentions of the group of grant makers when you brainstorm mutually beneficial ways to solve problems. In actuality, you are simply brokering your assets!

5. SUPPORTING CONSORTIA AND SUBCONTRACT EFFORTS WITH OTHER COLLEGES, UNIVERSITIES, AND PROFIT AND NONPROFIT PARTNERS

Consortia and subcontract opportunities are out there. It simply takes an assessment of your college or university's programs, labs, faculty/staff, and skills to initiate the concept. Support for consortia and subcontract efforts can be provided by a specially designated office, your grants office, or through any of your related centers or institutes. What the concept requires is a formal or informal structure that makes your faculty and staff aware that a function exists on campus to promote and assist in the development of relationships that get external or off-campus groups involved in grants. This may necessitate hiring a full-time person, sort of a consortia/sub-contract ombudsman, or adding additional functions to an existing job description. In addition, you could

- provide information about the development of consortia and subcontract efforts on your Web site, and/or
- develop and disseminate a special brochure on this subject to both on- and off-campus potential partners.

Whoever heads this initiative should have an in-depth knowledge of your college or university's resources and have, or be willing to develop, community linkages. In order to work effectively off-campus, this individual must become, if they aren't already, an active member of local industrial trade associations, the chamber of commerce, business incubator groups, and other nonprofit organizations in your community. In addition to the development of local and regional partnerships, this individual could even employ techniques to explore national collaborations. For example, he or she could use the search function of the Community of Science Funding Opportunities database to locate potential national partners with the necessary skills. Because this type of program is likely to have great appeal to your corporate nonprofit community, you may even be able to initially fund the consortium/subcontract ombudsman position on a grant from one or more of these sources, and a two-year project could result in the generation of enough indirect costs to eventually pick up the position.

6. PROGRAMS TO SUPPORT GRANT-SEEKING OPPORTUNITIES

In addition to the strategies already discussed, you may want to consider initiating special programs aimed at furthering grant opportunities on your campus. For example, Western Michigan University (WMU) in Kalamazoo, Michigan has two such programs—the Research Development Award (RDA) Program and the Graduate Opportunity for Long-term Development (GOLD) Program.

Prior to the development of these programs, the Office of the Vice President for Research at WMU offered many grant and contact-related seminars and training programs for faculty and staff. While these seminars and training programs were presented by several different consultants, Dr. Eileen Evans of the WMU office became particularly interested in those offered by my company, David G. Bauer Associates, Inc. Her initial interest came from viewing videotapes of my grant-seeking seminar. Then once I began to present grant-seeking seminars at her institution, the overwhelming positive seminar evaluations and the results attributed to the seminars furthered her interest. In particular, she began to associate positive grant-seeking behavior to a technique I use in my seminars entitled "90-Day Self Learning Contracts." This technique involves the development of a written contract for change relative to grant-seeking skills. Throughout my seminar, participants are provided with techniques to improve their grant-seeking skills. When they hear a technique they would like to initiate, they jot it down on two-part carbonless paper that is provided to them at the onset of the seminar.

By the end of the seminar, they have a list of grant-related action steps they hope to achieve within 90 days. They then keep one copy of the contract and place the other copy in an envelope that the participant addresses to himself or herself. I collect the envelopes and then mail them back to the participants in 90 days. When they receive their envelopes, they open them and check off the tasks they have completed, and make new agreements with themselves to complete those they have not.

What Dr. Evans discovered through follow-up with seminar participants is that many found the 90-Day Self Learning Contract process very worthwhile and wanted to meet with me again to develop new 90-day plans. After brainstorming how we could best address their needs, a new program evolved—the Research Development Award (RDA) Program.

WMU'S RESEARCH DEVELOPMENT AWARD (RDA) PROGRAM

Western Michigan University's RDA program is now in its sixth year. The program was designed to assist the participants in overcoming the grant-seeking–related barriers that they had experienced the most difficulty with, including

- searching lists of grantees to develop profiles of successful grant winners,
- establishing preproposal contact with grantors, and
- assuring the submittal of high-quality proposals.

To address these barriers, the program includes, among other things,

- the mandatory selection by each participant of a grant recipient mentor to be emulated;
- funds in the participant's RDA account to support grant-seeking–related activities;
- travel money to meet with funding source personnel for the purpose of preproposal contact or follow-up if the RDA participant's proposal has been rejected; and
- putting proposals through a quality circle or mock review before submittal (see chapter 8) and requiring program participants (research development associates) to take part in the quality circles of others.

The program calls for each research development associate (RDA) to develop

- a five-year career plan that includes their personal goals and how they relate to external funding,
- a one-year plan to move them toward their five-year career plan, and
- a 90-day plan to move them toward their one-year plan.

Every 90 days the RDAs meet with me to review the accomplishments of their plan, explore problems they are encountering, and develop a new 90-day plan to keep them moving forward.

To date, 75 percent of the RDAs have moved toward their plan and attracted outside support. In fact, the program has been credited as one of the contributing factors in WMU's nearly doubling of grant awards in the past five years. In addition, the program has become a recruiting tool to attract and keep new faculty.

One RDA made the following comments concerning the program: "The experience was excellent. There were many lessons taught that would have taken me years to learn (the hard way). The most positive aspect was the two funded proposals that we had to evaluate. That really brought things to focus." Another commented that the most positive aspects of the program were dealing with funding agencies (preproposal visits) and funding for travel to the agencies.

Western Michigan University has been gracious enough to allow me to include the latest information on their program in this book. Review exhibit 6.2 for more details on their Research Development Award Program, including eligibility requirements, award specifications, application process, selection criteria, review process, and deadlines. This information could be very useful in helping you develop and tailor a program that works for your institution.

WMU'S GRADUATE OPPORTUNITY FOR LONG-TERM DEVELOPMENT (GOLD) PROGRAM

In an effort to extend the benefits of the RDA Program to graduate students, Western Michigan University initiated a new program—the Graduate Opportunity for Long-term Development (GOLD) Program in May of 2000. The conceptual framework is the same as in the RDA program, although the program is aimed at graduate students. In addition, funding for grant-seeking–related activities, and some expectations, have been reduced, Funding for the GOLD program comes from the Office of the Vice President for Research, while funding for the RDA program comes from the Office of the Vice President for Research and the college. Expectations differ in that the proposal is the desired outcome of the GOLD program.

Exhibit 6.3 provides a detailed description of Western Michigan University's GOLD program. One interesting note on this newly instituted program is that all of the current participants were encouraged and sponsored to apply for the program by faculty who have participated in the Research Development Associates Program. One participant made the following comments: "I'm really glad I was invited to participate in the program. I'm impressed that my university invests its time and money in their graduate students in this manner . . . The most positive aspect of being involved in the GOLD Program is being treated as if I have potential to contribute to the university and to science . . . "

THE COMMUNITY GRANTS RESOURCE CENTER

In an attempt to further support grant opportunities, your office could also develop a program aimed at providing a central grant-opportunity focus for the community—such as a community grants resource center.

The grants resources necessary to operate a grants resource center are expensive, and there is usually duplication of these tools within nonprofit organizations in your community.

WESTERN MICHIGAN UNIVERSITY

Research Development Award Program
FY 2000-2001

The Research Development Award Program assists early-career faculty and professional staff in advancing their research plans by providing a series of development activities designed to facilitate the process of securing federal funding for their projects. Under the conditions of the program, the vice president for research makes as many as 20 awards annually.

Eligibility

Eligible faculty members are all Western Michigan University bargaining-unit members in a tenured or tenure-track appointment (a) who have been awarded a terminal degree appropriate for their discipline, (b) whose date of hire is between July 1, 1996, and August 31, 1999, (c) who will have completed at least two academic terms by the start of the program, and (d) who demonstrate interest in grant seeking through such means as submission of proposals for external funding, submission of proposals for FRACASF, or serving in some role on funded projects. Previous Research Development Award recipients may not reapply. Eligible professional/administrative staff will have demonstrated an interest in grant seeking in ways such as gathering data for a proposal, serving as reviewers for proposals, or being employed in some role on funded projects.

Award

Three components comprise the RDA award:

1. The vice president for research will award each RDA faculty and staff member $2,000, established in a research account to support expenses related to grantseeking and research. The award shall be used for travel to visit a mentor. Equipment, student employees, postage, and supplies are examples of approved uses of the award; salary for the RDA faculty or staff member is not.

WMU: RESEARCH DEVELOPMENT AWARD PROGRAM

EXHIBIT 6.2

2. The college or vice presidential unit will also award each of its participants $1,000, in the same manner and for the same purpose.
3. The vice president for research will support one visit to a federal sponsor by the RDA participant. The amount, not to exceed $625, shall reimburse transportation and lodging expenses, and is in addition to the sum of $3,000 awarded.

Program

RDA program participants agree to complete the following program activities during the period of May 2000 through December 2001:

1. A two-day workshop on seeking federal grants (Wednesday and Thursday, May 10 and 11, 2000)
2. A one-day workshop on seeking foundation grants (Friday, September 15, 2000, tentatively)
3. Four individual meetings with Dave Bauer, grant-seeking consultant, to define a research plan and assess progress in achieving goals
4. Develop a mentoring relationship with a faculty or staff member at another institution in order to establish a network of key colleagues. At least one meeting with the mentor shall occur on the mentor's campus
5. Participate in two or more quality circle reviews of proposals
6. Submit two proposals for federal support before December 2001
7. Submit interim reports on December 15, 2000, and April 30, 2001, to the Vice President for research

Application Process

Deans will notify eligible faculty members, and Vice Presidents will notify eligible staff members to invite applications for the 2000-2001 competition. All applications are made to the appropriate dean or vice president.

The Application

The application consists of:

1. a description of the research problem for which funding is being sought, including its significance, a brief review of current research or programs in the area, the scope of work necessary to address the problem, and the result or benefit to society (three pages maximum);
2. a statement of sponsored funding goals, quantified by number of proposals and award amounts, for three years beginning in 2000-2001 (one page maximum);
3. evidence of demonstrated interest in research and grant seeking (e.g. proposals submitted, member of grant review panel, publications in refereed journals, theses or dissertations advised, professional service as editor of journal) (one page maximum); and

WMU: RESEARCH DEVELOPMENT AWARD PROGRAM

EXHIBIT 6.2 (continued)

4. expertise profile available on the Community of Science database.

Criteria

Proposals of merit will demonstrate that:

1. study of the proposed research problem advances the research plans of the college or unit.
2. the research is feasible, given available fiscal, physical, and human resources.
3. federal funding exists for the proposed research.
4. interest in grantseeking convincingly demonstrates likelihood of full RDA program participation.
5. the applicant's academic preparation and experience indicate appropriate expertise.

Review Process

Deans and Vice Presidents will solicit RDA applications from a pool of eligible applicants that they identify (deans will identify faculty, Vice Presidents will identify professional/administrative staff). Deans and Vice Presidents will then review their college or unit applications according to the criteria and forward to the Vice President for Research a rank-ordered listing of applications for funding and copies of the proposals. In the event that the number of applications exceeds the number of awards available, the Vice President for Research reserves the right to determine distribution of awards.

Deadline

Proposals for FY 2000-2001 awards must be submitted to the dean or appropriate Vice President no later than 5 p.m. on Monday, March 27. Applications are due in the Office of the Vice President for Research until 5 p.m. on Monday, April 3, 2000. Awards will be announced on Monday, April 10. Please direct questions to Dr. Eileen B. Evans, associate dean, the Graduate College, at 387-3593.

WMU: Research Development Award Program

EXHIBIT 6.2 (*continued*)

Considerable savings could be realized by housing all of these resources in one area. Because your college or university already has access to many grants resources, why not open up your office and invite the community to participate? In addition to saving costs, sponsoring a community grants resource center will represent your institution as a concerned, sharing organization.

While developing a college grants program, I first surveyed the community for the grants resources that were available. Then I wrote a grant to a community foundation to purchase additional materials. When I finally received these new resources, I made them available to the community free of charge. Naturally, they were housed at my college grants office. Many

WESTERN MICHIGAN UNIVERSITY

Graduate Opportunity of Long-term Development (GOLD) Program

The Vice President for Research and Dean of The Graduate College is pleased to announce the establishment of The Graduate Opportunity for Long-term Development Program. This competitive program has multiple purposes, including increasing awareness of external opportunities among graduate students; engaging graduate students in the hands-on process of grantseeking; and enhancing external support for graduate student research.

Eligibility

Western Michigan University graduate students enrolled and in good standing in one of the University's graduate curricula, whose areas of research and scholarship are appropriate for external support, are eligible. Students must be enrolled in four contiguous semesters - two prior to the start of the program and two during the program. A spring and summer session count as one semester.
External sponsors have individualized eligibility requirements that students are required to meet. It is expected that students will consult with their graduate advisors, faculty mentors, and the appropriate research officer in Research and Sponsored Programs to identify external funding opportunities.

Award

The Vice President for Research and Dean of The Graduate College will award selected graduate students $2,000, placed in a research account to support expenses related to grantseeking. Establishing a relationship with a peer research mentor is important for student success as it provides insight into the process of competing for fellowships. Toward that end, a portion of the award is dedicated to travel expenses. (Peer mentors are those individuals who have successfully competed in external competitions and can offer the graduate student targeted advice.) Word processing

WMU: GRADUATE OPPORTUNITY FOR LONG-TERM DEVELOPMENT (GOLD) PROGRAM

EXHIBIT 6.3

support, preparation of graphics, and postage are examples of approved uses of the award; educational expenses such as tuition and fees are not supported by the award.

Program

The Graduate Opportunity for Long-term Development Program participants agree to complete the following program activities during the period of May 2000 through December 2001:

1. Attend a two-day workshop on seeking federal grants (Wednesday and Thursday, May 10 and 11, 2000).
2. Attend a one-day workshop on seeking foundation grants (Friday, September 15, 2000, tentatively).
3. Complete two discipline-based meeting with David Bauer, grantseeking consultant, to plan a grantseeking strategy.
4. Prepare a five-year research agenda.
5. Cultivate a peer mentoring relationship with an individual (at another institution) who has received funding from the intended competition or a similar competition.
6. Submit draft application for quality circle review during Fall 2000 semester.
7. Submit one application for external support during the period of September 2000 to December 2001.
8. Submit one copy of the application to The Graduate College.

Application Process

The application for The Graduate Opportunity for Long-term Development Program consists of:

1. A description of the research problem including its significance, a brief review of current research or programs in the field, the scope of work necessary to address the problem, and the result or benefit to society (three pages maximum);
2. A brief rationale justifying the appropriateness of the grant program to which the applicant is seeking funding;
3. A timeline for conducting the research;
4. Letters of support from the graduate student's (a) WMU faculty mentor and (b) graduate advisor assessing the student in terms of the quality of the proposed research, the importance of the proposed research to the field, the proposed timeline, the appropriateness of the targeted competition, and the student's ability to complete the program. (In cases where the faculty and graduate advisor are the same only one letter is required.)

WMU: Graduate Opportunity for Long-Term Development (GOLD) Program

EXHIBIT 6.3 (continued)

Criteria

Proposals of merit will demonstrate that:

1. Study of the proposed research problem advances research in the field.
2. The research is feasible, given available fiscal, physical, and human resources.
3. An appropriate match exists between the proposed research and the External sponsor.
4. The applicant's academic preparation and experience indicate appropriate expertise.
5. The timeline provided is feasible.

Review Process

Graduate advisors and faculty mentors will invite applications from eligible students within their programs and will ensure the GOLD application is complete. In consultation with chairs and departmental faculty they will review their unit's applications according to the listed criteria and forward to the college dean a rank-ordered listing of the College's selections with the GOLD applications attached. In the event that the number of applications exceeds the number of awards available, the Vice President for Research and Dean of The Graduate College reserves the right to determine distribution of awards.

Deadline

Proposals for FY 2000-2001 awards must be submitted to the appropriate college dean no later than 5 p.m. on Thursday, April 6, 2000. Applications are due in the Office of the Vice President for Research by 5 p.m. on Thursday, April 13, 2000. Awards will be announced on Thursday, April 20, 2000. Please direct questions to Dr. Eileen B. Evans, associate dean, the Graduate College, at 387-3593.

WMU: GRADUATE OPPORTUNITY FOR LONG-TERM DEVELOPMENT (GOLD) PROGRAM

EXHIBIT 6.3 (*continued*)

nonprofit organizations came to my office to use the materials. Their visits often resulted in the sharing of ideas. Gradually these groups began to use my college staff and faculty in their proposals for curriculum assistance, help with evaluation of their projects, statistical assistance, training, and so on. The assistance we provided the nonprofit community groups was so well accepted that several got together, formed a coalition, and then asked my office to provide more help. We encouraged the coalition to sponsor a student assistant, which they agreed to do. They paid the tuition of the student (this was a state college and tuition was low at the time) and in return the student provided grants assistance at their site. Our grants office trained the student, maintained the resource center, and provided the coalition with access to our online searching services. (Because it was the State University of New York, this included the SPIN system, which was created there.)

Eventually the program grew to include ten student assistants. Students lined up to participate in the program because it not only paid their tuition, but it also positioned them with potential employers in the community, and provided them with saleable skills in the nonprofit marketplace. My faculty and staff benefitted through the opportunities that were provided through inclusion in grants, contracts, and consulting. Our grants office became a one-stop grants asset for the community, saved my budget funds, and was an employment bonanza for my faculty and our students.

Naturally, this concept could be expanded to the for-profit community as well, to assist them in locating government contracts.

If the idea of sponsoring a community grants resource center appeals to you, review the following Letter Proposal. You may tailor it to your institution and submit it to an appropriate local foundation or corporation for funding.

LETTER PROPOSAL
COMMUNITY GRANTS RESOURCE CENTER

The Need

Our area, like many cities across the United States, relies on its nonprofit organizations to provide many vital human services. These organizations depend on philanthropic support for survival and find it more difficult each year to raise needed funds.

However, the situation is far from hopeless. Grants support from foundations, corporations, and the federal government represents an opportunity for these organizations to dramatically improve their financial situation and increase services to and/or continue to serve their communities. Over $100 billion is granted by these three sources each year. Unfortunately, few agencies have the time, expertise, or resources needed to develop support from grants. A great opportunity is missed, and worthwhile programs go undeveloped.

When they do apply for grants, local organizations often fail because their skills are not professional enough to face today's stiff competition for grant dollars. In many cases, grant failures can be turned into successes by training, more complete grant-research facilities, and attempts to create consortia projects sponsored by two or more local organizations.

We propose to develop a Community Grants Resource Center at _____ to fill these needs. It will be a conveniently located resource center for all grant-seeking organizations in and around the _____ area.

The Community Grants Resource Center will include a library of reference materials, files on granting agencies, newsletters, and a computerized search system. It will be staffed by a highly skilled grants coordinator who will assist area grant seekers to locate funding sources and prepare quality proposals. The coordinator will also serve as an advocate for local programs, visiting funding sources, and attending conferences at which funding officials meet. The coordinator will also seek out opportunities for incorporating the professional staff at our college/university and setting up learning opportunities for our students.

In short, the Community Grants Resource Center will give local organizations the tools they need to increase their levels of support. The center will give support in four main areas:

- *information*—on funding sources gathered and maintained in an extensive library
- *training*—given by the grants coordinator through seminars, state-of-the-art videotape series, etc.
- *advocacy*—the grants coordinator will maintain contact with grant makers, locate funding opportunities for local agencies, and help these agencies develop and present their ideas to funders
- *consulting and student sponsorship*—in grant-seeking

The Community Grants Resource Center will serve as a meeting place for local nonprofit agencies. It will be a place where they can discuss their work and initiate cooperative projects that make the most effective use of their resources.

GOALS OF THE COMMUNITY GRANTS RESOURCE CENTER

1. Increase the number and quality of proposals submitted for funding by nonprofit organizations.
2. Improve the acceptance rate of the proposals submitted.
3. Encourage coordination between local nonprofit organizations. This includes the sharing of information on funding sources and the creation of consortia projects pooling the resources of two or more local groups.
4. Help local organizations save time, money, and energy by teaching them to focus on only the most appropriate funding sources for their projects.
5. Serve as a center where local agencies, with the help of trained staff, can learn to improve their grant-seeking skills, find information on funding sources, and write more effective grant proposals.

FIRST-YEAR OBJECTIVES OF THE COMMUNITY GRANTS RESOURCE CENTER

1. Sponsor and submit grant proposals during the first year of operation.
2. Enlist several organizations as charter members of the office. Members will be charged a nominal fee based on their use of center resources (depends on funder's wishes).
3. Form a comprehensive grants library for the use of grant seekers.
4. Have the capacity to become 50 percent self-sufficient through membership/user fees after the first year. The remaining 50 percent will come from grant support and fund-raising methods.
5. Publish twelve monthly newsletters on subjects related to grantsmanship, alert local organizations to funding opportunities, and keep members/users informed of the local funding picture.
6. Create a complete filing system, including information on funding sources as well as user experience with those funders. Files will be open to all members/users of the resource center. This will facilitate the sharing of experiences and the improvement of approaches to funding sources. The filing system will be in place and working after the first month of operation.
7. Place community projects in the college/university database to search for funding sources. (Place appropriate projects on automatic e-mail alert system.)

WHAT THE COMMUNITY GRANTS RESOURCE CENTER WILL DO

The Community Grants Resource Center will be staffed by a grants coordinator and a full-time secretary. Once the center is set up, the coordinator and secretary will share responsibility for the following:

1. Setting up a Web site and organizing and running a grants library with online resources; Setting up an office with computers to serve those groups that require assistance and to house database access that is not able to be put on the Web site
2. Working with applicants to turn ideas into fundable proposals
3. Reviewing grants to avoid duplication of effort
4. Serving as a resource to anyone with questions about grant funding
5. Alerting organizations in the community about funding opportunities
6. Developing a skills bank of people who can be resources to grant applicants, then operating a referral service that matches resource people with appropriate applicants
7. Providing planning tools and other instructional aids to grant applicants
8. Maintaining extensive research files on funding sources that make grants in the community, including basic data, lists of grants, guidelines, and records of other organizations' experiences in developing support
9. Providing a community forum for funding-source representatives to inform grant applicants about the current funding scene
10. Maintaining a grants telephone hotline to answer immediate questions about funding regulations and deadlines
11. Collecting sample proposals, both successful and unsuccessful, to serve as guides for future grant applicants
12. Maintaining an extensive research system for the purpose of "webbing" the interconnections between and affiliations of various funding officials
13. Providing standard forms for grant applicants to use that incorporate the key elements of successful approaches to funding sources (e.g., feasibility forms, research forms, evaluation forms, etc.)
14. Purchasing additional database access and reports from professional research firms that are of interest to local organizations. (These reports would normally be too expensive for just one organization to purchase.)
15. Producing and distributing a confidential newsletter for members including practical how-to information. Newsletters will also keep users of the office up-to-date on status of proposals submitted and grants received
16. Helping form special-interest committees to stimulate grants in specific subject areas and to help with specific grant programs. Typical committees could be in research, health, culture, education, youth projects, and so on.
17. Starting a Grants Commission. Members would help in researching specific funding sources, introducing applicants to personal contacts, and informing applicants about current trends in government funding and legislation.
18. Maintaining contact with funding sources through e-mail, written correspondence, telephone, and personal visits (state, regional, and national funders)
19. Acting as a funding catalyst, suggesting new ideas for proposals, especially with regard to new and developing programs
20. Providing training programs and consultation to applicants on proposal writing and grant-application procedures
21. Reviewing preliminary drafts of proposals for clarity and adherence to guidelines
22. Assisting applicants in preparation of budgets and final drafts
23. Expediting and following up on proposals after submission

24. Monitoring progress of grants after award, including verifying grant payments
25. Assisting in preparation of interim and final project reports and evaluations

EVALUATION

The success of the Community Grants Resource Center will be measured in two ways. First, we will compare our status at the end of year one with our stated objectives.

We also plan to conduct a survey of the members/users of the center. This survey will ask specific questions in the following three areas:

- How effective are grant applications now as compared with before the existence of the center?
- How valuable was the assistance of the grants coordinator in grants solicitation activities?
- How valuable were the resources at the center, and which ones were most helpful?

We will tally the survey results and then prepare a final report of the first-year results of the Community Grants Resource Center based on both aspects of the evaluation. This report will also include statistical analysis of the success rate of the proposals submitted for funding through the Community Grants Resource Center.

FUTURE FUNDING

This proposal is a request for the first two years of funding for the Community Grants Resource Center. After the first year, operation of the office should be less expensive, as the following startup costs will have been paid:

- basic library expenses (not including ongoing costs such as journal subscriptions and research-updating services)
- the purchase of office equipment

After year one of the program, we plan to develop support from the following three sources:

- 50 percent membership/user fees;
- 35–45 percent government, corporate, and foundation grants; and
- 5–15 percent fund-raising methods such as major gift and mail solicitation.

Budget Yearly Costs	Year 1	Year 2
Grants Coordinator Salary	$50,000	$52,500
Office Manager/Secretary Salary	$20,000	$21,200
Employee Benefits	$21,000	$22,110
Library	$10,000	$ 4,000
Office Rent	$ 9,600*	$ 9,600*
Office Equipment and Maintenance	$5,000	$ 500
Telephone (Regular & Hotline)	$ 6,000*	$ 6,000*
Printed Newsletter & E-mail Alert System	$ 6,000*	$ 6,000*
Printing	$ 5,000*	$ 5,000*

Web Site Development and Maintenance	$ 3,000*	$ 3,000*
Travel (New York City & Other Locations)	$ 5,000	$ 5,000
Memberships in Professional Associations	$ 1,000	$ 1,000
Conference and Seminar Registrations/		
Attendance	$ 3,000	$ 3,000
TOTAL	$144,600	$138,910

Note: Member/user fees should provide approximately 50 percent of the total budget during the second year. The more frequent the usage, the higher the fee. Also, the starred (*) items could possibly be donated or contributed in-kind by the college/university.

Obviously, there are other programs out there in the 3,000-plus colleges and universities designed to increase grant opportunities and help faculty and staff realize more of their grants potential. We invite you to share your programs and the other successful techniques you have employed to develop more grant opportunities for your faculty and staff with David G. Bauer Associates, Inc., and, with your permission, we will place your examples on our Web site and in future editions of our work. Please see ordering information at the end of this book for Bauer Associates address and phone number.

Exhibit 6.4 provides a list of questions you may use to survey your faculty for feedback on your institution's existing grants opportunity research system. Completing exhibit 6.5 will help you incorporate this important component into your office's overall grants plan.

	Yes	No
1. Are you aware of our Grants Office newsletter?	____	____
a. If you are aware of it, have you read it?	____	____
b. Is it informative (does it provide useful information)?	____	____
c. Is it interesting (do you enjoy reading it)?	____	____
d. Do you think it encourages grant writing activity?	____	____
e. Does it recognize faculty and staff efforts?	____	____
	Yes	No
2. Are you aware of the _____ database?	____	____
a. If you are aware of it, have you used it in the past year?	____	____
b. If you are aware of it and have not used it, why not?		

SURVEY QUESTIONS—EVALUATING AND IMPROVING YOUR GRANT OPPORTUNITY RESEARCH SYSTEM

EXHIBIT 6.4

If you have used the _____ database in the past year, please answer the following:

	Yes	No
c. Was it easy to use?	_____	_____
d. Have you found potential funding opportunities by using it?	_____	_____
e. Have you written a proposal as a result of a search of the database?	_____	_____
f. Were you funded from a grant opportunity found on the database?	_____	_____

3. Are you registered for a computer-based e-mail alert service that notifies you of any new funding opportunities within your area of interest?

Yes	No	Don't Know
_____	_____	_____

  a. If "no," why not?

If "yes",

	Yes	No
b. Did you receive assistance with your selection of key words?	_____	_____
c. Do you receive as many announcements as you would expect?	_____	_____
d. Are the announcements relevant to your interests?	_____	_____
e. Have you followed up on any announcements received?	_____	_____
f. Are you eligible for all the announcements you receive?	_____	_____
g. Have you updated your keywords in the last year?	_____	_____
h. Are you registered for any other funding databases?	_____	_____
i. If you are registered for other funding databases, which ones?		

4. What additional services could the grants office provide to assist you in locating grant opportunities?

SURVEY QUESTIONS—EVALUATING AND IMPROVING YOUR GRANT OPPORTUNITY RESEARCH SYSTEM

EXHIBIT 6.4 (*continued*)

For Each Activity/Item listed, Check Status

Activity/Item	Reviewed, Appropriate Part of Grants Office	Reviewed, Appropriate Part of Other Office (List)	Reviewed, Not Applicable	Reviewed, Inappropriate Needs Action	Non-existent, Needs Action
1. Computer Software Programs and Internet-Based Grantor Research Systems (List): • •					
2. Other Grants and Contracts Research Tools (List): ___ ___ • •					

Complete this Section for Each Activity/Item Needing Action

What Needs to be Accomplished?	By Whom? (Office/Person)	By When? (Time Frame)	Resources Required—Personnel, Supplies, Equipment, Programming, etc.	Estimated Costs

GRANTS OFFICE INVENTORY—EVALUATING AND IMPROVING YOUR GRANT OPPORTUNITY RESEARCH SYSTEM

EXHIBIT 6.5

For Each Activity/Item listed, Check Status

Activity/Item	Reviewed, Appropriate Part of Grants Office	Reviewed, Appropriate Part of Other Office (List)	Reviewed, Not Applicable	Reviewed, Inappropriate Needs Action	Non-existent, Needs Action
3. Grants Newsletters					
4. Strategies for Involving your Grant Seekers with Funding Sources (List): _____ _____ _____ • • •					
5. Strategies for Supporting Consortia and Sub-contract					

Complete this Section for Each Activity/Item Needing Action

What Needs to be Accomplished?	By Whom? (Office/Person)	By When? (Time Frame)	Resources Required— Personnel, Supplies, Equipment, Programming, etc.	Estimated Costs

GRANTS OFFICE INVENTORY—EVALUATING AND IMPROVING YOUR GRANT OPPORTUNITY RESEARCH SYSTEM

EXHIBIT 6.5 (continued)

For Each Activity/Item listed, Check Status

Activity/Item	Reviewed, Appropriate Part of Grants Office	Reviewed, Appropriate Part of Other Office (List)	Reviewed, Not Applicable	Reviewed, Inappropriate Needs Action	Non-existent, Needs Action
Efforts (List): • _____ • _____ • _____ • _____ 6. Programs to Support Grant Opportunities (List): • _____ • _____ • _____ • _____					

Complete this Section for Each Activity/Item Needing Action

What Needs to be Accomplished?	By Whom? (Office/Person)	By When? (Time Frame)	Resources Required—Personnel, Supplies, Equipment, Programming, etc.	Estimated Costs

GRANTS OFFICE INVENTORY—EVALUATING AND IMPROVING YOUR GRANT OPPORTUNITY RESEARCH SYSTEM

EXHIBIT 6.5 (*continued*)

CHAPTER 7

The Role of the Grants Office in Contacting Funding Sources

While the grants administrator supports programs and services that assist grant seekers with the best strategies and techniques to help sustain them, he or she must also constantly look out for the institution's well-being. He or she must act as an administrator with responsibilities to the institution's mission, while considering the grants interests of the institution's prospective grant seekers. In addition, the grants administrator must report to a senior administrator who has his or her own grants agenda.

Although the job is difficult, the grants-office administrator must seek to maintain a balance between all of the differing interests. The job is made easier when the institution has a grants-office mission statement that sets priorities for the grants effort and outlines a plan to accomplish these priorities. In the absence of such a statement understood by all staff, the grants administrator is forced into an imbalance in the win-win formula. This may result in siding with the senior administrator (the power and authority) at the expense of the faculty and staff (the idea generators). The mission of the institution is thus compromised and everyone is a potential loser. To keep this from occurring, one must remember that all parties can win—and not at the expense of one faction over another.

The potential for a conflict of interest is glaringly evident in the policies related to preproposal contact with potential grantors. Working for over thirty years in grant seeking with private and public funding sources has demonstrated to me time and time again the value of maintaining personal contact with grantors. Surveys of successful grantees repeatedly verify the importance of keeping apprised of the nuances of the federal grants scenario by making one or two visits to Washington, D.C. each year to meet with program officials to discuss how changes in priority and emphasis will affect re-application and new proposal ideas. While e-mail and electronic contact have yet to be formally evaluated in terms of the role they play in preposal contact and grants success, informal surveys and my experience have demonstrated that while face-to-face meetings are the best, well-designed phone contacts and e-mails are close seconds at providing grant seekers with the information they need to maximize their success.

Contact with federal grantors is not intended to "buy" any special treatments or advantages. Contact is designed to take advantage of the grantor's staff's perspective concerning where the program is heading and what types of projects are likely to appeal to the reviewers.

The optimum way to view proposed projects would be to incorporate the data retrieved from preproposal contact with the grantor. That would, of course, assume that the college or university would propose the project most likely to be funded versus what the college or university would like to get funded. That is where the dilemma of preproposal contact lies. Do we send the grantor what they want or what the institution wants? The grants administrator could approach this concept from a variety of perspectives. The astute administrator includes an evaluation of the linkages that the grant seeker has to the potential grantor. Even when the potential grantee has a linkage to the grantor, the following questions arise:

- Whom should the institution endorse as its grantee of choice to fund?
- What if several proposals are submitted to the grantor? How will the grantor know which one has the institution's support?
- Should the institution's grants office suggest the development of a system of identification and support of linkages to grantors?

In today's competitive grants marketplace, it would seem ludicrous not to suggest that potential grant seekers develop and keep up with who in the grants world might support their research and demonstration grants.

The institution's grants system must deal proactively with these issues and questions. The institution's development officials (as opposed to only grants or academic officials) must be included and a system of checks and balances on endorsement of preproposal contact must be developed. While many institutions hope these issues of priority and personal contact will just go away, I can assure you that grant seekers are making contacts daily with little concern for the larger picture. So why not place the issue on the table and suggest the development of a system for recording these linkages?

DEVELOPING A WEBBING AND LINKAGE SYSTEM FOR PRIVATE AND PUBLIC FUNDING SOURCES

One important function that your grants office may provide to your faculty and staff is recording and monitoring who knows specific funding officials, foundation trustees, and/or corporate board members. Because whom you know may be more important than what you know or how you write a proposal, the institution that has a system to record and retrieve linkages operates from a significant advantage.

A friend of the college or university with a link to a potential funding source can

- help you discover the hidden agenda of the funding source,
- arrange an opportunity for you to meet with the funding source to discuss the project, and
- attend such a meeting with you or for you.

There is no substitute for a well-designed project submitted by a credible institution to an appropriate funder. When you also have an advocate for your institution whom the funder already knows and trusts, you have the best possible chances of success.

Who are these linkages? Where do you find them? Some links to funders may already be part of your system. With a little cultivation and the building of trust, more will come forward and allow your institution to use their linkages and contacts to further your mission.

The first step is teaching your faculty, staff, volunteers, advisory group members, and advocates that your institution's ability to attract grants funds depends directly on preproposal communication with funding sources. Let them know that there is a 300 to 500 percent increase in success through preproposal contact with grantors. Make sure they are aware of the role that the friends of the institution can play in such contact. Ask people to think about whom they know, whom their spouses know, and whom their close friends know that can be related to state, federal, foundation and/or corporate support. Use electronic means, newsletters, meetings, and so on to raise awareness of this concept.

Before you ask the friends of your institution to reveal their linkages, they should know how the information they provide will be used. The following are the basic rules to a good webbing and linkage system.

1. Let the friends of your institution know that the information they provide will be kept secure and that only a few people will have access to it. Give them the names of the people who will have access to the linkage data.
2. Assure them that they will be contacted to discuss their endorsement of the project and for approval before their name is used with any funding source. Let them know that they will be given the opportunity to approve or disapprove the plans to contact the funding source. (See exhibit 7.1, the Webbing and Linkage Sample Cover Letter.) You will use them to contact their linkage to get your "foot in the door."

Researchers, faculty, and staff should be encouraged to develop their own linkage system because such a system will support them throughout their careers. One way they can begin building their base of contacts is for you to ask them to distribute a worksheet (exhibit 7.2, Webbing and Linkage Worksheet 1) with a list of those funding sources they are currently considering pursuing for grants to their friends. Their friends should then review the list for possible linkages. For government prospects, they should list program officers, contact people, directors, staff members, and even past grantees and reviewers that their research has uncovered. For foundation and corporate sources, they should list funding-source staff, the board members/trustees, directors, contributions officers, and contact people. They may also want to add space or a separate worksheet for other funding-source contacts.

Another way to gather this linkage data is to distribute a questionnaire that requests the desired information but does not provide a list of funding sources (exhibit 7.3, Webbing and Linkage Worksheet 2). While this approach is initially less time-consuming, my experience has shown that the return of useful information is much greater when there are specifics on the webbing and linkage worksheet. Also, it is easy to omit a linkage when the worksheet is open-ended. One advocate I worked with thought he would be embarrassed if I saw him playing golf with a potential contact whose name he had not given. He much preferred a ready-made list containing funding source names.

Date

Name
Title
Address

Dear _____:

Our proposal-development effort has developed several approaches to meeting the need(s) of _____.

Our success in receiving a grant to fund a proposal in this area is greatly enhanced when we contact the funder before we write the proposal.

Please review the attached list of proposed funding sources and designate those to which you may have a linkage. (Or please list any funding sources to which you have a linkage.) The linkage may be through you directly or indirectly through a relative, acquaintance, or corporate/business affiliation.

You will always be approached for us for your approval and assistance in contacting the funding source *before* contact is actually made. Your responses will be strictly confidential and access of this information will be limited to _____.

Your sharing of this information may be worth thousands of dollars in grants. It may also save hundreds of hours of time spent in preparing proposals for the wrong funders.

Sincerely,

Name
Title
Phone Number

WEBBING AND LINKAGE SAMPLE COVER LETTER

EXHIBIT 7.1

The best response to requests for linkage information occurs when the faculty, staff, advisory committee members, and volunteers seek to gather this data. One organization I belong to has a linkage committee headed by a few of the board members: the vice-president of a major bank (from the trust department), a corporate board member, and a foundation trustee. These people have the respect of the other board members, the staff, the volunteers,

Foundation

Name_____   Staff Members _____
Address _____   _____
Director _____   _____
Contact Person _____   Board Members/Trustees _____
Notes _____   _____
_____   _____
_____   _____

Corporation

Name_____   Staff Members _____
Address _____   _____
Contributions Officer _____   Board Members_____
_____   _____
Notes _____   _____
_____   _____

Government Agency

Agency _____   Staff Members _____
Address _____   _____
Program Officer_____   _____
Contact Person _____   Past Grantees _____
Director _____   _____
Notes _____   Past Reviewers _____
_____   _____
_____   _____

Other Funding Source Contacts

_____
_____
_____
_____
_____

WEBBING AND LINKAGE WORKSHEET 1

EXHIBIT 7.2

Your Name:
Address:
Phone Number: Fax: E-mail:

1. On what foundation or corporate boards are you or your spouse?

2. Do you know anyone who is on a foundation or corporation board?
If so, please list.

3. Does your spouse know anyone on a foundation or corporation board?
If so, please list.

4. Have you served on any government committees?
If so, please list.

5. Do you know any government funding contacts?
If so, please list.

6. Please list the fraternal groups, social clubs, and/or service organizations in which you are involved.

You may also ask questions on educational background, military service, religious affiliation, political preference, job title and description, and ability to travel for business. Please note, however, that it is optional to ask for personal data.

WEBBING AND LINKAGE WORKSHEET 2

EXHIBIT 7.3

and the advocates, and their requests for information result in responses. Developing and recording linkages can be looked at as

- a faculty/staff responsibility,
- an activity to be undertaken by deans and department chairs with their advisory groups, and
- the responsibility of center and/or institute directors.

In my first attempt at developing a webbing and linkage committee, the banker of our group turned to a local foundation trustee and said, "Will your foundation grant our organization $10,000 to get started on a linkage system?" Her answer was "yes." In fact, she verbally granted us the money without even having a letter proposal, although we needed to submit a letter proposal for initiating a webbing and linkage system (see exhibit 7.4) for her files. The initiation of a linkage system was funded because key individuals perceived the usefulness and impact such a system could have on our grant seeking. Because these key individuals have "bought in" to the project monetarily and conceptually, they will be motivated to convince others to contribute to the linkages database.

This particular group has decided to embark on a multi-phase program to build its linkage base. The foundation area will be addressed in the first phase, and the webbing and linkage program will stress "getting our foot in the door" of these private funding sources. Separate questionnaires aimed at uncovering linkages have been developed for board members, advisory committee members, staff, and volunteers.

The second phase will involve corporate linkages; then state and federal contacts will be researched in phase three. Two types of linkages will be examined in phase three: elected officials to assist in grant appropriation and contact with funding sources, and bureaucrats, especially those related to government grant programs.

To initiate a system, you only need rudimentary computer equipment. A linkage system can eventually provide the funds for added capacity, new programs, and equipment. By giving your institution the ability to effectively use the linkage information, a donor may take credit for the grant monies generated by the system.

Your grants linkage system will gain acceptance quickly and easily, as long as it is kept separate from fundraising. In the grants marketplace, the money you are going after *must* be given away. The money disseminated in a grant does not come from an *individual*. In fundraising you are asking an individual for his or her own money. Do not mix your grants-linkage system with fundraising or you will find that your linkages are severely reduced.

The grants linkage system can be organized around a particular grant area, program, or department, or it can be organized around your entire institution. Because individuals have a tendency to relate to causes, problems, or particular problems or solutions, it may be easiest to capitalize on these focused interests in building support for your linkage system as opposed to the whole college/university.

The individual with the appropriate linkage may assist you in contacting a certain funding source, or go with you or your project director to see the funding source. Be aware, however, that when your linkages become involved in endorsing a project or proposal, they may take liberty in negotiating the grant amount or changing the project to fit the funder without checking with the grants administrator or project director. While involvement and endorsement is encouraged, the need to move to close the gap between what is and what

Date

Foundation Name:
Foundation Address:

Dear _____:

We at _____ are grateful for your past support. In fact, your grant of $ _____ in _____ has accomplished _____ _____. Your continued support of the area of _____ accounted for _____ percent of your past year's grants. It is with our knowledge of your commitment to this area, and your interest and support of our institution, that I approach you with this proposal. (Start with a statement reflecting the giving pattern of the foundation as it relates to your institution and the need you must reduce.)

Our area is fortunate to have _____ foundations and _____ major corporations that consistently demonstrate their philanthropic support of local educational organizations and other nonprofits. This support has contributed to the growth and maturation of our institution. To sustain our development, we are now seeking to secure grant funds from the larger base of regional and national corporate and private foundations.

Although we have the projects and ability to prepare outstanding proposals that could draw monies into our local area, we lack a track record and familiarity with these foundations. What we are missing is a system to determine individuals who could help us contact these funding sources. A study in *Grants Magazine* reported that organizations that contacted funding sources *before* they wrote proposals experience a 500-percent increase in grant-proposal acceptance. As you can see, knowing "whom you know" could be worth its weight in gold (grants).

We invite the _____ Foundation to invest with us in the development of a computerized webbing and linkage system. First, we will survey the faculty, staff, advocates, and friends of our college/university to ascertain whom they know on major corporate and foundation boards and/or staffs. The results of this survey will then be entered into a personal computer retrieval system. Individuals and their linkages will be held in the strictest confidence, and no one from our staff will contact a funder without prior approval from the individual supplying the linkage. In some instances, an individual will be invited to accompany a member of our institution on a personal visit to the funding source.

LETTER PROPOSAL FOR INITIATING A WEBBING AND LINKAGE SYSTEM

EXHIBIT 7.4

Last year foundations granted over _____ billion dollars, and corporate grants totaled _____ billion. We know that part of this _____ billion dollars could be a grant to our area of _____. This project seeks to discover how much of these funds might be granted to us and who could assist us in this endeavor.

We are uniquely suited to put a system of linkages to use. We have a distinguished and motivated faculty, staff, and advocate base.

We are requesting $_____ from the _____ Foundation. These funds will be used for the following:

Personal Computer $_____
Laser Printer $_____
Software $_____
Data Entry $_____

TOTAL $_____

You can be confident that your investment will provide a return worthy of your support and will truly be a gift that keeps on giving.

                              Sincerely,

                              Name
                              Title
                              Phone Number

LETTER PROPOSAL FOR INITIATING A WEBBING AND LINKAGE SYSTEM

EXHIBIT 7.4 (*continued*)

should be is what the linkage is endorsing. The program or project design is the purview of the experts and program initiator.

Another problem that surfaces when a linkage system is developed is that you may be tempted to write a proposal to a funder that you discovered a linkage to, even though the proposal is not a priority. In fact, it may not even move your institution toward meeting its mission. Be careful of this. Remember, the reason for the linkage system is to locate linkages to funders that you have identified as interested in your proposals. If you have a strong linkage to a funding source that is clearly inappropriate for your proposal/project, explain the need for the project to the funder, mention that you know the project is not a priority of the funder's, and ask if they know of an appropriate funding source and could assist you in contacting them. This could result in a positive relationship with the initial funding source and improve your institution's image, because the source will know your college/university does its grants homework.

CONTACTING AND MONITORING PUBLIC FUNDING SOURCES

The use of the grants office as the control center for monitoring contact with funding sources is vital to maintaining a positive image of the institution in the grants marketplace. It is risky to allow any employee of the institution to carry the name of the college/university or imply knowledge and consent for contact and ideas unless he or she is designated to hold that authority.

Many well-intentioned grant seekers have misrepresented their institutions by

- taking inferior-quality proposals to funders,
- requesting inappropriate grant amounts,
- submitting a proposal to a funding source without knowing if other proposals from their institution have recently been submitted to the same source, and
- visiting a funding source to discuss a proposal and running into another grant seeker from their institution in the reception area.

In order to demonstrate to a funder that you will be able to attend to the details of administering a proposal after it is awarded, it is important to show adequate administration of the preproposal phases of grant seeking. To maintain a high-quality image of your institution, evaluate your preproposal-contact controls and procedures, and determine the role and function of your grants office in this area.

The importance of preproposal contact with government funding sources cannot be overemphasized. In a study of 10,000 federal proposals, the only significant variable separating the funded and rejected proposals was preproposal contact with the funding source. As previously stated, chances for success go up from 300 to 500 percent when contact is made with the funding source *before* the proposal is written. Remember, you must not write the proposal until you are knowledgeable about the funding source. Having information on the funding source, such as past grantees, reviewers, and so on, will pay off because you will be viewed as a knowledgeable partner in the grants process.

Contact by e-mail, letter, phone, and when possible, a personal visit should be encouraged. One way to encourage yourself to follow a systematic method of approaching funding sources is to set up a schedule of preproposal contact. For example:

Week 1: E-mail or write to two funding sources.

Week 2: E-mail or write to two more funding sources.

Week 3: Call the two funding sources you e-mailed or wrote to during Week 1 and ask for an appointment.

Week 4: Call the two funding sources you e-mailed or wrote during in Week 2 and ask for an appointment.

Week 5: Follow up on appointments from phone conversations.

In some institutions, contacting prospective funders is the sole purview of the grants office; in others, individual grant seekers are encouraged to initiate preproposal contact. In either case, the following letters and worksheets offer guidance on how to address this important aspect of grant seeking, and you are encouraged to provide your grant seekers with assistance in securing the information required to develop a productive grants strategy.

The Sample Letter to a Federal Agency for Mailing List and Past Grantees (exhibit 7.5), Sample Letter to a Federal Agency for a List of Reviewers (exhibit 7.6), and Sample Letter to a Federal Agency for an Appointment (exhibit 7.7) have been designed to assist you in organizing your preproposal-contact effort and to help you develop a procedures manual for this area. Please note that, if your research provides you with e-mail addresses for the federal agencies you are interested in, you may e-mail these letters rather than sending them through the U.S. Postal Service.

Date

Name
Title
Address

Dear _____:

Our institution is developing a project that we would like to have funded under your program _____.

Please add me to your mailing list to receive the necessary application forms, program guidelines, and any other information you feel would be helpful to me in this endeavor. A list of last year's grant recipients under this program would be very much appreciated. In addition, I would like to know how many applications you received in your last solicitation. I noticed that a total of_____ proposals were funded last year.

I have enclosed a self-addressed envelope for your convenience in returning the list of successful grantees, or you may e-mail the information to me at _____. Thank you for your cooperation and assistance in this matter.

Sincerely,

Name
Title
Phone Number

SAMPLE LETTER TO A FEDERAL AGENCY FOR MAILING LIST AND PAST GRANTEES

EXHIBIT 7.5

Date

Name
Title
Address

Dear _____:

I am presently developing a proposal for (CFDA # Program Title)
administered by your office. I would like to base the writing of my proposal on
the level, expertise, and diversity of the reviewers. Therefore, I would greatly
appreciate a list of last year's reviewers. Information on the composition of the
review committee will help me prepare a quality proposal based upon the
reviewers' backgrounds. I would also appreciate it if you could advise me if
the makeup or background of the review committee will change significantly in
the next funding cycle.

It is my intention to have my colleagues participate in a mock review of my
proposal before I submit it, and I would like the mock review to follow your
agency's actual review process as closely as possible. Therefore, I am also
requesting information on the review process and the scoring system used and
a copy of the reviewers information materials from last year.

While I have been able to gather some of this information through my
research, I would like to verify the information I have and obtain more detailed
information if it is available. I have enclosed a self-addressed label for your
convenience in responding to my request, or you may e-mail the information to
me at _____. I appreciate your effort to provide me with this
information.

Sincerely,

Name
Title
Phone Number

SAMPLE LETTER TO A FEDERAL AGENCY FOR A LIST OF REVIEWERS

EXHIBIT 7.6

Date

Name
Title
Address

Dear _____ :

My research on your funding program indicates that a project we have
developed would be appropriate for consideration by your agency for funding
under (CFDA # Program Title).

I would appreciate five to ten minutes of your time to discuss my project. Your
insights, knowledge, and information on any grants that have been funded
using a similar approach that my research has not uncovered would be
invaluable. My travel plans call for me to be in your area on _____,
but my plans are flexible.

I will phone /e-mail you to confirm a date and time to meet with you to discuss
this important proposal.

Sincerely,

Name
Title
Phone Number

SAMPLE LETTER TO A FEDERAL AGENCY FOR AN APPOINTMENT

EXHIBIT 7.7

USING E-MAIL TO CONTACT PUBLIC FUNDING SOURCES

When researching federal or state grant prospects, you will usually be able to locate the
names and telephone numbers of program officers. Sometimes you will also be given their
e-mail addresses. If you cannot find an e-mail address, go to the agency's Web site and look
at its directory of personnel. If you do use e-mail to contact a government program officer,
make sure your e-mail reflects your knowledge of their program and asks one or two
questions. Government bureaucrats will most likely respond to an e-mail request for
information. However, if you do not receive a response, try sending another e-mail or a
combination of an e-mail and a telephone call.

USING THE TELEPHONE WITH PUBLIC FUNDING SOURCES

Telephoning federal and state funding sources can be very frustrating. Often the contact
name or telephone number derived from preliminary research is incorrect. Again, check the

personnel directory on the agency's Web site for more accurate information. If the information you gather proves incorrect and you do not reach the program officer, ask your questions to the individual you do reach. Ask who the actual contact person is and how to reach him or her. Also, if all else fails, you can enlist the services of the individual in your congressperson's office designated to assist people in your district with grants.

Naturally, the best preproposal-contact approach is to see the funding source in person. If you cannot do so, however, try to gather the same information over the phone that you would face to face. Although it is more difficult to "read" what the funding source is saying over the phone than on a personal visit, you want the same results. Your goal is to increase your chances of success by finding out how to meet the needs of the funding source. Review the suggested questions found in exhibit 7.8, Questions to Ask a Program Officer.

MAKING AN APPOINTMENT WITH A PUBLIC FUNDING SOURCE

Objective: To obtain an interview with the highest-ranking person in the program

Step 1:   Call and ask for the program officer. If the program officer is not available, leave a phone message, briefly stating your interest in visiting them during trip to their area.

Step 2:   If you can, get the program officer's assistant's or secretary's name and ask when his or her boss can be reached. You could also try to contact them by e-mail. Use the agency's Web site and its listing of personnel to get e-mail information and, in some cases, you can figure out who may work for or report to the program officer.

Step 3:   Call back or e-mail again. Try person-to-person. Alternative plans would be to ask an advocate to set up the appointment, to get congressional help in making the appointment, and/or try going in cold early in the week to get an appointment for later in the week. (They may prefer to see you then to get you out of the way.)

Step 4:   If all of the above steps fail, ask the individual answering the telephone who else can answer technical questions concerning the program. You may get an appointment with a screen, but it will be better than talking to yourself!

Step 5:   When you finally get a program person on the phone, introduce yourself and give a *brief* description of your institution and project, research, and so on. Let the program person know that you believe the need for your project or research is extremely important and worthwhile in your field, that your institution is uniquely suited to conduct the research or project, and that you understand that the funding source's program deals with these needs. Tell him or her that you would like an appointment to discuss the program and your approaches. Be sure to mention that you are planning a trip in the vicinity and that you have a flexible schedule.

When you get an appointment, stop talking and hang up. If no appointment is possible, say that you have some questions that you can ask over the phone and request five minutes of his or her time now or later. Ask the same questions you would ask in person (see exhibit 7.8, Questions to Ask a Program Officer).

- Do you agree that our project addresses an important need?

- What do you expect to be the average size of your grant awards this year?

- How will successful grantees from last year affect people submitting new or first applications? Will last year's grantees be in competition with me, or have their funds been set aside? If so, how much is left for new awards?

- Are there any unannounced programs or unsolicited proposals available to fund an important project like ours?

- What is the most common mistake or flaw in proposals submitted to you?

- Are there any areas you would like to see addressed in a proposal that may have been overlooked by the other grantees or applicants?

- We have discussed several approaches to this needs area. You may know whether any of these have been tried. Could you review our approaches and provide us with any guidance?

- Do you review or critique proposals if they are developed early?

- Would you recommend a previously funded proposal for us to read for format and style? (Remember, you are entitled to read *any* funded proposal, but don't be too pushy.)

- Is your program geared toward a specific type of grant (e.g., consultant, demonstration, evaluation)?

- The guidelines call for _____ copies of the proposal. Could you use more? May I bind the copies in inexpensive binders?

- Are there any problems created by my use of tabs to separate the different sections of the proposal?

QUESTIONS TO ASK A PROGRAM OFFICER

EXHIBIT 7.8

THE VISIT: FACE-TO-FACE CONTACT WITH A PUBLIC FUNDING SOURCE

The object of face-to-face contact with a representative of a government funding source is to discover as much as possible about the program and how it awards grants. With this information, you can produce a proposal that reflects a sensitivity to their program priorities. Before you make a visit, review your Funding-Source Staff Profile (exhibit 7.9), and after you make contact, fill in the Public Funding Source Contact Summary Sheet (exhibit 7.10). In some cases, you or your grants staff may be making this visit for several of your faculty or staff, or you may accompany them, or instruct them on visiting alone. In any case, completion of the summary sheets as soon as you (or your faculty/staff) return from the visit is recommended.

Before each visit to a funding source, review this sheet to be sure you are bringing the correct faculty, staff, advocates, and materials.

Funding source _____
Agency director _____
Program director _____
Contact person _____
Title _____

Profile

Name_____
Date of birth_____ Place of birth _____
Education: college _____
    postgraduate _____
Work experience _____
_____
_____
_____

Military service _____
Service clubs _____
_____
Interests/hobbies _____
_____
Publications _____
_____
_____
Comments _____
_____
_____
_____
_____
_____
_____

FUNDING-SOURCE STAFF PROFILE

EXHIBIT 7.9

The image you create through your personal contact can place your institution in a positive position for years. You want the grantor to respect you, to be your advocate with reviewers, and to do so, you must look and talk like the funder thinks you should. Remember, the more you differ from what the funder expects and desires, the greater the problems with communication and agreement. Dress is a critical factor in establishing your credibility. If you do not know the source's expectations on dress, play it safe and read

Add to this sheet each time you contact a public funding source.

Project title _____

Agency name _____

Program _____

Contacted on (date) _____

Contacted by whom _____

Contacted by: Letter ___ Phone ___ E-mail ___ Personal contact _____

Faculty, staff, and/or advocates present _____

_____

Discussed _____

_____

_____

_____

_____

_____

Results _____

_____

_____

_____

_____

_____

PUBLIC FUNDING SOURCE CONTACT SUMMARY SHEET

EXHIBIT 7.10

John T. Molloy's *New Dress for Success* (New York: Warner Books, 1988) and/or his *New Women's Dress for Success* (New York: Warner Books, 1996). (Molloy's initial research on dress was carried out under a grant.)

To ensure presenting a proper image, review guidelines for dress and other aspects of personal contact with funders. The grants office may suggest that faculty and staff report their intentions to visit a federal program officer so you that you can apprise the grant seeker of other faculty or staff who have made a visit to or plan to visit the grantor. You may wish to incorporate the following suggestions in your guidelines for contacting funding sources.

1. Encourage two people to visit the funding source. Consider sending an advocate or graduate of your program rather than a paid staff member.
2. Bring materials that help demonstrate the need in the specific field of interest. Bring your Proposal Development Workbook (see Chapter 5) as well as audiovisual aids, CD or computer-based presentations, or videotapes that focus on the need for the project or research, rather than on your institution. A presentation on a laptop computer is a great way to see and hear your project and institution.
3. Role-play with your team member. Know who will take responsibility for the different parts or segments of your presentation.

4. Have information on your proposal, but *never* leave a proposal with the funding executive. Preproposal contact is based on the premise that you are there to gather information that you will use in your proposal preparation. By leaving a proposal, you are demonstrating that you had no intention of using the time that he or she invested in you to improve your proposal.

COORDINATING CONTACT WITH PAST GRANTEES AND REVIEWERS

By now you have located a list of previous grantees on the Internet or have requested one from the funding source via e-mail or U.S. mail. You may have also requested the list again by phone. If necessary, you could politely remind the funding source that you are entitled to know who received funding under the Sunshine Law or Freedom of Information Act. You may also ask you congressperson to obtain the list for you.

Once you have the list, your office may assist the grant seeker in selecting a grantee to call who is not in close proximity to you. Your grant seeker may need your help in calling the grantee and explaining to that person where you got his or her name. Ask to speak to the director or person who worked on the proposal. In general, past grantees will feel flattered that you called. In some cases, you may find it useful to contact the grants office of the institution and talk to the grants staff person who worked on the proposal. If your office cannot fulfill this function, provide your grant seeker with these instructions and the following list of questions to ask the previous grantee:

- Did you e-mail, write to, telephone, or go see the funding source before writing your proposal?
- Whom on the funding source's staff did you find most helpful?
- Did you have the funding source review or critique your proposal before its final submission?
- Did you use consultants to help you on the proposal?
- Was there a hidden agenda to the Request for Proposal (RFP)?
- When did you begin the process of developing your application and contacting the funding source?
- What materials did you find the most helpful in developing your proposal?
- Did the funding source come to see you for a site visit before the proposal was awarded? After it was awarded? Who came? What did this representative wear? Approximately how old was he or she? Would you characterize him or her as a conservative, moderate, or liberal? Did anything in the process surprise you?
- How close was your initial budget to the awarded amount? (You can verify this information by looking at the grantee's proposal when you visit the funding source.)
- Who negotiated the budget?
- What would you do differently next time?

QUESTIONS FOR PAST REVIEWERS

You have requested a list of reviewers. Again, by the Sunshine Law, you can demand one, but don't. Tell the funding source you are concerned about the makeup or background of the reviewers because you prepare your proposal based on their perspective of the problem.

If they are reluctant to give names, try to get general information on the reviewers and the peer review process. Most federal and state grants staff are very concerned about the quality of the proposals submitted to their program, and they will relate very positively to your request for reviewer scoring or evaluation criteria to help you carry out a review before your grant seeker submits his or her proposal. Once you get a profile of the reviewers, ask if your grant seeker could be considered for selection as a reviewer.

Unfortunately, some federal program officers frown on contact with past reviewers. However, remember that discussions with past reviewers can be very beneficial, and let the program officer know why you need to develop your understanding of the process and how you will use the information.

Again, experience demonstrates that most grant seekers will be reluctant to make this contact and that they will need your office's assistance. You may e-mail or telephone a past reviewer. Start your conversation by identifying yourself and telling the individual that you understand he or she was a reviewer for the program. Then proceed with the following questions:

- How did you get to be a reviewer?
- Did you review proposals at the funding source's location or at your home?
- What training or instructions did the funding source give you?
- Did you follow a point system? If so, please describe it.
- What were you told to look for?
- How would you write a proposal differently now that you have been a reviewer?
- What were the most common mistakes that you saw?
- Did you meet other reviewers?
- How many proposals were you given to read?
- How much time did you have to read them?
- How did the funding source handle discrepancies in point assignments?
- What did the representative of the funding source wear, say, and do during the review process?
- Did you know about a staff review to follow your review?

CONTACTING AND MONITORING PRIVATE FUNDING SOURCES

As with government funding sources, contact with private funding sources before you write proposals is crucial to a successful proposal. Preproposal contact enables you to gather information concerning the funding source, including their needs and particular approaches or methods they find interesting. You can use this information to tailor your proposal specifically to the funding source.

However, because 50,000 foundations employ fewer than 4,000 individuals, many private funding sources are short on staff and it may be difficult to arrange contact with them. Often you will find that addresses for these sources are actually those of trust departments of banks. Your best bet for establishing contact may be using your webbing and linkage connections to secure a visit with a trustee or board member. *The Foundation Directory* is cross-referenced by names of board members to aid you in the process of determining who knows whom.

Although difficult to achieve, personal contact with a private funding source is possible if you arrange it in an organized, strategic manner. The process should consist of e-mailing or writing a letter, making a telephone call, and visiting the funding source.

PRIVATE FUNDING SOURCE WEB SITES

When this book went to print, fewer than 2,000 of the 50,000 foundations had a Web site and less than one dozen allowed electronic transmittal of proposals. With new changes in federal disclosure rules for foundations, this group is now able to comply with public information requirements by placing their IRS 990AR tax returns on the Web. My guess is that most of the 50,000 foundations will set up Web sites and electronic transmittal procedures over the next two years. In the meantime, check to see if the foundation you are interested in has a Web site, and if it does, review it to see if the Web site contains information on the foundation's proposal process.

THE INQUIRY LETTER

After checking for available Web site information, you may find that you still need to request basic information such as application guidelines and current priority statements in writing either through postal mail or e-mail. This contact should be made before you send a letter or an e-mail to the foundation or corporate funding executive requesting an appointment. Exhibit 7.11, The Sample Letter to a Private Funding Source for Basic Information (Inquiry Letter) illustrates how to word this type of correspondence.

THE APPOINTMENT LETTER

It's always a good idea to arrange an initial interview with a funding source before you submit a proposal. The best way to set up such a meeting is through your webbing and linkages. Then you will not need to contact the funding source, but your linkage will. However, if you are not able to use a linkage, the Sample Letter to a Private Funding Source for an Appointment (exhibit 7.12) will help you develop your request. Again, this letter can be sent via the postal service or e-mailed if you have the funding source's e-mail address. Please note, however, that the information you obtain from sending or e-mailing your initial inquiry letter may indicate that visits by prospective grantees are not allowed, and that the funding source simply requires the submittal of a one- to two-page letter proposal summarizing your request.

TELEPHONING A PRIVATE FUNDING SOURCE FOR AN APPOINTMENT

If you do not have a linkage or if your linkage was unable to set up an appointment for you, and you have a phone number for the funding source, you may decide to call to set up an appointment. But what do you say when you make the call?

- Ask for the funding official by name, if possible.
- Tell the official you will be in the area and would like to meet with him or her briefly to discuss a project that your research indicates the source would be interested in.
- Ask for an appointment.

Date

Name
Title
Address

Dear _____:

We have developed a project that benefits _____. Your support of this project would constitute a significant contribution in this field, which we understand is one of the important concerns of _____.

We would appreciate receiving information on your desired format for proposals, current priority statements, and other guidelines. Please add us to your mailing list or e-mail list for annual reports, newsletters, and other materials you think might be useful to us as we work on this and related projects. Our e-mail address is _____.

I will be calling you in the near future to discuss our opportunities to work together. Thank you for your cooperation.

Sincerely,

Name
Title
Phone Number

SAMPLE LETTER TO A PRIVATE FUNDING SOURCE FOR BASIC INFORMATION (INQUIRY LETTER)

EXHIBIT 7.11

If the funding official agrees to see you, make the necessary arrangements and hang up.

If the funding official will not grant you an appointment because the foundation or corporate policy does not allow visits by prospective grantees, arrange a phone interview for a later date (see the following section on telephone interviews), and/or ask if his or her travel schedule would allow them to visit your site to see your program. If one of your advocates is going to be talking to a funding source board member, you should let the funding official know. He or she will probably be more willing to talk with you in order to be able to field questions from the board member.

If the official will not grant you an appointment because of a lack of interest in your project, tell them about the data your research uncovered that prompted you to contact them. But don't be surprised to find out that their interests are no longer the same as what your research indicated. Unfortunately, it can take years for changes in the interests of funding sources to show up in resource tools. Also, ask if they are aware of other sources who may still be interested in your area. Funding sources often know one another and have inside knowledge of who is funding what.

Date

Name
Title
Address

Dear _____:

I am interested in meeting with you to discuss an important project that deals
with _____. In researching
this field, I have noticed serious, active interest on the part of _____
_____. Because we are analyzing several
possible approaches, your input at this time would be most valuable in our
formal proposal development. A few minutes of your time would enable us to
more closely meet both your concerns and our interest in this field.

I will call you to arrange a brief meeting at your convenience.

Sincerely,

Name
Title
Phone Number

SAMPLE LETTER TO A PRIVATE FUNDING SOURCE FOR AN APPOINTMENT

EXHIBIT 7.12

If you can't get through to a funding official at all, use the intermediaries and ask them intelligent questions (see exhibit 7.13, Questions to Ask a Funding Source at the First Meeting). In addition, make sure to let them know that you *will* call back. Most people try once and give up. You must be persistent.

THE TELEPHONE INTERVIEW

It is often difficult to get a foundation or corporate funding official to give you the time for an face-to-face meeting to discuss your project, or it may be inconvenient and/or expensive to set up such a meeting. While a face-to-face contact is the first choice, in those cases when it is not an option, conduct a phone interview with the funding official.

The following checklist details a four-step process to follow each time you discuss your project over the phone with a funding source. The data you would like to obtain or validate from the phone call include

- the funding source's current granting priorities;
- specific information on how you should change your project and/or proposal to make it more attractive to the funding source;

1. Having received last year's guidelines, will there be any changes? If so, what?

2. Our research shows that last year there were _____ proposals funded for a total of $_____. How many applications were those awards selected from?

3. Last year the amount of funds awarded by your organization to our type of project was approximately $_____, and the average grant size was $_____. Is this accurate and will this remain consistent?

4. Our research indicates that your deadlines were _____ and _____. Will they be the same this year?

5. Do proposals that are submitted early receive favorable treatment?

6. Whom do you use to review proposals? Reviewers? Outside experts? Board Members? Staff?

7. Are these your current granting priorities? (Give the funding official a copy of your research sheet.)

8. How do you look upon the submission of more than one proposal in a funding cycle?

9. Is this project eligible for funding under your guidelines?

10. Is our budget estimate realistic?

11. Would you look over our proposal if we finished it early?

12. Can you suggest other funding sources appropriate for this project?

13. May I see a proposal you have funded that was well liked for its style and/or format?

QUESTIONS TO ASK A FUNDING SOURCE AT THE FIRST MEETING

EXHIBIT 7.13

- proposal-format guidelines or, if there are no guidelines, information on the format preferred by the board members; and
- the most appropriate grant size to request.

Keep in mind the following tips:

- Phone midweek. Avoid Mondays and Fridays because they are filled with e-mails and are the start and end of the work week.
- Use the funding executive's name.
- Mention who referred you to the funding source.
- Refer to any correspondence you have already sent to the funding source.
- Request five minutes. Let the official know you will call back if it is not convenient at that time.

THE VISIT: FACE-TO-FACE CONTACT WITH A PRIVATE FUNDING SOURCE

A face-to-face interview is the most effective and direct way of making contact with a funding-source executive. It is an invaluable tool in developing a relationship with that funding source. Your chances of making a good impression and of understanding the information you are given are much greater in person than on the phone.

For this meeting, you have called or written ahead and have probably already shared some general introductory information.

Once you have arranged your appointment, consider the following questions (see also exhibit 7.13, Questions to Ask a Funding Source at the First Meeting).

1. *Who is (are) the best person(s) to represent us at the meeting?* Your representative at the first meeting should be an articulate member of your institution. He or she should also be a high-ranking member of your institution and a prime mover in the project you are trying to fund. One of the best approaches is to use an advocate from your advisory committee who is not and will not be paid by your college or university on this project. The time and concern of the unpaid advocate will give you instant credibility. No more than two people should be sent, or you will scare the funding source. The dress of the people sent is more important in private philanthropy than public (although it is important there also). Dress to create the image that your research suggests the funding source would like you to have. (By calling a past grantee, you may be able to find out the age and personal interests of the funding official.)

2. *What materials should be brought to the meeting?* The materials needed are best collected and organized in your proposal-development workbook (see chapter 8). You may want to bring additional materials to document the need for the project or research. Because this meeting is usually carried out with a single representative of the foundation or corporation, a laptop computer with pictures and sound that document the problem and the uniquenesses of your campus, laboratories, or consortium can be very effective at acquainting the prospective grantor with your project and institution's special qualities. Keep the presentation short (two to three minutes) and commensurate with your request. For instance, a full-motion video and professional sound would surely dwarf a $5,000 request! Visuals should be used to demonstrate need and develop agreement on the importance of meeting the need. The funding source needs to know that you have developed several possible approaches to meeting the need and that you are there to learn which approach they are most interested in. Remember, you are not there to sell or convince them on one particular approach. And most important, be ready to demonstrate the cost efficiency of the proposed approaches, your research on the grantor's past giving, and your readiness and organization by using your proposal-development workbook (see chapter 8) to answer such questions as, "Why should we give the money to you instead of another institution doing work in your field?"

PRIVATE FUNDING SOURCE REPORT FORM

Each time a member of your institution contacts a funder by e-mail, in person, or over the telephone, he or she should complete a Private Funding Source Report Form (exhibit 7.14) and a copy of the form should be put in your files. The faculty or staff member can e-mail or even fax you a copy, but your office should definitely have one.

Complete this form after each contact with a private funding source.

Name of Funding Source _____

Address of Funding Source _____

Name of Person Spoken to/e-mailed at Funding Agency _____

_____

Title of Person Spoken to/e-mailed at Funding Agency _____

_____

Phone Number and Extension of Person Spoken to/e-mailed _____

e-mail Address of Person Spoken to/e-mailed _____

Date of Contact _____

Type of Contact: _____ Phone _____ e-mail _____ In Person _____

Name of Person Who Made Contact _____

Phone Number and Extension of Person Who Made Contact _____

e-mail Address of Person Who Made Contact _____

Objective of Contact _____

_____

_____

_____

_____

_____

_____

Results of Contact _____

_____

_____

_____

_____

_____

_____

_____

PRIVATE FUNDING SOURCE REPORT FORM

EXHIBIT 7.14

This simple procedure has a number of important benefits:

- You do not have to reinvent the wheel each time you speak with the funding source, or worry about damaging your image by discussing issues you have already discussed with the funder.
- You always have a source of current information on the funding source.
- You do not have to waste time locating people in your institution who have contacted the funder to ask them basic questions such as amount to request, name of person to whom you should submit the proposal, and proposal emphasis.

- You avoid the embarrassment of contradicting something said by a colleague in a previous contact with the funder.

A blank copy of this form should be placed on your Web site (see chapter 15), e-mailed, or sent to all advocates who may make contact with funders. Completed forms should be filed under the names of the funders and referred to before subsequent contacts with those funders.

Remember, one of your main objectives is to uncover the hidden agenda of the funding source and any information on priorities and how they affect you.

COORDINATING CONTACT WITH ADVOCATES

Advocates can increase the credibility of the organization and provide valuable assistance to your funding effort. The development of an advocacy file will help you coordinate contact with your advocates. An advocacy file will provide for the one-stop location of

- lists of advocates used by the institution,
- lists of advisory committee members,
- advocate endorsement letters, and
- a directory of interested individuals with various skills who will represent the institution on potential advisory committees, etc.

The lack of coordination in this important area can result in advocacy "burnout" created by

- multiple requests to individual advocates for endorsement letters from several grant seekers,
- repeated requests due to lost or misfiled letters, or
- the requesting of an advocate to become a member of an advisory committee when he or she is already on one or more.

The most logical site for storing and managing information on advocates and dean and department chair advisory groups is the grants office, because it is the office that seeks to maximize the use of this information.

Most colleges and universities do not elicit feedback on how their many advocates and advisors feel about their utilization. However, input from these individuals should be solicited and processed in order to meet their expectations and increase their desire to involve themselves with your institution. Share the survey questions listed in exhibit 7.15 with your counterparts and use them to generate feedback, which can be used in the development of your new or improved program.

Once when I surveyed the members of a corporate advisory group for a dean, we were surprised to find out that the group's major complaint was that they felt we were not taking full advantage of the group's linkages to individuals who could help the institution!

Preproposal contact is one variable which is definitely related to grant success. If your success rate is down, brainstorm the inclusion of the techniques discussed in this chapter with a relevant group of individuals, and be sure to include preproposal contact when diagraming the factors related to developing a successful grants strategy (see chapter 1). Complete exhibit 7.16 so that you can be certain that the role of the grants office in contacting funding sources is adequately addressed in your overall plan.

Questions for Volunteers, Advocates and Advisory Committee Members

1. How would you rate the overall usefulness of your participation at (institution) as a volunteer, advocate, or advisory committee member?

   _____ of little usefulness _____ somewhat useful _____very useful

2. Which of the following functions have you participated in as an advisory committee member, advocate, or volunteer of the institution?
   _____ providing feedback on existing program
   _____ planning new program
   _____ developing new program
   _____ providing opinions
   _____ supplying information on potential opportunities for the college/university
   _____ raising funds for the college or university
   _____ providing list of webbing and linkages
   _____ contacting potential funding sources on behalf of the college/university
   _____ visiting potential funding sources on behalf of the college/university

3. What other functions could you have supplied assistance with but were not asked?

4. Would you recommend serving as a volunteer, advocate, or advisory committee member at the institution to others in our community?
   _____Yes _____ No

   Why or why not?

5. What was the most positive aspect of your participation?

6. What was the most negative aspect of your participation?

SURVEY QUESTIONS—THE ROLE OF THE GRANTS OFFICE IN CONTACTING FUNDING SOURCES

EXHIBIT 7.15

Questions for Faculty and Staff

7. How would you rate your grants office's assistance in providing you with the names of alumni, volunteers, advocates, advisory committee members, and/or other faculty and staff who have a relationship (linkage) with your potential grantor?

   ___ non-existent
   ___ inadequate
   ___ adequate
   ___ more than adequate

8. If you have ever been provided with the name of a linkage and have contacted him or her, how useful was the information you gathered?

   ___ of little value
   ___ somewhat valuable
   ___ very helpful

9. Has the grants office ever helped you in the area of pre proposal contact with *public* (federal and state) grantors?

   _____ Yes _____ No

   If yes, please rate the helpfulness of their assistance in the following areas. (If assistance not provided, please leave blank.)

	Of Little Value	Somewhat Helpful	Very Helpful
a. Assistance with telephone contact	_____	_____	_____
b. Assistance with e-mail/written contact	_____	_____	_____
c. Assistance with personal visit	_____	_____	_____
d. Assistance with coordinating contact with past reviewers	_____	_____	_____
e. Assistance in being invited to become a reviewer	_____	_____	_____
f. Assistance in obtaining a list of past grantees	_____	_____	_____
g. Assistance in getting guidelines and published rules	_____	_____	_____
h. Assistance in obtaining scoring and/or other evaluation information	_____	_____	_____
i. Assistance in identifying advocates and obtaining letters of support	_____	_____	_____

SURVEY QUESTIONS—THE ROLE OF THE GRANTS OFFICE IN CONTACTING FUNDING SOURCES

EXHIBIT 7.15 (*continued*)

10. Has the grants office ever helped you in the area of preproposal contact with *private* (foundation and corporate) grantors? _____Yes _____No

If yes, please rate the helpfulness of their assistance in the following areas. (If assistance not provided, please leave blank.)

	Of Little Value	Somewhat Helpful	Very Helpful
a. Assistance in writing letter of inquiry and/or other written contact including e-mail	_____	_____	_____
b. Assistance making contact by phone	_____	_____	_____
c. Assistance with personal visit	_____	_____	_____
d. Assistance obtaining guidelines on format, application forms, annual reports, tax returns, etc.	_____	_____	_____
e. Assistance in identifying advocates and obtaining letters of support	_____	_____	_____

SURVEY QUESTIONS—THE ROLE OF THE GRANTS OFFICE IN CONTACTING FUNDING SOURCES

EXHIBIT 7.15 (*continued*)

For Each Activity/Item listed, Check Status

Activity/Item	Reviewed, Appropriate Part of Grants Office	Reviewed, Appropriate Part of Other Office (List)	Reviewed, Not Applicable	Reviewed, Inappropriate Needs Action	Non-existent, Needs Action
1. Webbing and linkage system • record of "friends" of in-stitution • method or system to ascertain links between friends and funders (questionaires, etc.) • computerized system to record, store, update,					

Complete this Section for Each Activity/Item Needing Action

What Needs to be Accomplished?	By Whom? (Office/ Person)	By When? (Time Frame)	Resources Required— Personnel, Supplies, Equipment, Programming, etc.	Estimated Costs

GRANTS OFFICE INVENTORY—THE ROLE OF THE GRANTS OFFICE IN CONTACTING FUNDING SOURCES

EXHIBIT 7.16

For Each Activity/Item listed, Check Status

Activity/Item	Reviewed, Appropriate Part of Grants Office	Reviewed, Appropriate Part of Other Office (List)	Reviewed, Not Applicable	Reviewed, Inappropriate Needs Action	Non-existent, Needs Action
maintain and retrieve linkage information • linkage committee with some board representation 2. Preproposal contact controls or a systematic method for approaching funding sources					

Complete this Section for Each Activity/Item Needing Action

What Needs to be Accomplished?	By Whom? (Office/ Person)	By When? (Time Frame)	Resources Required— Personnel, Supplies, Equipment, Programming, etc.	Estimated Costs

GRANTS OFFICE INVENTORY—THE ROLE OF THE GRANTS OFFICE IN CONTACTING FUNDING SOURCES

EXHIBIT 7.16 (continued)

For Each Activity/Item listed, Check Status

Activity/Item	Reviewed, Appropriate Part of Grants Office	Reviewed, Appropriate Part of Other Office (List)	Reviewed, Not Applicable	Reviewed, Inappropriate Needs Action	Non-existent, Needs Action
• standardized e-mail/ letters for: getting on mailing lists, requesting lists of reviewers, obtaining an appointment, getting basic information • sample lists of questions to ask: funding officers, past grantees, past reviewers					

Complete this Section for Each Activity/Item Needing Action

What Needs to be Accomplished?	By Whom? (Office/ Person)	By When? (Time Frame)	Resources Required— Personnel, Supplies, Equipment, Programming, etc.	Estimated Costs

EXHIBIT 7.16 (*continued*)

CHAPTER 8

The Role of the Grants Office in Promoting an Organized Proposal

The grants office has a dramatic effect on the perception that prospective grant seekers have of the grants process. Does your office make proposal preparation appear organized, controllable, and accomplishable? Or is the process chaotic, confusing, and out of control?

Developing and distributing grants-office procedures to all staff members will educate them about the role of your office. Whether this user information is presented to your faculty and staff in newsletters, through e-mails, a manual, or on your Web site, its distribution will aid in promoting an organized, proactive image of your office. In addition to a description of how your grants office processes grants, consider distributing a computerized package of helpful checklists and worksheets to each grant seeker. Ultimately, increased organizational skills and accurate expectations will assist the grant seeker in producing a better proposal and reflect positively on your grants office.

Review the following worksheets, checklists, and grant tools and identify those items that you can use to assist the grant seeker with idea generation, grant writing, budget preparation, and so on. *The "How To" Grants Manual*, the companion book to this book, contains more detailed information on the areas mentioned in this chapter and is available through Oryx Press. Please note that, while the techniques suggested in *The "How To" Grants Manual* are aimed at the individual grant seeker, many of the same techniques are included in this book but are presented from a grants system perspective.

ORGANIZING PROPOSAL IDEAS FOR MARKETING/PROPOSAL DEVELOPMENT WORKBOOK

One function of the grants administrator's job is to help prospective grant seekers develop and organize their proposal ideas. This assistance must be rendered in such a way that it

- supports the monitoring and quality-control functions of the grants office;
- provides the tools necessary for the marketing of proposals;
- organizes the process, and thus saves time for the institution, the administration, and the proposal developer.

Grant writers often find the proposal development process complex and difficult because it is often expected to be accomplished during "spare time" or integrated into a demanding job description. Many grant writers become overwhelmed because they look at the big picture only—the completed proposal. As a result, they procrastinate and avoid approaching the application until the deadline is close and it is too late to incorporate successful concepts and do an adequate job.

The Swiss cheese concept, developed in Allan Lakein's book *How to Get Control of Your Time and Your Life*, is a time-management strategy that can help your grant seekers make the process of preparing and applying for grants more organized and less overwhelming.[1] The proposal developer can be thought of as a mouse who is faced with a large piece of cheese. Rather than attempting to eat the cheese in one sitting, the mouse would do well to eat holes in the cheese one little piece at a time. The grant seeker can take a similar approach; he or she must divide the grants process into pieces and tackle each piece individually until the task is completed. Taken one step at a time, the proposal-development process will not be overwhelming.

The steps necessary to organize and produce a grant application are logical and follow a definite order. These steps provide the basis and chapters in *The "How To" Grants Manual*, and the purpose of mentioning them here is not to replicate what is contained in that book but to provide you with a context in which to explore the development of your grants system. By focusing on the steps or activities leading to the finished proposal, proposal preparation seems more accomplishable. The steps are listed below. The first ten assist the proposal developer in putting ideas in written form, developing reactions to these ideas, and evaluating the original idea and variations on that idea to produce the most fundable project.

1. Develop and evaluate your project ideas.
2. Redefine your project ideas.
3. Document the need for your project.
4. Determine your institution's uniquenesses.
5. Develop your case statement.
6. Use advocates.
7. Organize a project-advisory committee.
8. Choose the correct funding source.
9. Research your chosen funding-source marketplace.
10. Contact your prospective funding sources.

The next eight steps assist the grant writer in developing his or her proposal.

11. Develop your problem/needs statement.
12. Write your objectives.
13. Develop your methods.
14. Develop your project planner.

15. Evaluate.
16. Explore future funding.
17. Disseminate.
18. Budget.

The remaining ten components assist the proposal developer in the significant tasks of writing and submitting the proposal.

19. Proposal Introduction
20. Title Page
21. Summary Abstract
22. Attachments
23. Cover Letter
24. Letter Proposal
25. Proposal-Review Committee
26. Submission: Private Source
27. Submission: Public Source
28. Outcome and Follow-up

Before tackling these steps, it is helpful for the grant seeker to set up a proposal-development workbook, or Swiss cheese book, for each of his or her major areas of interest.

A proposal-development workbook consists of a three-ring binder with a tab or divider for each of the steps or activities outlined above. The proposal writer places information collected over time in the appropriate sections. This will reduce the time wasted frantically searching for information at the last minute. In addition, you can arrange to have standard information about your institution inserted into the proper sections (e.g., case statement). By placing helpful information in the workbooks in advance, you will enhance your image as an organized and efficient partner in the grant-seeking process and show your faculty and staff that you are sensitive to the time they invest in the grants process and value their efforts. I estimate that the use of the proposal-development workbook will save up to 50 percent of the time ordinarily spent in proposal preparation.

In addition, the proposal-organizing workbook provides the grant seeker with information to answer the funding official's questions during preproposal contact. Finally, when personal contact by the proposal developer is not possible, the grants administrator can do a more credible job representing the prospective grant seeker to funders by consulting the grant seeker's workbook.

NEEDS STATEMENT/OBJECTIVES/METHODS

The following is a brief discussion of the needs statement and objectives and methods section of a proposal. The Grant-Writing Checklist (exhibit 8.1) and the Tailoring Worksheet (exhibit 8.2) that follow will assist the grant seeker in designing and writing his or her proposal.

Needs Statement

Most grant seekers feel strongly about the need for their project. Too many assume that funding sources share the same feelings of concern and forget that the funding source has to

The proposal must be organized in the exact manner prescribed by the funder. Do not change the order requested. Identify the sections by the same language and terms that the grantor uses.

The order in which the proposal is submitted is rarely the order in which it is written. As you write each of the main sections of your proposal, make certain that you have addressed the following items:

Needs Statement/Search of Relevant Literature

_____ Statement is clear and concise
_____ Well-chosen, documented statistics
_____ Motivating and compelling—sense of urgency
_____ Objective with a variety of sources cited
_____ Documentation of gap between what is and what ought to be
_____ Documentation matched to reader/reviewer

Hypothesis/Specific Aims/Objectives

_____ Measurement indicators established
_____ Performance indicators established
_____ Time frame for completion established
_____ Cost estimate in objective

Methods/Activities/Protocol

_____ Written clearly
_____ Sequence and relationship of activities clear
_____ Project personnel's time allocated by activities
_____ Time frames for activities outlined

GRANT-WRITING CHECKLIST

EXHIBIT 8.1

choose between many interesting proposals and several areas of concern. To increase their chances of funding, grant seekers must document the existence of a problem or need that is viewed by the funding source as a state of affairs that can be made better, improved, or different. Essentially, the grant seeker must show that there is a gap between what is and what ought to be.

The grant seeker should search the relevant literature in his or her project area, collect data that demonstrates need, and keep it in a Proposal-Development Workbook. When he or she is ready to write a tailored proposal, the proposal developer can select the items he or she thinks will be the most convincing to their particular funding source.

The development of research proposals follows an analogous route to model and demonstration grants. There must be a clearly defined problem, question, gap, or need to be addressed.

---

1. Project Title:
2. Funding Source Selected:
3. The Approach Most Likely to Meet with Success (based on research and contact with funding source):

4. Grant Request Size (range):
5. Evaluation Criteria or Points Assigned to Each of the Following Parts of the Proposal and Page Limitations to Each Component:
    a. Needs Statement—

    b. Methods/Activities—

    c. Evaluation—

    d. Background of Principal Investigator/Project Director—

    e. Attachments—

TAILORING WORKSHEET

EXHIBIT 8.2

Researchers are inoculated with the same virus that all grant seekers share—the "why" virus. (Why does this happen? What can we do to change it?) The researcher asks a question and then must search the literature in the field to determine what is already known and who would care if the question were answered. (What is the value or benefit? Who would value the closing of the gap?) For example, the question of whether treatment X or Y influences the healing time of a pressure sore (bedsore) is subject to a search of the literature to see what work has already been done in this area and to determine the importance of the question. (What exists now? What is the incidence or extent of the problem, and the future impact of not addressing the question?) If there is no compelling or motivating reason to use grant monies to answer the question, the researcher is not likely to be successful.

The research question must be specific and focused. Many researchers are overly optimistic and select too broad a question or too many questions to investigate. This sets them up for failure because they cannot control the situation. In other words, they have too many forces or variables to deal with that can influence the outcome.

Researchers must develop their questions into either a null hypothesis or an alternative hypothesis. The null hypothesis predicts that there is no basic difference between the two selected areas. For example, "There is no difference between pressure sores treated with X or Y." The researcher sets up the study to measure the outcome, or the *dependent* variable (increased healing of pressure sores). The researcher manipulates or changes the intervention, or the *independent* variable (use of treatment X or Y), to observe the effect of the two treatments on the dependent variable. Just as behavioral objectives contain a measurement indicator for success (increasing reading scores from the 80th to the 90th percentile as measured by the Flockman reading scale), the researcher must select a statistical evaluation model, before data are collected, that will be used to evaluate the differences in the intervention. When there are significant differences between two treatments, the null hypothesis is disproved and the results are based on differences in treatment rather than on chance.

The alternative hypothesis predicts that there is indeed a difference between the two treatments and suggests the direction of that difference. For example, "Treatment X will result in a healing rate that is 50 percent faster than treatment Y."

Irrespective of whether your grant seeker is writing a proposal for a research, model, or demonstration grant, the grants office's role in this process is to encourage the grant seeker to use all existing resources to search for relevant literature. The goal of the search is to gather articles, studies, and statistics to demonstrate and document a compelling need.

Objectives

Because on occasion the grants office will be asked to help a grant seeker to develop proposal objectives and methods, the office should have subject material on these areas.

Objectives are measurable steps taken to narrow or close the gap between what is and what ought to be. Objectives must follow the need statement, because one cannot write an objective unless the need is documented.

To write an objective, the proposal developer must first determine the results area, measurement indicators, performance standards, time frame, and cost frame, and then combine all of this information into a standard format. The standard format for a nonresearch objective is "To (action verb and statement reflecting the measurement indicator) by (performance standard) by (deadline) a cost of no more than (cost frame)." For example, "To reduce hospital readmissions of people over sixty-five in Boise by 10 percent by the seventh month of the project at a cost of no more than $15,000."

A well-written objective reflects the amount of change wanted in a result area. If an objective does not reflect the amount of change desired, chances are that the measurement indicator is wrong or the performance standards are too low. Remember, objectives should emphasize the end result (the ultimate benefit of the program's work), not tasks or methods.

Methods

The methods or activities section of a proposal is the detailed description of what will actually be done to meet the objectives. The methods section should

- describe the program activities in detail;
- describe the sequence, flow, and interrelationships of the activities;
- describe the planned staffing of the program;
- describe the client population and the method of determining client selection, and
- present a reasonable scope of activities that can be accomplished within the stated time frame and with the resources of the organization.

It should also

- make reference to the cost/benefit ratio of the project,
- discuss why success is probable,
- describe the uniqueness of the methods and overall project design, and
- assign responsibility to specific individuals for each part of the project.

By encouraging grant seekers to use the project planner discussed in the following section, the grants office can be sure that the methods section will reflect a well-conceived plan for the accomplishment of the objectives.

PROJECT PLANNER

You may choose to use a project planner (exhibit 8.3) to assist the proposal writer in developing the relationship between the methods/activities and the costs. The project planner was developed in my grants office at a university to assist me in understanding the grant writer's intentions and in developing a format that would lead to a realistic, defensible budget.

The project planner forces the grant writer to establish a relationship between the project personnel, space, equipment, consulting expense, and supplies and each method or activity proposed to meet each objective. Such task analysis allows the grants-office administrator to help the writer negotiate the final award and administer the funded proposal.

The project planner allows for the development of quarterly cash forecasts, documentation of in-kind or matching commitment, and monitoring of milestones or progress indicators. Whether these tasks fall under the purview of your grants office or not, the project planner outlines the key areas that will enhance your institution's credibility with the funder.

Review the Project Planner Instructions (exhibit 8.4) on how to complete this spreadsheet and develop an example that is tailored to your college or university and your fiscal system. Reproduce the instructions and your example, and distribute them to your prospective grant seekers to assist them in understanding their proposal, the budget, and the importance of demonstrating to the funding source that their project is organized and that the proposed results are attainable. The project planner also positions your college or university as an institution that will be capable of administering the funds after the award is made. (Please note that the disk that accompanies this book includes an electronic project planner that can be used with Microsoft Excel.)

BUDGET AND CASH FORECASTS

Grant offices normally assist grant seekers in some way with budget preparation. Many potential problems can be avoided by establishing and implementing standardized budget procedures.

The advantages of providing budget assistance are directly related to how early it is provided in the proposal-preparation process. Some institutions review the budget just prior to sign-off. Unfortunately at this point, there is little time for significant restructuring. Therefore, the earlier in the process, the better.

PROJECT PLANNER™

PROJECT TITLE: _____

A. List Project objectives or outcomes A. B. B. List Methods to accomplish each objective as A-1, A-2, A-3 . . . B-1, B-2 . . .	MONTH		TIME	PROJECT PERSONNEL	PERSONNEL COSTS		
	BEGIN	END			SALARIES & WAGES	FRINGE BENEFITS	TOTAL
	C / D		E	F	G	H	I

© David G. Bauer Associates, Inc.
(800) 836-0732

TOTAL DIRECT COSTS OR COSTS REQUESTED FROM FUNDER ▶

MATCHING FUNDS, IN-KIND CONTRIBUTIONS, OR DONATED COSTS ▶

TOTAL COSTS ▶

PROJECT PLANNER

EXHIBIT 8.3

Sheet _____ of _____

Proposal Developed for _____

PROJECT DIRECTOR: _____ Proposed starting date _____ Proposal Year _____

CONSULTANTS • CONTRACT SERVICES			NON-PERSONNEL RESOURCES NEEDED SUPPLIES • EQUIPMENT • MATERIALS				SUB-TOTAL COST FOR ACTIVITY	MILESTONES PROGRESS INDICATORS	
TIME	COST/WEEK	TOTAL	ITEM	COST/ITEM	QUANTITY	TOT. COST	TOTAL I. L. P	ITEM	DATE
J	K	L	M	N	O	P	Q	R	S
								T		◄ % OF TOTAL
									◄
								100%	◄

PROJECT PLANNER

EXHIBIT 8.3 (*continued*)

1. List your objectives or tasks in Column A. Not all funding sources are interested in particularly well-written objectives. Just give them what they want. Some contracts require tasks or enabling objectives.

2. In Column B, list the activities or methods necessary to meet the objective. These are the tasks that will meet the need.

3. In Column C/D, place the date you will begin the task and the date you will end it.

4. In Column E, designate the number of person weeks needed to accomplish the task. You may use person hours, person days, or person months instead.

5. Use Column F to designate the personnel that will spend measurable or significant amounts of time on the task. The determination of key personnel is critical for the development of job descriptions. By listing the activities or tasks that the key personnel are responsible for and the minimum qualifications or background required, you will have a job description. Call a placement agency to get an estimate of the salary needed to fill the position. The number of weeks or months of work will determine whether the position is part- or full-time.

   By completing this portion of the project planner, you will be able to quickly access how many hours of work are assigned to a given time span. If you have your key personnel working more than 160 hours a month, you may need to change Column E—the number of person weeks necessary to accomplish this task.

6. Columns G, H, and I are for personnel costs. Special care should be taken to determine whose time on your staff (or in your institution) will be donated. This may be a requirement for the grant, or you may want to use this contribution to demonstrate your good faith to the funding source.

   Put an asterisk (*) by each person you donate to the project and be sure to include the donation of fringes for each person with donated wages.

7. Columns J, K, and L are for consultants and contract services. These three columns should be used for services that are most cost efficiently supplied by individuals who are not in your institution's normal employ. Note that there are no fringes paid to these individuals.

8. Columns M, N, O, and P are where you list the nonpersonnel resources needed to complete this activity and achieve your objective. Be careful not to underestimate the materials and supplies necessary for the successful completion of the project. Grant seekers sometimes lose out on potential donated or matching items simply because they do not ask themselves what they *really* need to complete each activity.

9. Column Q can be completed in one or two ways. Each activity can be subtotaled or several activities can be subtotaled together within each

PROJECT PLANNER INSTRUCTIONS

EXHIBIT 8.4

objective. In either case, lines should be drawn designating amounts requested, amounts donated, and total amounts so that the funding source can clearly see the in-kind contributions.

10. Under Column R, Milestones, record what the funding source will receive as progress indicators. Progress indicators should show the funding source that you are working toward your objectives.

11. Column S lists the date on which the funding source will receive the milestone or progress indicator.

12. INDIRECT COSTS—At the bottom of the project planner you will see a section on indirect costs. Indirect costs are usually a critical part of federal grants. Unfortunately, they are often poorly understood by *many* grant seekers. The concept involves repaying the recipient of a federal grant for costs that are indirectly attributable to the grant but are difficult to break down individually. Indirect costs are calculated by using a formula provided by the Federal government and include such things as

- heat and lights for an office,
- upkeep of the building,
- maintenance staff, and
- the payroll department.

The formula is expressed as a percentage of the total amount requested from the funding source (total from Column Q of your project planner) or as a percentage of the personnel costs (total from Column I of your project planner).

PROJECT PLANNER INSTRUCTIONS

EXHIBIT 8.4 (*continued*)

The grants office can help the grant seeker estimate costs accurately and save time by developing files on common grant-related costs, such as

- project personnel and consultants,
- costs for computers and phone lines,
- indirect costs,
- rental and lease agreements on grant equipment, and
- square-footage costs for off-campus rental space.

In addition, the grants office input can be especially helpful in estimating matching or donated costs.

Although budget requirements and forms vary, the basic information required is generally the same. Careful construction of your project planner will help you prepare your budget with a cost estimate for each activity. However, remember that your project planner is not the budget—it is an analysis of what has to be done and the costs involved in each step of the process.

The Grants Office Time Line

The Grants Office Time Line (exhibit 8.5) is a valuable tool. It helps to maintain the institution's image and credibility with the grantor by providing an understanding of the relationship between activities, their timing and their cost. It will also assist the grants administrator in meeting the milestones (progress indicators) listed on columns R and S of the project planner.

The grants office should have a copy of the time line of each grant in progress. In addition, the project director or principal investigator should also have a copy. This will help to avoid problems such as late reporting, overlooked reports, and the over- or under-expenditure of funds, which can all severely damage the grantee's credibility with the prospective funder.

THE BUDGET FOR PUBLIC FUNDING SOURCES

Public funding sources typically require that several detailed budget sheets be submitted in the source's own specific format. Generally, the budget section is located several sections away from the objectives and methodology sections. To assist in budget negotiation and for other reasons already discussed, a project planner should be completed and used to help develop the budget. The figures derived from this process should be put in whatever format is requested by the funder.

One of the more common federal budget forms for nonconstruction projects is Standard Form (SF) 424A (exhibit 8.6). However, when completing a budget for a specific program, you must use the forms provided in the particular agency's proposal guideline package.

The information requested on the budget summary and budget categories may be retrieved from the project planner.

The Grants Office Time Line can be used to develop the required information on cash forecast. Each activity or method has a project begin and end date. One can also determine the cost of each activity or method by adding together the cost of all the elements needed to complete the activity. With a little extrapolation on the cost of each activity and when it will begin and end, you can help your grant seeker develop a rough idea of the quarterly cash flow.

THE BUDGET FOR PRIVATE FUNDING SOURCES

Budget formats for private funding sources vary widely. Most foundations and corporations do not provide a suggested format. Some leave this item up to the discretion of the applicant; others do not require a budget at all—just the total amount requested.

You may use the format of the Sample Project Budget (exhibit 8.7) in those instances when the funding source does not provide or suggest a format. If attachments are allowed, include a project planner in your proposal. This can be very beneficial, because space is often limited to two to five pages in the private proposal system, and the project planner succinctly tells the whole story. The project planner documents the budget request (sometimes referred to as the budget narrative), and in some cases the planner may be viewed by private funding sources *as* the budget and the budget narrative. It also appeals to those readers/reviewers who are visually oriented.

GRANTS OFFICE TIME LINE

ACTIV-ITY NO.	1	2	3	4	5	6	7	8	9	10	11	12	TOTAL COST FOR ACTIVITY

	1st QUARTER	2nd QUARTER	3rd QUARTER	4th QUARTER	TOTAL

QUARTERLY FORECAST OF EXPENDITURES ▲

Grants Office Time Line

EXHIBIT 8.5

BUDGET INFORMATION - Non-Construction Programs

OMB Approval No. 0348-0044

SECTION A - BUDGET SUMMARY

Grant Program Function or Activity (a)	Catalog of Federal Domestic Assistance Number (b)	Estimated Unobligated Funds		New or Revised Budget		
		Federal (c)	Non-Federal (d)	Federal (e)	Non-Federal (f)	Total (g)
1.		$	$	$	$	$
2.						
3.						
4.						
5. Totals		$	$	$	$	$

SECTION B - BUDGET CATEGORIES

6. Object Class Categories	GRANT PROGRAM, FUNCTION OR ACTIVITY				Total (5)
	(1)	(2)	(3)	(4)	
	$	$	$	$	$
a. Personnel					
b. Fringe Benefits					
c. Travel					
d. Equipment					
e. Supplies					
f. Contractual					
g. Construction					
h. Other					
i. Total Direct Charges *(sum of 6a-6h)*					
j. Indirect Charges					
k. TOTALS *(sum of 6i and 6j)*	$	$	$	$	$
7. Program Income	$	$	$	$	$

STANDARD FORM 424A—BUDGET INFORMATION—NON-CONSTRUCTION PROGRAMS

EXHIBIT 8.6

SECTION C - NON-FEDERAL RESOURCES

(a) Grant Program	(b) Applicant	(c) State	(d) Other Sources	(e) TOTALS
8.	$	$	$	$
9.				
10.				
11.				
12. TOTAL *(sum of lines 8-11)*	$	$	$	$

SECTION D - FORECASTED CASH NEEDS

	Total for 1st Year	1st Quarter	2nd Quarter	3rd Quarter	4th Quarter
13. Federal	$	$	$	$	$
14. Non-Federal					
15. TOTAL *(sum of lines 13 and 14)*	$	$	$	$	$

SECTION E - BUDGET ESTIMATES OF FEDERAL FUNDS NEEDED FOR BALANCE OF THE PROJECT

(a) Grant Program	FUTURE FUNDING PERIODS (Years)			
	(b) First	(c) Second	(d) Third	(e) Fourth
16.	$	$	$	$
17.				
18.				
19.				
20. TOTAL *(sum of lines 16-19)*	$	$	$	$

SECTION F - OTHER BUDGET INFORMATION

21. Direct Charges:	22. Indirect Charges:

23. Remarks:

Authorized for Local Reproduction   Standard Form 424A (Rev. 7-97) Page 2

STANDARD FORM 424A—BUDGET INFORMATION—NON-CONSTRUCTION PROGRAMS

EXHIBIT 8.6 (*continued*)

Project Name:	Expediture Total	Donated/ In-Kind	Requested From This Source
I. PERSONNEL			
A. Salaries, Wages			
B. Fringe Benefits			
C. Consultants/Contracted Services			
PERSONNEL SUBTOTAL			

SAMPLE PROJECT BUDGET

EXHIBIT 8.7

Project Name:	Expediture Total	Donated/ In-Kind	Requested From This Source
II. NONPERSONNEL			
A. Space Costs			
B. Equipment			
C. Supplies (Consumables)			
D. Travel			
Local			
Out of Town			
E. Telephone			

SAMPLE PROJECT BUDGET

EXHIBIT 8.7 (*continued*)

Project Name:	Expediture Total	Donated/ In-Kind	Requested From This Source
F. Other Nonpersonnel Costs			
NONPERSONNEL SUBTOTAL:			
PERSONNEL SUBTOTAL:			
PROJECT TOTAL:			
PERCENTAGE:			

NOTES:

SAMPLE PROJECT BUDGET

EXHIBIT 8.7 (*continued*)

An estimate of the cash forecast can be made from the Grants Office Time Line. Follow the same procedure as that for federal funds.

CREATING YOUR PROPOSAL ONLINE

The increasing advances in technology are having a dramatic effect on grant writing. This does not just refer to the incorporation of electronic submittal which is discussed in chapter 10, but also the creating, organizing, and writing of proposals. Many federal agencies are in the midst of planning systems that allow for the creation of proposals online using the agency's standard forms. In fact, a new law promises what agencies have been talking about for years—streamlining federal grants, mainly through electronic means. Public Law 106-7, the Federal Financial Assistance Management Improvement Act of 1999, requires agencies to create a common system for simplifying application, administrative, and reporting procedures for grants through electronic processing. While some agencies will have difficulty meeting the law's requirements in a timely fashion, some are already doing so. For example, the Department of Education recently started using an electronic format known as e-GAPS, or Electronic Grant Application Package System. The program provides the proposal developer with grant packages specific to each Department of Education program or competition. The e-GAPS Web site (http://e-grants.ed.gov) provides the applicant with templates with which they can create their proposal, techniques to cut and paste, and the capability to add attachments from word processing files. The system is initiated by the applicant who registers by selecting a user identification number (ID). Once given an ID, the applicant is referred to as the application manager. The application manager may share his or her ID with other members of his or her grant-writing team or consortium, thus allowing for multiple individuals to work on separate sections of a proposal simultaneously. This system and others under development from other federal agencies will provide the the college or university grants effort with the ability to:

- keep within space and page limitations. The templates force the proposal writer to deal with these limitations, which reduces the time it takes for grants offices to keep track of each solicitor's particular rules and to tactfully handle reducing the number of words in someone else's proposal.
- prepare budgets on the correct federal forms. This avoids problems that occur when forms vary from agency to agency.
- easily submit proposals, thereby reducing the need for commercial delivery.
- reduce costs associated with paper, printing, and the personnel needed to photocopy, collate, staple, etc.

The e-GAPS system is now an integral part of the Department of Education's Central Application Processing System (EDCAPS) and includes the Grants Administration and Payment System (GAPS). This multi-layered system already provides for funds to be drawn electronically for efficient project utilization and soon will be used to electronically distribute applications to reviewers for scoring and evaluation. Currently, applicants must use their own spell and grammar checks, and proposals are returned online for changes. However, who knows what the future will hold.

What is really interesting is that these new electronic proposal organizing opportunities have yet to be explored for their impact on grants administration. For example, what are the checks and balances regarding sign-off from the appropriate institutional officials? The Department of Education says it will still require some written signatures on funded projects, but what about on applications? One thing is for sure: there will always be a few entrepreneurs on campuses who will figure out the weaknesses of the new systems and exploit them to their own advantage.

In any event, this new area presents a unique opportunity to implement feedback mechanisms virtually from the onset of the programs. Evaluation early on in any of these developing electronic proposal organizing systems will increase efficiency and reduce potential abuse.

PROPOSAL-IMPROVEMENT COMMITTEE

One of the most effective techniques for encouraging staff to produce well-organized proposals is to encourage the development and use of a proposal-improvement committee to critique proposals prior to submittal. The techniques suggested are adaptations of Walter Edward Deming's work with quality circles to improve production in the corporate world.[2] The purpose of this committee is to increase the fundability of proposals by reviewing them in the same way that actual reviewers and board members will review them, make changes and corrections before the proposal is submitted, and therefore, increase the score and attract funding.

The strategy can be implemented at the department level by a proactive department chair, but generally the impetus for quality emanates from the grants office. Therefore, it is my contention that the development and use of a proposal-improvement committee is best encouraged and managed by the grants office. Because the grants effort and its evaluation is always related to the college or university's proposal success rate, you are, after all, the administrator inexorably involved in quality.

Research and preproposal contact should provide the information necessary to duplicate, as closely as possible, the actual reviewing process. For example, if the research indicates that the review process takes two hours, send the committee members a draft of the proposal prior to the committee meeting with a note outlining the amount of time the reviewers actually spend on each proposal and a sketch of their backgrounds. (However, please note that many proposals are reviewed in less than one hour and that in those cases you may review the research on the funding source and the time limitations, distribute the proposal, and conduct the review at the committee meetings.) Request that your mock reviewers score the proposal following the system that the actual reviewers will use and bring their comments and scores to the meeting.

The proposal-improvement committee should be comprised of your most promising grant writers. I initiated the idea of an improvement committee by inviting potential members to my grants office for lunch. I explained the activities of the committee to them and assured everyone present that the meetings would not last longer than one hour and would include a free lunch. After several months of meetings and a rotation of committee members, former committee members who realized the value of this exercise were actually organizing their own committees without the involvement of the grants office.

The greatest impetus for the use and acceptance of a proposal-improvement committee came when several letter proposals to private funders, each less than five pages long, received funding. The proposal initiators gained valuable insight into how foundation and corporate board members read and reacted to proposals that were not being evaluated by a strict set of criteria like those for federal proposals. It also helped to have a corporate friend of the college and a foundation trustee volunteer to serve on the committee. Committee members and staff began to feel that if these proposals could bring in money, so could theirs. They also learned that the background of reviewers, as well as writing style and proposal organization, were important factors in the process that could not be forgotten in the zeal to tell the funding source what he or she *wanted*.

Western Michigan University in Kalamazoo is just one institution that has put this technique to good use. At WMU, the impetus for performing a quality circle is encouraged and supported by the grants office, and one staff person from the grants office is responsible for the following functions associated with the process:

- assisting the proposal developer in obtaining the necessary reviewer scoring and evaluation information;
- organizing a group of volunteer mock reviewers;
- reproducing the draft proposal and scoring system materials;
- setting up a room for the quality circle to occur;
- arranging breakfast, lunch or dinner for the volunteer mock reviewers.

In summary, the implementation of a proposal-improvement committee can

- result in a greater sensitivity and understanding of the funding source's values;
- increase the number and quality of the proposals that come from the members of the committee; and
- foster a positive atmosphere for suggesting proposal improvements and reduce the negative, fault-finding atmosphere that a proposal-critiquing exercise can often produce.

The following three worksheets should be used by the proposal-improvement committee:

- the Proposal-Improvement Committee Worksheet (exhibit 8.8), which explains the task of the committee and the proposal-review procedure;
- the Proposal-Improvement Committee—Funder Profile (exhibit 8.9); and
- the Proposal-Improvement Committee—Scoring Worksheet (exhibit 8.11).

Exhibit 8.10 is a sample of a completed Proposal-Improvement Committee—Funder Profile.

PROVIDING AN OUTSIDE CRITIQUE

In the event that your office has not yet organized a proposal-improvement committee or instituted the quality circles concept, your grant seeker may benefit by having your grants office pay for a review from an individual who has a similar background as the actual reviewers'. In these cases, utilization of an outside expert is preferable, because the grants office staff should not be expected to possess the technical expertise required in each specific field, nor be able to review hypotheses, specific aims, objectives, formulas, and statistical analysis techniques.

Thank you for assisting us in our efforts to produce quality proposals that enhance our institution's image. Your task is to review each proposal and identify those elements that are positive and should be retained in the final version of the proposal, and those elements that need to be improved. Your suggestions for improving weak areas would be appreciated.

It is critical to the success of this exercise and ultimately to the acceptance of this proposal that you review it from a viewpoint that closely matches that of the real reviewer's. To assist you in this task, we have included a summary of our research on the prospective funders. Remember, please make your suggestions from the funder's point of view!

Instructions

- Review the funding-source description and role-play how you would see our proposal from their eyes.

- Read the proposal and indicate with a plus (+) those elements you feel may be appealing to the funding source.

- Indicate with a minus (-) those elements that might be viewed negatively by the funding source.

Because we are simulating the way in which this proposal will be read by this funding source, please follow the time constraints that our research has uncovered. Remember, the funders do not always pore over every word. Although some spend several hours, most skim the proposal in ten minutes.

PROPOSAL-IMPROVEMENT COMMITTEE WORKSHEET

EXHIBIT 8.8

The time frame required to take advantage of this type of review must be agreed upon early in the proposal-preparation process. The dates for sending a draft to the outside reviewer must allow for adequate time for review, return of the proposal to the developer, and evaluation and incorporation of the suggestions.

One of the major problems with this type of review is that outside consultants often do not read proposals from the perspective of the actual reviewers. They frequently spend more time reading the proposals than would the actual reviewers and do not use the same scoring system or evaluation criteria utilized in the actual review. You can avoid some of these problems by providing the consultant with the actual evaluation criteria and/or scoring system prior to his or her review.

If your office pays a stipend or an honorarium to the outside consultant/reviewer, avoid using a friend or colleague of the proposal developer's for this task. Instead, you can work

PROPOSAL TITLE: _____

PROSPECTIVE FUNDING SOURCE: _____

AREAS OF INTEREST TO FUNDING SOURCE: _____

SAMPLE OF GRANTS IN INTEREST AREAS:

PROPOSAL REVIEW PROCEDURE

PROPOSALS ARE
READ BY:

	X	Time	Educational Background	Socioecon. Background	Known Biases or Viewpoints	Other
FUNDING OFFICIAL						
FUNDING STAFF						
REVIEW COMMITTEES						
BOARD MEMBERS						
OTHER						

GENERAL FUNDING SOURCE INFORMATION
NUMBER OF PROPOSALS RECEIVED IN 20_____:
NUMBER FUNDED IN 20_____:
AMOUNT OF $ DISTRIBUTED IN 20_____:

APPLICATION PROCESS & GUIDELINES
PROPOSALS REVIEWED: ___ MONTHLY ___QUARTERLY ___ ANNUALLY
                    ___ AS NEEDED ___ OTHER
PROPOSAL FORMAT & LENGTH:

ATTACHMENTS ALLOWED:
OTHER:

PROPOSAL-IMPROVEMENT COMMITTEE—FUNDER PROFILE

EXHIBIT 8.9

PROPOSAL TITLE: _Summer Success: Preparing Girls for Transition to College_

PROSPECTIVE FUNDING SOURCE: _Caldwell Foundation_

AREAS OF INTEREST TO FUNDING SOURCE: Colleges/Universities (Education), Science Hospitals (Health)

SAMPLE OF GRANTS IN INTEREST AREAS: $15,000 Improve College of Curriculum
$20,000 Increase women in science
$25,000 Bioengineering research

PROPOSAL REVIEW PROCEDURE

PROPOSALS ARE
READ BY:

	X	Time	Educational Background	Socioecon. Background	Known Biases or Viewpoints	Other
FUNDING OFFICIAL						
FUNDING STAFF						
REVIEW COMMITTEES						
BOARD MEMBERS	X	5–10 Minutes	M.B.A. B.S. Degrees	Upperclass	Like to help people & themselves	
OTHER						

GENERAL FUNDING SOURCE INFORMATION
NUMBER OF PROPOSALS RECEIVED IN 2000: 150
NUMBER FUNDED IN 2000: 12
AMOUNT OF $ DISTRIBUTED IN 2000: $180,000
ANTICIPATED DISTRIBUTION IN 2001: $200,000

APPLICATION PROCESS & GUIDELINES
PROPOSALS REVIEWED: __X__ MONTHLY ___QUARTERLY ___ ANNUALLY ___ AS NEEDED ___ OTHER

PROPOSAL FORMAT & LENGTH: 1 page letter proposal

ATTACHMENTS ALLOWED: None
OTHER:

SAMPLE PROPOSAL-IMPROVEMENT COMMITTEE—FUNDER PROFILE

EXHIBIT 8.10

LIST AREAS IDENTIFIED	INITIALS							TOTAL POINTS PER AREA	RANK
INDIVIDUAL TOTAL								GROUP TOTAL	

PROPOSAL-IMPROVEMENT COMMITTEE—SCORING WORKSHEET

EXHIBIT 8.11

with your proposal developer to select a past reviewer and/or grant seeker in his or her field. The amount of the honorarium or stipend depends upon the grants area. In other words, you will need to offer more in some areas of study than others. Generally, because you are only asking for a few hours of the reviewer's time, $200 to $500 is the normal range. The results will be well worth the investment.

As a final note, you may want to have the consultant sign/notarize an agreement that states that he or she is aware of the fact that the proposal is the intellectual property of the proposal developer.

GRANTS OFFICE EDITING AND PROPOSAL ASSEMBLY

If your grants office has assisted the grant seeker in taking part in a proposal-improvement committee quality circle/mock review or has hired an outside consultant to review the proposal, the major work of editing should be taken care of. However, most grants offices provide for a staff person who reads the proposal thoroughly and edits it for spelling, grammar, budget-related math errors, and layout. The layout includes everything from visual presentation to proofing the exhibits and attachments.

Reproduction and assembly are critical aspects of the process because they have much to do with how the proposal and your grants office will be viewed. Reviewers never forget proposals that are submitted with upside-down, missing, and/or blank pages. Even with electronic submittal, your staff should be allowed to proof each proposal, send it to one of your own terminals, and print it out to ensure that it looks good. One of the most common complaints of reviewers is that proposals are often plagued with mistakes such as

- not following the funding source's rules/directions on allowable font and number of pages,
- proposal components out of sequence,
- suggesting too much change for the amount of funding requested, and
- budgets that do not add up.

Many times, fine-tuned editing can take place while a copy of the proposal is being circulated for sign-off. Errors in spelling, grammar, the budget, and slight changes in presentation are not the issues being addressed in sign-off; release time, space requirements, and in-kind or matching contributions are.

The grants office is the place to examine proposal presentation and ensure that funding source rules have been complied with. From the number of characters (including spaces) in the title, to the number of key words underlined in the abstract or summary, the quality of the printing, the binding used, and the placement of the staple, your office is the last stop before transmittal. Essentially, the buck stops with your office!

Exhibit 8.12 provides a list of questions to be used in gathering feedback on the way your office promotes and could better promote the development of organized proposals; exhibit 8.13 is designed to help you keep track of the status of the activities and items aimed at your office's efforts in this area.

REFERENCES

1. Allen Lakein, *How to Get Control of Your Time and Your Life* (New York: New American Library, 1996).
2. Gary Fellers, *The Deming Vision: SPC/TQM for Administrators* (Milwaukee: ASQC Quality Press, 1992).

1. Are you aware that the grants office is available to assist you in any aspect of proposal development, including design and evaluation?

    _____ Yes   _____ No

    Please evaluate the following grants office services. (If services not used, please leave blank.)

	Inadequate	Adequate	More than Adequate
a. Assistance with concept development	_____	_____	_____
b. Providing techniques for organizing proposal ideas	_____	_____	_____
c. Assistance with literature searches	_____	_____	_____
d. Helping you develop your needs statement	_____	_____	_____
e. Assistance securing/reviewing program guidelines	_____	_____	_____
f. Helping you tailor your proposal to the funding source	_____	_____	_____
g. Assistance with budget development & cash forecasts	_____	_____	_____
h. Assistance with the development of objectives, methods, & protocol	_____	_____	_____
i. Assistance with the development of your hypothesis	_____	_____	_____
j. Helping to design your evaluation component	_____	_____	_____
k. Proposal editing	_____	_____	_____
l. Proposal assembly	_____	_____	_____
m. Assistance in reviewing proposals with reviewers will prior to submittal	_____	_____	_____
n. Final proposal review	_____	_____	_____
o. Assistance creating your proposal online when possible	_____	_____	_____

2. What suggestions do you have for improving the grants office's services?

3. What additional services could the grants office provide to assist you in proposal development?

4. If you feel the grants process is currently chaotic and/or confusing, how could the grants office help to make it more organized, controllable, and accomplishable?

SURVEY QUESTIONS—THE ROLE OF THE GRANTS OFFICE IN PROMOTING AN ORGANIZED PROPOSAL

EXHIBIT 8.12

For Each Activity/Item listed, Check Status

Activity/Item	Reviewed, Appropriate Part of Grants Office	Reviewed, Appropriate Part of Other Office (List)	Reviewed, Not Applicable	Reviewed, Inappropriate Needs Action	Non-existent, Needs Action
1. Grants office procedures—suggestions, forms and worksheets for: • organizing proposal ideas (Swiss cheese concept, workbook, etc.) • writing needs statements, objectives and methods					

Complete this Section for Each Activity/Item Needing Action

What Needs to be Accomplished?	By Whom? (Office/ Person)	By When? (Time Frame)	Resources Required— Personnel, Supplies, Equipment, Programming, etc.	Estimated Costs

GRANTS OFFICE INVENTORY—THE ROLE OF THE GRANTS OFFICE IN PROMOTING AN ORGANIZED PROPOSAL

EXHIBIT 8.13

For Each Activity/Item listed, Check Status

Activity/Item	Reviewed, Appropriate Part of Grants Office	Reviewed, Appropriate Part of Other Office (List)	Reviewed, Not Applicable	Reviewed, Inappropriate Needs Action	Non-existent, Needs Action
• tailoring proposals to funding sources (tailoring worksheet) • developing budgets & budget formats (project planner) • estimating cash forecasts (time line) • editing					

Complete this Section for Each Activity/Item Needing Action

What Needs to be Accomplished?	By Whom? (Office/Person)	By When? (Time Frame)	Resources Required— Personnel, Supplies, Equipment, Programming, etc.	Estimated Costs

GRANTS OFFICE INVENTORY—THE ROLE OF THE GRANTS OFFICE IN PROMOTING AN ORGANIZED PROPOSAL

EXHIBIT 8.13 (*continued*)

For Each Activity/Item listed, Check Status

Activity/Item	Reviewed, Appropriate Part of Grants Office	Reviewed, Appropriate Part of Other Office (List)	Reviewed, Not Applicable	Reviewed, Inappropriate Needs Action	Non-existent, Needs Action
• assisting in proposal assembly • reviewing proposal presentation 2. Proposal improvement committee (or other system for re-viewing proposals in the					

Complete this Section for Each Activity/Item Needing Action

What Needs to be Accomplished?	By Whom? (Office/ Person)	By When? (Time Frame)	Resources Required— Personnel, Supplies, Equipment, Programming, etc.	Estimated Costs

GRANTS OFFICE INVENTORY—THE ROLE OF THE GRANTS OFFICE IN PROMOTING AN ORGANIZED PROPOSAL

EXHIBIT 8.13 (*continued*)

For Each Activity/Item listed, Check Status

Activity/Item	Reviewed, Appropriate Part of Grants Office	Reviewed, Appropriate Part of Other Office (List)	Reviewed, Not Applicable	Reviewed, Inappropriate Needs Action	Non-existent, Needs Action
same manner the actual reviewers will prior to submittal)					

Complete this Section for Each Activity/Item Needing Action

What Needs to be Accomplished?	By Whom? (Office/ Person)	By When? (Time Frame)	Resources Required— Personnel, Supplies, Equipment, Programming, etc.	Estimated Costs

GRANTS OFFICE INVENTORY—THE ROLE OF THE GRANTS OFFICE IN PROMOTING AN ORGANIZED PROPOSAL

EXHIBIT 8.13 (continued)

CHAPTER 9

The Role of the Grants Office in Assurances, Certifications, Institutional Reviews, and Research Compliance

After World War II, the federal government became the major funding source for research in the United States. Federal agencies were created and authorized by Congress to award research funds to nonprofit organizations. In 1996, federal research and development grants to colleges and universities alone totaled $14.3 billion.

Over the years federal agencies have broadened their scope to include monitoring of ethical standards for research. Institutions that receive funds from federal agencies are required to adhere to federal, state, and local statutes, as well as agency policies governing research projects. Specific guidelines regulating the conditions of research at institutions of higher education have been issued by the Public Health Service (PHS), the Food and Drug Administration (FDA), and the National Institutes of Health (NIH). All of these agencies work under the auspices of the U.S. Department of Health and Human Services (DHHS), and other federal and state funding agencies accept the DHHS, PHS, and NIH guidelines as the standard requirements for research. These guidelines stipulate minimal criteria and are not intended to deter a college or university from establishing more stringent regulations or from adhering to additional professional or legal guidelines.

ASSURANCES AND CERTIFICATIONS

Although the principal investigator has primary responsibility for conducting his or her research according to legal and ethical guidelines, it is the role of the grants office to make sure that investigators are aware of applicable statutes and regulations and to assure government funding sources that all rules, guidelines, and stipulations have been followed.

Your grants office should have a checklist of assurances and certifications for each type of funding source. The appropriate individuals and offices should review the checklist and sign off on the assurances and certifications as they are met. The appropriate individuals and offices should receive special instructions to make sure that the office has complied with certain rules. For example, it should be noted if the personnel office must comply with assurances regarding the manner in which job openings are advertised, fair employment procedures followed, and positions filled.

In some colleges and universities the business office or accounting department may control purchasing or supplies, materials, or equipment. Federal and state grants and contracts are known for their rules and regulations in this area. In addition to rules on requiring bids on purchases, there are assurances that the grantee allow minority businesses to compete. If the business office is not aware of the regulations and does not sign off on the checklist of assurances and certifications, the institution may inadvertently be in violation of these rules.

Block-grant recipients who accept federal pass-through dollars sign assurances that they will treat the administration of the funds as if the ultimate grantee received the funds directly from the federal government. (In the early 1980s, many categorical federal programs were condensed into block grants, or pass-through monies, and given to states for distribution.) This means that the recipients must abide by the federal rules that govern the purchase, rental, and lease of equipment; personnel practices; record keeping; and so on.

Unfortunately, many institutions deal with the area of assurances only after there is a problem (for example, when a federal audit reveals a large error in the administration of funds). Remember, pleading ignorance is no excuse.

The grants office is the logical choice for informing individuals and offices within the organization of their particular responsibilities in dealing with the funders' restrictions. Proper education by the grants office will result in a planned, preventive system that will maintain the institution's present and future credibility.

A partial Checklist of Assurances and Certifications that apply to grants is provided in exhibit 9.1. Some of the assurances and certifications listed may not be applicable to your type of organization or your investigators' projects and programs. Further, certain federal awarding agencies may require applicants to certify additional assurances. Therefore, it is imperative to contact the grantor's program officer to obtain the specific rules, regulations, and guidelines.

INSTITUTIONAL REVIEWS AND RESEARCH COMPLIANCE

Most colleges and universities have committees to conduct institutional reviews in each of the major categories of research compliance. Each committee has a single set of review criteria to promote the same ethical standards for all research whether it is funded or not. The same review process provides consistent procedures for all research and eases record keeping for the grants office.

Although the multiple review of proposed research projects by a variety of committees may seem to create an unnecessary layer of bureaucratic paperwork, the reviews are vehicles for ensuring that ethical consideration is given to each aspect of the research and that research questions do not take precedence over safety and ethical issues.

Many of the federal, state, and local statutes governing research apply to five major categories:

- the use of human participants as research subjects,
- the use of animal subjects,

Some of the assurances and certifications listed below may not be applicable to your project, program, or type of organization. Further, certain federal awarding agencies may require applicants to certify additional assurances. For specifics, always contact the awarding agency.

Assurance/Certification   **In Files**
Human Subjects—45 CFR 46, P.L. 93-348
Vertebrate Animals—PHS Policy on Human Care and Use of Laboratory
     Animal Welfare/ Laboratory Animal Welfare Act of 1966, P.L. 89-544
Recombinant DNA—NIH Guidelines for Research Involving Recombinant
     DNA Molecules
Research Misconduct—42 CFR Part 50, Subpart A, 42 CFR 94
Radiation Safety—Nuclear Regulatory Commission

Employment/Labor
Debarment and Suspension—45 CFR 76
Drug-Free Workplace—Drug-Free Workplace Act of 1988, 45 CFR 76
Lobbying**—45 CFR Part 93
Intergovernmental Personnel Act of 1970 (Merit Systems)
Hatch Act (Political Activity of Employees)

Construction Subagreements
Davis-Bacon Act
Copeland Act
Contract Work, Hours and Safety Standards Act

*Non-Discrimination**
National Labor Relations Act of 1935
Federal Communications Act
Title II of the Civil Rights Act of 1964
Title VI of Civil Rights Act of 1964
Title IX of the Civil Rights Act of 1870, Civil Rights Act of 1964
Civil Rights Act of 1866
Apprenticeship Amendments of 1973
Age Discrimination in Employment Act of 1975
Section 504 of the Rehabilitation Act of 1973
Title IX of the Education Amendments of 1972

Historical
National Historic Preservation Act of 1966
Archaeological and Historic Preservation Act of 1974

CHECKLIST OF ASSURANCES AND CERTIFICATIONS

EXHIBIT 9.1

Environmental Protection
Flood Disaster Protection Act of 1973
National Environmental Policy Act of 1969
Protection of Wetlands
Coastal Zone Management Act of 1972
Clean Air Act of 1955
Safe Drinking Water Act of 1974
Endangered Species Act of 1973
Wild and Scenic Rivers Act of 1968
Lead-Based Paint Poisoning Prevention Act

Miscellaneous
Delinquent Federal Debt—OMB Memorandum M-87 32, "Certification
     of Nondelinquency by Applicants for Federal Assistance"
Financial Conflict of Interest—42 CFR Part 50, Subpart F
Privacy Act of 1974
Freedom of Information Act/Regulation—45CFR Part 5
Single Audit Act Amendment of 1966/OMB Circular No. A-133
Patents & Copyrights

*One of the necessary Assurance of Compliance Forms (form HHS 690) is
available from GrantsInfo, e-mail: GrantsInfo@nih.gov, (301) 435-0714.

**Standard Form LLL, "Disclosure of Lobbying Activities" is available from
GrantsInfo, National Institutes of Health, e-mail: GrantsInfo@nih.gov,
(301) 435-0714.

CHECKLIST OF ASSURANCES AND CERTIFICATIONS

EXHIBIT 9.1 (*continued*)

- the use of recombinant DNA,
- the use of radioactive material, and
- research misconduct.

1. Human Participants as Research Subjects—All federal and state-funded projects that involve human participants as research subjects must comply with Title 45 Code of Federal Regulations (CFR), Section 46 regarding the protection of human subjects involved in research, development, and related activities. Subpart A of 45 CFR Section 46 is also known as the common rule because it serves as the federal regulation for 17 major federal agencies. The CFR is a codification of the general and permanent rules published in the Federal Register by the executive departments and agencies of the federal government. You can obtain the CFR online at http://www.access.gpo.gov/nara/cfr. Once there, you can retrieve Title 45, Section 46, Subpart A by citation. These regulations are also available from the Office for Protection from Research Risks (OPRR), National Institutes of Health, Rockville, MD 20892, (301) 496-7041 and online at http://grants.nih.gov/grants/oprr/ human subjects/45cfr46.htm.

You may also obtain a guidebook which outlines the specific requirements of institutions engaging in research using human subjects from OPRR. This *1993 Protecting Human Research Subjects Institutional Review Board Guidebook* can be obtained online at http:// grants.nih.gov/grants/oprr/irb/irb_guidebook.htm and contains, among other things, information on the required composition of institutional review boards and a discussion of research projects exempt from review.

Colleges and universities are required to have Institutional Boards for the Protection of Human Subjects to review all federal and state-funded projects that use human participants as subjects. Institutional Boards for the Protection of Human Subjects should review all projects (even those that are not government-funded) that include research with children, other vulnerable populations, and populations that present more than a minimal risk (e.g., elderly people, pregnant women, institutionalized individuals, and prisoners).

The review of research protocols by the IRB focuses on possible risk of physical, psychological, or social injury to participants resulting from the research. If there are any apparent risks, the participants must receive adequate protection and the potential benefits to them and to humankind in general must be great enough to justify their participation.

Before applying for external funds for a research project involving human subjects, the researcher must apply to the IRB and receive approval. The chair of the IRB works very closely with the research administration office. Often the chair is a staff member from the office. All proposals involving human subjects must include a letter approving the project, signed by the IRB chair. Because projects can be approved for only one year, investigators must resubmit yearly for a new approval. The IRB's record keeping and correspondence system is quite extensive, so secretarial assistance must be provided for this committee.

In most instances, human subjects must sign a written, informed-consent form approved by the IRB. (The only time the IRB may waive the requirement for a signed consent form is if the form is the only record linking the subject to the research or if the research presents no more than minimal risk of harm to subjects and involves no procedures for which written consent is normally required outside of the research context.) The detailed requirements for a consent form are described in OPRR Reports and in the *IRB Guidebook* previously mentioned. To review consent forms and consent form checklists developed by various institutional sponsored research offices, visit the National Council of University Research Administrators (NCURA) Web site at http://www.ncura.edu, click on "resources," and then "university departmental and sponsored research offices." The NCURA Web site will also provide you with agency forms and sample university and institution policies and agreements.

Besides establishing an IRB, colleges and universities using human subjects in research must also submit an assurance of compliance with the approved guidelines for the use of human subjects in research to the Department of Health and Human Services (DHHS). The institution then receives a multiple-project assurance code, which is required on all proposals involving human subjects.

Even the questions you choose to ask from the survey questions contained in this book should be reviewed and approved by your IRB before the process is initiated. Please note that the sample surveys included in the last chapter were approved by the IRBs at the institutions that developed them.

If you want to know more about human subject protection, Institutional Review Boards, or related assurances, visit the Office for Protection from Research Risks Web site at http://grants.nih.gov/grants/oprr/oprr.htm.

2. Animal Subjects—The Office for Protection from Research Risks of the National Institutes of Health has issued the *Public Health Service Policy on Human Care and Use of Laboratory Animals*. A reprint of the original policy can be found online at http://grants.nih.gov/grants/oprr/phspol.htm. The document requires that institutions establish protocol to ensure appropriate care and use of all animals involved in research, research training, and biological testing activities conducted or supported by the PHS. It also requires that institutions submit an assurance of compliance statement to PHS. The statement must be approved and the institution issued an assurance number, which is then required on proposals to all PHS agencies.

The policy requires that an institution conducting research funded by PHS have an institutional animal care and use committee (IACUC), appointed by the president or chief executive officer of the institution. This committee must consist of a veterinarian, one active scientist, one community member with no affiliation to the institution, and one nonscientist. More than one role can be filled by any individual committee member, but the committee is not to be made up of fewer than five individuals. The IACUC is charged with reviewing all protocols for using animals in research. Each investigator is required to submit information on animal use to the IACUC and receive approval prior to beginning any research involving animals or submitting a proposal requesting external funds.

The IACUC reviews only the protocol involving the use of animals. It may approve the project as submitted or request that the investigator make changes in the protocol. The IACUC is primarily concerned that the research avoid unnecessary discomfort, pain, or anxiety to the animal. The committee must also consider whether the anticipated results will be for the good of society, whether the work will be performed by a qualified scientist, and whether the appropriate species has been chosen for this particular research project.

In general, the IACUC is a collegial group working with the scientist to ensure the best possible protocol for the research project, thus protecting the animal's welfare without interfering with the design of the research. The IACUC works with the investigator to make appropriate changes when desired rather than inhibiting or stopping a research project. However, if it is not possible to reach an agreeable solution, the IACUC is authorized to prohibit the research.

Once a project has been approved, the IACUC monitors the research through visits to the laboratories. Investigators may not make any changes in protocol without first receiving the permission of the IACUC.

Any college or university seeking external funds for research involving animals will probably establish its own IACUC. However, if only a few projects are being conducted on the campus, it is permissible to have research projects reviewed by a PHS-approved IACUC at another university, research institution, or hospital. All proposals requesting external funds must have a letter signed by the chair of an approved IACUC indicating approval of the project before funds will be awarded for the research.

In addition to requiring IACUC approval of research, the PHS policy also requires that institutions appoint an animal assurance officer, who is ultimately responsible for maintaining compliance. In medium-sized institutions, the assurance officer is likely to be a qualified faculty administrator who works in the research administration office. By looking at samples of animal use protocol forms, you can get a better understanding of the kinds of information needed for an IACUC review. To review forms used by a variety of university sponsored research offices, visit the NCURA Web site at http://www.ncura.edu, click on "resources," and then "university departmental and sponsored research offices."

3. Recombinant DNA—If a research project involves the use of recombinant DNA molecules, the research protocol must be reviewed and approved by an Institutional Biosafety Committee (IBC). This committee concerns itself with the safe use and disposal of recombinant DNA. All research involving recombinant DNA techniques that is supported by the DHHS must meet the requirements outlined in the *NIH Guidelines for Research Involving Recombinant DNA Molecules.* The current guidelines and announcements of modifications and changes to the guidelines are available on the NIH Web site at http://www.nih.gov/od/oba or from the Office of Biotechnology Activities, National Institutes of Health, Bethesda, MD 20892, (301) 496-9838. The guidelines emphasize that it is the responsibility of the institution to adhere to the intent of the guidelines as well as to the specifics.

The institutional biosafety committee has to be made up of at least five individuals who have expertise in recombinant DNA technology, biological safety, and physical containment. Two members shall not be affiliated with the institution and are appointed to represent the interest of the community.

The IBC reviews research protocols to assess the safety of recombinant DNA experiments and any potential risk to public health or the environment. All principal investigators proposing to work with recombinant DNA molecules must provide proof of ability to work with the substance without creating a harmful situation in the research laboratory or endangering the environment.

Institutions must appoint a biological safety office (BSO) if they engage in recombinant DNA research at the BSL3 or BSL4 containment level. The BSO is a member of the IBC with specific responsibilities: reporting problems, developing emergency plans, and providing technical advice.

The biosafety review committee considers whether laboratory personnel have received adequate training, whether hazardous materials will be handled properly, and whether facilities are adequate to support the proposed project. In addition to judging the proper use of hazardous materials, the IBC also determines that method of disposal is safe for the environment. The chair of this committee is often a faculty member with expertise in handling and disposing of hazardous substances.

4. Radioactive Material—Colleges or universities that have research projects using radioisotopes or teach using radioisotopes must have a license from the U.S. Nuclear Regulatory Commission (http://www.nrc.gov/). The license lists the names of every researcher at the institution who is eligible to use radioactive materials in research, specifies the kind and amount of isotopes that can be used, and describes the accepted methods of disposal.

To initiate a research project using radioactive materials, a researcher must submit an application to the Radiation Safety Committee of the institution and be added to the existing license. Investigators who are not listed as radioisotope users on the existing license cannot submit a proposal using radioactive materials.

If an institution does not have a license, it must apply to the Nuclear Regulatory Commission for one. The license requires a quarterly review of all materials used to ensure that the institution stays within the guidelines. All proposed research projects are still reviewed by the radiation safety committee to ensure that the research protocol is within the guidelines specified by the institution's license.

The research administration office is responsible for ensuring that all research projects using radioisotopes receive approval. The institution must also appoint a radiation safety officer, who receives and distributes all radioactive materials to the individual research laboratories, updates the license regularly, and prepares for inspections from the Nuclear Regulatory Commission.

5. Research Misconduct—Misconduct review is a procedure required by the Public Health Service to ensure ethical research procedures and reporting. Each institution that receives or applies for a research, research training, or research-related grant or cooperative agreement under the Public Health Service Act must certify that the institution has established administrative policies as required by 42 CFR Part 50, Subpart A, "Responsibilities for PHS Awardee and Applicant Institutions for Dealing with and Reporting Possible Misconduct in Science," and 42 CFR 94, "Public Health Service Standards for the Protection of Research Misconduct Whistleblowers." Further, each covered institution must certify that it will comply with those policies and the requirements of the final rule. The regulations can be obtained online at http://www.access.gpa.gov/nara/cfr or http://ori.dhhs.gov/89rule.htm.

Misconduct is defined as serious deviation—such as fabrication, falsification, or plagiarism—from accepted practices in carrying out research or in reporting the results of research. In addition, the failure to comply with federal requirements affecting specific aspects of the conduct of research, as discussed in this chapter, may also be considered misconduct.

The other procedures described in this chapter require that a review take place before submitting a research proposal. Because misconduct in research is only an issue after the research is under way, no prior review is required. However, institutions are required to assure the PHS that they have policies and procedures for conducting an inquiry into any allegation of misconduct and that, when warranted, a full-scale investigation of the alleged misconduct will be conducted. Inquiries should be completed in no more than 30 days, and if an investigation is required, the institution is expected to complete it within 120 days. A report of the findings must then be prepared. Notification to NIH or DHHS is not required when an inquiry begins; however, if an investigation is considered necessary, the NIH program officer must be informed before it begins. The name of the person involved may then be added to the PHS alert file. The PHS alert file includes information from NIH and other PHS agencies.

For further information on research misconduct review, contact the Office of Research Integrity, Division of Policy and Education, Rockwall II, Suite 700, 5515 Security Lane, Rockville, MD 20852, (301) 443-5300, Fax: (301) 594-0042 or (301) 445-5351, or visit their Web site at http://ori.dhhs.gov.

PERSONNEL REQUIREMENTS AND PROCEDURES

The acceptance of federal funds requires the signature of assurances relating to federal nondiscrimination laws. The following federal nondiscrimination laws are listed here because of their general applicability to grants. However, they are not meant to be inclusive of the rules governing this area.

1. *The National Labor Relations Act of 1935.* Prohibits discrimination in certain employment practices on the bases of race and sex. This includes private employers and subcontractors.
2. *Federal Communications Act.* Prohibits discrimination in employment on the base of race, color, national origin, sex, or religion. This is relevant to all organizations and entities regulated by the Federal Communications Commission (broadcasters, common carriers, cable-television operators, and private firms).
3. *Title II of the Civil Rights Act of 1964.* Prohibits discrimination in the use of public accommodations on the base of race, color, religion, or national origin. This is pertinent to all private organizations providing public accommodations.
4. *Title VI of the Civil Rights Act of 1964.* Provides that no person in the United States shall, on the base of race, color, or national origin, be excluded from the participation in, be denied benefits of, or be subjected to discrimination under, any programs or activity receiving federal financial assistance.
5. *Title IX of the Civil Rights Act of 1870, Civil Rights Act of 1964.* Prohibits use of state custom or law to deprive individuals and organizations in the United States of civil rights for any reason.
6. *Civil Rights Act of 1866.* Prohibits discrimination in real estate transactions on the base of race or color. Refers to all organizations and individuals engaged in real estate transactions.
7. *Apprenticeship Amendments of 1973.* Prohibits discrimination in employment on the base of race, color, religion, sex, or national origin. Refers to apprenticeship programs registered with the Department of Labor.
8. *Age Discrimination in Employment Act of 1975.* Prohibits discrimination in employment on the base of age. Refers to private employers, state and local government, and labor organizations.
9. *Section 504 of Rehabilitation Act of 1973.* Provides that no otherwise qualified handicapped individual in the United States shall solely by reason of the handicap be excluded from any program receiving federal financial assistance.
10. *Title IX of Education Amendments of 1972 (Section 901).* Prohibits age discrimination in education programs receiving federal financial assistance.

INTELLECTUAL PROPERTY ISSUES

The grants office serves as the contact point for faculty and staff concerns related to the protection of products that are created from internally and externally supported work. This includes providing protection in the form of advice, sample agreements for working with consultants, co-investigators, and consortia partners on issues related to noncompetition agreements, patent rights, copyrights, and other questions related to intellectual properties.

The grants staff should not be expected to provide legal advice to grant seekers, but they can provide standard college and university forms created by the institution's legal counsel. The grants staff should refer principal investigators and project directors to the appropriate legal counsel in these areas and act as a facilitator in the process. If there are requirements made by a grantor or subcontractor related to these areas, they must be signed off by the institution's appropriate legal counsel.

Review the questions in exhibit 9.2 to gather feedback on how you might be able to improve your system in the areas of assurances, certifications, institutional reviews, and research compliance. Complete the grants office inventory (exhibit 9.3) to help you develop a plan that works for your office, your institution, your grant seekers, and your funding sources.

---

1. If you have had contact with one or more of your college or university's institutional review boards, how would you rate your experience?

   ___very good   ___good   ___okay   ___bad   ___very bad   ___indifferent

2. If you have not had contact with one or more of your college or university's institutional review boards, are you aware that you must receive, before submittal, approval for any projects or research that involve:

	Yes	No
human participants as subjects?	_____	_____
animal subjects?	_____	_____
recombinant DNA?	_____	_____
radioactive material?	_____	_____

3. If you are aware of one or more of these requirements, how were you made aware of them?

4. If you are unaware of one or more of these requirements, how and when do you think these requirements could have been effectively transmitted to you?

SURVEY QUESTIONS—THE ROLE OF THE GRANTS OFFICE IN ASSURANCES, CERTIFICATIONS, INSTITUTIONAL REVIEWS, AND RESEARCH COMPLIANCE

EXHIBIT 9.2

5. How knowledgeable do you feel you are about the assurances that federal awarding agencies require applicants to certify?

	no knowledge	little knowledge	somewhat knowledgeable	very knowledgeable
human subjects	_____	_____	_____	_____
vertebrate animals	_____	_____	_____	_____
recombinant DNA	_____	_____	_____	_____
research misconduct	_____	_____	_____	_____
radiation safety	_____	_____	_____	_____
employment/labor	_____	_____	_____	_____
construction sub-agreements	_____	_____	_____	_____
nondiscrimination	_____	_____	_____	_____
historical	_____	_____	_____	_____
environmental protection	_____	_____	_____	_____
other miscellaneous	_____	_____	_____	_____

SURVEY QUESTIONS—THE ROLE OF THE GRANTS OFFICE IN ASSURANCES, CERTIFICATIONS, INSTITUTIONAL REVIEWS, AND RESEARCH COMPLIANCE

EXHIBIT 9.2 (*continued*)

For Each Activity/Item listed, Check Status

Activity/Item	Reviewed, Appropriate Part of Grants Office	Reviewed, Appropriate Part of Other Office (List)	Reviewed, Not Applicable	Reviewed, Inappropriate Needs Action	Non-existent, Needs Action
1. Assurances • Checklist of assurances for each type of funding source and policy for sign-off on assurances as they are met • Policy for informing individuals and offices of their particular responsibilities in deal-					

Complete this Section for Each Activity/Item Needing Action

What Needs to be Accomplished?	By Whom? (Office/Person)	By When? (Time Frame)	Resources Required—Personnel, Supplies, Equipment, Programming, etc.	Estimated Costs

GRANTS OFFICE INVENTORY—THE ROLE OF THE GRANTS OFFICE IN ASSURANCES, CERTIFICATIONS, INSTITUTIONAL REVIEWS, AND RESEARCH COMPLIANCE

EXHIBIT 9.3

For Each Activity/Item listed, Check Status

Activity/Item	Reviewed, Appropriate Part of Grants Office	Reviewed, Appropriate Part of Other Office (List)	Reviewed, Not Applicable	Reviewed, Inappropriate Needs Action	Non-existent, Needs Action
ing with the funder's restrictions					
2. Animal research • Approved assurance statement					

Complete this Section for Each Activity/Item Needing Action

What Needs to be Accomplished?	By Whom? (Office/Person)	By When? (Time Frame)	Resources Required—Personnel, Supplies, Equipment, Programming, etc.	Estimated Costs

GRANTS OFFICE INVENTORY—THE ROLE OF THE GRANTS OFFICE IN ASSURANCES, CERTIFICATIONS, INSTITUTIONAL REVIEWS, AND RESEARCH COMPLIANCE

EXHIBIT 9.3 (*continued*)

For Each Activity/Item listed, Check Status

Activity/Item	Reviewed, Appropriate Part of Grants Office	Reviewed, Appropriate Part of Other Office (List)	Reviewed, Not Applicable	Reviewed, Inappropriate Needs Action	Non-existent, Needs Action
• IACUC composition requirements • Notice of intent form available to investigators 3. Human subjects research • Human subjects					

Complete this Section for Each Activity/Item Needing Action

What Needs to be Accomplished?	By Whom? (Office/ Person)	By When? (Time Frame)	Resources Required— Personnel, Supplies, Equipment, Programming, etc.	Estimated Costs

EXHIBIT 9.3 (continued)

For Each Activity/Item listed, Check Status

Activity/Item	Reviewed, Appropriate Part of Grants Office	Reviewed, Appropriate Part of Other Office (List)	Reviewed, Not Applicable	Reviewed, Inappropriate Needs Action	Non-existent, Needs Action
assurance on file • IRB committee composition meets guidelines • Consent forms meet guideline requirements • Human subjects review form available to investigators • Guidelines available to investigators					

Complete this Section for Each Activity/Item Needing Action

What Needs to be Accomplished?	By Whom? (Office/Person)	By When? (Time Frame)	Resources Required—Personnel, Supplies, Equipment, Programming, etc.	Estimated Costs

GRANTS OFFICE INVENTORY—THE ROLE OF THE GRANTS OFFICE IN ASSURANCES, CERTIFICATIONS, INSTITUTIONAL REVIEWS, AND RESEARCH COMPLIANCE

EXHIBIT 9.3 (*continued*)

For Each Activity/Item listed, Check Status

Activity/Item	Reviewed, Appropriate Part of Grants Office	Reviewed, Appropriate Part of Other Office (List)	Reviewed, Not Applicable	Reviewed, Inappropriate Needs Action	Non-existent, Needs Action
4. Biosafety committee • IBC composition meets requirements • Biological safety officer • Regulations available to investigators 5. Radiation safety • Review committee composition meets requirement					

Complete this Section for Each Activity/Item Needing Action

What Needs to be Accomplished?	By Whom? (Office/ Person)	By When? (Time Frame)	Resources Required— Personnel, Supplies, Equipment, Programming, etc.	Estimated Costs

EXHIBIT 9.3 (*continued*)

For Each Activity/Item listed, Check Status

Activity/Item	Reviewed, Appropriate Part of Grants Office	Reviewed, Appropriate Part of Other Office (List)	Reviewed, Not Applicable	Reviewed, Inappropriate Needs Action	Non-existent, Needs Action
• Appointed radiation safety officer • Up-to-date license • Regulations available to investigators 6. Misconduct in research • Procedure for inquiry • Procedure for investigation					

Complete this Section for Each Activity/Item Needing Action

What Needs to be Accomplished?	By Whom? (Office/Person)	By When? (Time Frame)	Resources Required— Personnel, Supplies, Equipment, Programming, etc.	Estimated Costs

GRANTS OFFICE INVENTORY—THE ROLE OF THE GRANTS OFFICE IN ASSURANCES, CERTIFICATIONS, INSTITUTIONAL REVIEWS, AND RESEARCH COMPLIANCE

EXHIBIT 9.3 (*continued*)

For Each Activity/Item listed, Check Status

Activity/Item	Reviewed, Appropriate Part of Grants Office	Reviewed, Appropriate Part of Other Office (List)	Reviewed, Not Applicable	Reviewed, Inappropriate Needs Action	Non-existent, Needs Action
7. Personnel requirements and procedures • Designation of person or office to ensure compliance with federal nondiscrimination laws 8. Intellectual property procedures					

Complete this Section for Each Activity/Item Needing Action

What Needs to be Accomplished?	By Whom? (Office/Person)	By When? (Time Frame)	Resources Required—Personnel, Supplies, Equipment, Programming, etc.	Estimated Costs

GRANTS OFFICE INVENTORY—THE ROLE OF THE GRANTS OFFICE IN ASSURANCES, CERTIFICATIONS, INSTITUTIONAL REVIEWS, AND RESEARCH COMPLIANCE

EXHIBIT 9.3 (*continued*)

The Role of the Grants Office in Tracking Proposals, Sign-Off, Submission, and Follow-Up

GRANTS TRACKING SYSTEM

To help move proposals through your system and allow you to follow and identify where proposal are at all times, consider assigning an internal identification or logging number to each proposal as soon as the proposal idea is generated. A number identification system can do much more than just put your proposal submittals in chronological order. It can help make sign-off, submission, and follow-up go smoothly and provide your grants office with valuable information.

Because one function of the grants office is the generation of data relevant to the grants effort and the mission of the organization, it is necessary to keep a record of

- who is initiating proposals,
- the funding sources approached,
- pending grants, and
- the proposal success rate (funded proposal vs. submitted proposals).

A number identification system can supply this information, plus other information that can quickly designate the researcher and department or division. Early identification of the proposal idea can provide data on who follows through on proposal preparation and uses the resources of the grants office in preproposal activity. An identification number on a proposal idea will track the developing proposal through the institution. And because a proposal idea may have more than one title and may be referred to in different ways and with various abbreviations, an identification number can help avoid confusion. For example, at the end of each fiscal year my grants office report included a review of how many grant ideas were intiated, how many searches were provided, how many ideas progressed to sign-on, as well as how many proposals were submitted, pending, and approved. Each faculty member's grant idea was assigned a number. The true success of my institution's grants effort and how well my staff functioned was related to how effectively we moved from idea to funded project—not just how well we moved from submittal to funded project. An identification system that reflects the true beginning of the grants process will provide you with valuable insight into where your system is functioning well and where it needs improvement.

To develop your identification system, review your past submittals to determine which funding sources were sent the greatest number of your proposals. Arrange your identification numbers according to the most frequently used funding sources.

Sample Identification Systems (First Three Digits)

001–099   *ederal Funding Sources*
   001–020 = Education Programs
   021–030 = Department of Defense
   031–040 = National Science Foundation
   041–050 = National Endowment for the Arts

100–199   *Private Foundations*

   100–120 = National General Purpose
   121–130 = Special-Interest Health
   131–140 = Special-Interest Higher Education

200–299   *Corporations*

   200–220 = Light-Electronics Firms
   221–230 = Computer Software

300–399   *State Funding Sources*

   300–320 = State Department of Transportation

The number of categories can be expanded and divided so that you can determine if the proposal award is a contract or a grant, and letters can be added for greater identification. For example, you could use a letter code to designate the size of the proposal award.

   A = $500,000 and up
   B = $250,000–$499,999
   C = $100,000–$249,999
   D = $25,000–$99,999
   E = $5,000–$24,999
   F = $4,999 and under

Letters can also be used to designate departments and even the researcher or project director. For example, 201-FS-01/1 is a proposal submitted to a light-electronics firm. *F* indicates that the proposal request was less than $5,000. *S* designates your investigator, department, or division. The *01* of the 01/1 indicates the year (2001), and the *1* indicates that it was the first proposal submitted in 2001.

A numbering system also helps you keep accurate files, which will prove beneficial should the funding source call you and refer to a proposal. While you are looking for it, you can at least sound intelligent, as the system will allow you to identify the approximate dollar amount of the proposal, the grant writer, the area of interest that it addresses, and the department that submitted it.

Other variables that are important to your institution may also be included in your identification system. For example:

- the number of years a proposal is funded for
- the type of reimbursement system that will be used
- specific request of the funding source (e.g., secrecy, confidentiality)
- a possible patent-rights coding that may serve to remind all staff to place proposal in a locked file, etc.

In addition to statistical and record-keeping functions, the identification system will help track the progress of proposals through your organization. You might use your computer to provide daily or weekly updates of each proposal's stage of development.

Another effective way to easily identify and track developing proposals is to use washable, magnetic bulletin boards and reusable magnetic plastic strips. The grant I.D. number and other pertinent information can be listed on the special material that sticks to the magnetic bulletin board. As a grant moves through the stages of development, sign-off, submittal, and eventual award or denial, the magnetic strip can be moved and information added easily (funding source, logging number, etc.). The use of colored magnetic materials can let you see the necessary components or restrictions of any one proposal at a glance.

PROPOSAL SIGN-OFF PROCEDURES

Proposal sign-off is an area of major importance to funding sources. In fact, grant applications often have explicit instructions on who must sign the proposal and how many copies must have original signatures. Unfortunately, administrators find this area problematic because many proposal developers wait until the last minute to prepare proposals and procure appropriate signatures. This procrastination results in major difficulties when the individuals with the necessary signatures are out of the office, at out-of-town meetings, or on vacation. It is my belief that the last-minute, rush-rush, sign now-read later proposals are exactly the ones that deserve a closer look.

While you may think that everyone has a sign-off procedure, an organized method for recording and monitoring grant proposals, and a number identification system, this is not the case. Several of my clients who have requested grants-process audits could not tell me how many proposals their institution had submitted over the past year or the status of the submitted proposals (e.g., pending action, awarded, rejected). And in some cases, copies of proposals that had been submitted were incomplete or missing from files. In addition, many colleges and universities have entrepreneurial grant seekers who purposely circumvent the grants office and even the requirements of signatures. It they are successful in attracting the interest of the funders, these entrepreneurs seek the necessary signatures only after the proposal has been funded.

Without a mandatory sign-off procedure, it is difficult to document the progress of the grants office and track and retrieve important data such as matching funds and space and time commitments. Institutions without formal systems to record and monitor such data often find themselves being asked to explain things such as how 130 percent of a principal investigator's time could be allocated to grants.

Sign-off systems differ greatly from institution to institution. The following suggestions may help you develop or improve your own sign-off system and form.

The appropriate administrators, as well as those individuals who will be affected by the project, should be included in the final sign-off. Also include copies of the preproposal review forms with the final sign-off sheet to remind the signing parties of the initial conditions, concerns, and stipulations that the proposal developer/writer had to meet before gaining the individual's and organization's support. You may want to ask the proposal developer to include individual notes indicating where the necessary changes were made. This will speed up the signing process considerably.

Another method that expedites the sign-off process is the use of paper clips of different colors which correspond to the areas that must be signed by each individual. Include each individual's color clip on a copy of his or her preproposal review form for easy identification. Do not allow proposal developers to ask individuals to complete preproposal review forms at the same time they are signing off. This encourages the rush-rush approach and defeats the whole purpose of an organized sign-off system.

The rules for sign-off should be outlined in a cover sheet attached to your sign-off form. They may consist of

- who is to sign,
- when and where to sign,
- how much time the individual has to review the proposal,
- what the protocol is when signature is impossible owing to problems with the proposal,
- where to go with questions, and
- how the proposal should be moved to the next appropriate individual for signature.

Use your number identification system to help you monitor sign-off. You may want to use your computer screen or a dedicated monitor to track the progress of proposals that are in the sign-off process. Who has the proposal, who has signed off, and where and how the proposal will be transmitted to the next required signee is of critical importance and time is of the essence. Please note that it is necessary to track printed copies of proposals being signed off as well as the wave of the future—electronic version of proposals.

Earmark those proposals that must be expedited. You can use colored flags on printed versions and an outstanding cover page on electronic versions. Depending on time constraints, it may be necessary to designate an individual to be on call to move the signed proposal to the next administrator to sign, and/or to e-mail those administrators who have not responded in a timely fashion. When time is of the essence, nothing can be more upsetting than a required administrator who signs the proposal and places it in interoffice mail, resulting in a missed deadline. While your grants system may denounce the practice of submitting proposals at the last minute, the grants office should efficiently track every proposal through the sign-off procedure, whether it be of the rush-rush type or one being submitted early.

DOCUMENTING AND MONITORING MATCHING FUNDS

Because the Preproposal Review Form (see chapter 4) provides a space to record possible matching-funds needs, information concerning the funding source's requirements for matching or in-kind contributions should be known long before the final sign-off form is circulated. Even so, the final sign-off form should include information on the matching funds that must be committed to a project if it gets funded, and the grants-office administrator should provide this information to the individual responsible for the institution's commitment. Providing a printout to deans and/or department chairs reminding them of the matching funds or in-kind contributions can be easily tracked and e-mailed to these administrators periodically.

Of greater significance is the documenting and monitoring of this commitment when the proposal is funded, so that any possible audits will support the contribution. In-kind contributions of personnel services and space, as well as matching money, can best be recorded in the grants office, as it has the greatest knowledge of the funding source and its requirements. (Your grants office should have an Office of Management and Budget circular that outlines the federal guidelines for the documentation of matching funds. See chapter 12.)

A grants office that knows its success rate can more easily predict its matching funds needs. However, even with this information, predicting the exact requirements for matching funds can be difficult because not all grants call for matching contributions. In general, matching funds and in-kind resources should be allocated by organizational priorities and mission and the grants office's plan. Each grant-seeking priority is allocated a certain amount of matching funds. In addition, some colleges and universities allocate a specific amount for faculty and staff interests and some also allow for a contingency fund to be used in the event that the overall grants success rate is greater than anticipated.

Priority areas and their matching-funds budget should always be documented on both Preproposal Review Forms and sign-off sheets so that the appropriate administrators have the necessary information to make decisions. The following Matching Funds Checklist (exhibit 10.1) and Matching Funds Worksheet (exhibit 10.2) will help you in this area.

SUBMISSION

In some instances, the decentralized grants office is the office that submits proposals to outside funding sources. In other decentralized situations, submission is the responsibility of the centralized grants office. Irrespective of which office actually submits the proposal, the central grants office is responsible for ensuring that all proposals receive the proper internal sign-off as well as meet all of the funding source's requirements.

Submission to Public Funding Sources

Submission of proposals to public funding sources requires a much different and more complex procedure than submission to private funding sources. Because you are dealing

1. Do you have a definite matching funds allocation/budget?

2. Are matching funds allocated by an established priority?

3. Are all commitments for matching funds listed on preproposal review forms and/or sign-off sheets?

4. Are all matching funds commitments recorded by the grants office?

5. Can the grants office provide a running tally of matching funds commitments within minutes?

MATCHING FUNDS CHECKLIST

EXHIBIT 10.1

with public funds, procedures for submittal and deadlines must comply with public-information laws and give equal notice and opportunity to everyone.

Government officials cannot grant any leeway on deadlines. Proposal deadlines for federal programs are published in the Federal Register. (To access the Federal Register on the Internet visit http://www.nara.gov/fedreg/.) A change in deadline must be announced in the register 30 days in advance to allow ample time for all grant seekers to adjust to the new deadline date.

Whether your grants system is proactive (proposal development is initiated months before the deadline date) or reactive (proposal development is initiated a few hours before the deadline), the federal rules are clear and unyielding. Once the required signatures have been affixed to the proposal, it follows a definite system.

Read the guidelines carefully. Some government programs require a preapplication that, among other things, determines applicant eligibility. If this step is required, be sure to include all references to your approved eligibility when submitting the full proposal.

The federal government has made state review of federal grants to nonprofit organizations an option of each state. Some states may require this intergovernmental review process; however, local and state review of all federal programs is not necessary. Executive Order 12372 says that a state may require that federally funded proposed projects be

1. Total amount of matching funds available $ _____

2. Matching funds already allocated to accepted proposals:
    Proposal $ _____   Amount $ _____
             $ _____   _____
             $ _____   _____
                                                     Total $ _____

3. Remaining matching funds available $ _____
    (#1 minus total of #2)

4. Matching funds in pending proposals:

    Pending
    Proposal   _____   Amount $ _____
                _____ $ _____
                _____ $ _____
                _____ $ _____
                                                   Total $ _____

5. Estimate of success rate of pending proposals (%) _____

6. Estimate of matching funds needed for pending proposals
    (Apply percentage of #5 to total of #4)

Notes: _____
       _____
       _____
       _____
       _____

MATCHING FUNDS WORKSHEET

EXHIBIT 10.2

reviewed by appropriate local and state officials if they are potentially at cross-purposes to programs and priorities at the local and state levels.

To make sure that your proposal does not fall under your state's elective review, contact your governor's office or the federal agency to which you are applying, or check the Federal Register that published the grant's rules and regulations for the program in question. Once you locate the state office that is responsible for the checking procedure (called your "state single point of contact"), discuss the situation with a representative of the office to avoid any conflict. (To locate your state single point of contact visit http:// www.whitehouse.gov/ omb/grants/spoc.html on the Internet.) If your state requires a review, submit your proposal and your application to the funding source at the same time. Your state's review and comments will be submitted to the federal agency within 60 days.

The federal agency must either address the concerns outlined in your state's comments and follow the recommendations made or explain why it chose not to. The federal agency is not bound by the state's recommendation, and funds can be granted as the agency sees fit.

Follow all federal instructions carefully to ensure that your proposal is accurately addressed, labeled, and submitted. If you are delivering the proposal by hand or by messenger, be sure to check that it reaches the proper point. Federal programs use proposal logging centers. Many federal proposal packages contain a return card that is completed and mailed back to you. This means that your proposal reached the logging center but does not necessarily mean it has been delivered by the logging center to the appropriate funding program. While your proposal usually makes it from the logging center to the appropriate program, a follow-up call may be in order, and it is a necessity if you have not received a return card.

Most federal guidelines call for your proposal to be postmarked at a United States postal office before a certain date. Retain your receipt in case your proposal does not get to the appropriate program officer. A postmarked receipt will prove that your proposal has been lost and allow you to resubmit a copy.

It is becoming more common for federal programs to have their application forms available online and to encourage and accept (and even require) proposals submitted electronically over the Internet. For example, the National Science Foundation (NSF) uses an electronic submittal system known as FastLane to redesign and streamline the way it does business. (To obtain more information on FastLane visit http://www.fastlane.nsf.gov/.) In addition, the Department of Education recently unveiled a new system for creating and submitting electronic grants (see chapter 8). This system is known as e-GAPS (Electronic Grant Application Package System), and you can obtain more information on it by visiting http://e-grants.ed.gov on the Web. It is a good idea to always check with the program officer or contact person to determine if Internet transmittal is allowed and to confirm the preferred method of submission.

Submission to Private Funding Sources

An organization appears to be a poor steward of funds if it does not comply with deadlines. Therefore, be prompt when you submit your proposal. Find out if early submission will give you favorable treatment and how many copies of the proposal the funding source would like. Applications frequently instruct you to submit one or two copies when the funding source could actually use five.

The submittal process for private funding sources is not subject to the rules that govern federal agencies. Private funders have a variety of deadlines and frequently experience a time lag between submittal date and evaluation by staff and/or board members. Thus, failure to adhere to an exact deadline does not necessarily mean that your proposal will not be considered or will automatically be placed in the next funding cycle.

Follow the mailing instructions provided by the funder. Many funders enforce a strict length requirement for proposals, so be wary of placing a cover letter over your letter proposal. Record the submittal date of your proposal, and retain your postal receipt.

The number of foundations and corporations that accept proposals submitted electronically over the Internet will gradually increase as the number of foundations and corporations with Web sites increases. Estimates are that fewer than 25 of the approximately 50,000 foundations now accept electronically submitted proposals. However, do not expect this number to increase dramatically in the near future, because electronic submittal would mean that foundations would receive a greater number of proposals to read and process, and there is not much interest in this from the already understaffed private funding sources.

The following suggestions on how to submit proposals to private funders may be helpful to your grants office:

- Send the contacts that are uncovered through your webbing and linkage system an abstract of the proposal or a copy of the letter proposal.
- Ask friends of the funding source to push for your proposal at the board meeting.
- Ask friends of the funding source to use their contacts to try for a favorable decision.
- Minimize personal contact with the funding source once you have submitted the proposal.
- When it comes time to submit your request, consider delivering it in person if you are located near the funding source, or use an advocate or board member to deliver it for you. Hand delivery makes more of an impression on funding agencies, and it also helps you avoid problems with the postal service.

RESPONDING TO AND DEALING WITH THE FUNDER'S DECISION

The worksheets and checklists in the following sections are designed for the grants administrator to review and include as part of the grants-office procedures manual.

The grants office is the official sender of the proposal, but the funder may call or write to the individual listed as project director for questions or budget negotiations. While the grants office's goal is usually to encourage the grant writer to assume responsibility for the proposal, it is crucial for the office to know when the funder makes contact with your organization.

Dealing with the Decision of the Public Funding Source

You will receive a response to your proposal several months after its submittal. The response will be one of the following:

- accepted,
- accepted with budget modifications (i.e., let's talk about the budget),
- approved but not funded,
- supportable but not fundable, or
- rejected

Monitoring contact with funders becomes even more important when dealing with the decision on the proposal. To ensure that your organization's image will be upheld throughout this critical phase, only one office must be responsible for handling contact with the federal funding source.

Review the suggestions outlined under each possible response to your proposal in the Public Funding Decision Checklist (exhibit 10.3). Identify those suggestions that are *now* part of grants-office procedures and determine who is currently responsible for each of them. Then select which of the remaining suggestions will be added to your existing procedures. Note, however, that you should always request a list of the successful grantees and a description of the reviewers irrespective of the funding decision.

Two blanks correspond to each suggestion listed. Check the first box if the suggestion is *currently* one of your grants-office procedures. Check the second box if it is *not currently* a procedure but is one which you would like to incorporate in the *future*. At the end of each suggestion, indicate who is now responsible for implementing the suggestions or who will be responsible in the future.

Accepted

___ ___ 1. Send a thank-you letter.

___ ___ 2. Request a critique of your proposal to learn what the funding source liked about it.

___ ___ 3. Ask the funding source to visit you or set up a visit to them.

___ ___ 4. Request any completion forms to learn what records you need to keep.

___ ___ 5. Ask the funding source what are common problems with grants like yours and how to avoid them.

Accepted with Budget Modifications

___ ___ 1. Send a thank-you letter.

___ ___ 2. The funding source will probably call you. When they do, refer them to your project planner to negotiate the budget items.

___ ___ 3. Select the methods you would consider eliminating, and isolate the associated costs.

___ ___ 4. Reduce the amount of change predicted in the objectives or the number of people to be served by the project.

___ ___ 5. Be prepared to turn down the funds before you enter into an agreement that will cause you to lose your credibility later.

Approved but Not Funded

___ ___ 1. Send a thank-you letter.

___ ___ 2. Call the funding source and ask them how far from the funding cut-off point you were.

___ ___ 3. Ask what you could have done better.

___ ___ 4. Request the reviewers' comments.

___ ___ 5. Try to get additional appropriations. Remember that federal bureaucrats get their funds from appropriations and anything you can do to increase those funds will earn you great respect by funding sources. Additional funds may mean a better chance of getting your proposal funded.

___ ___ 6. Ask if there are any discretionary funds left over for unsolicited proposals.

PUBLIC FUNDING DECISION CHECKLIST

EXHIBIT 10.3

Rejected

—	—	1. Send a thank-you letter.
—	—	2. Request the reviewers' comments. (Enclose a self-addressed stamped envelope for convenience.)
—	—	3. Ask the funding official for his or her suggestions.
—	—	4. Ask if the proposal could be funded as a pilot project, needs-assessment study, or some other way.
—	—	5. Ask if there are any ways the funding source could assist you in getting ready for the next submission.
—	—	6. Ask what your chances are if you try again and what you would have to change to increase your chances of success.
—	—	7. Ask if you could become a reviewer to learn and become more familiar with the review process.

PUBLIC FUNDING DECISION CHECKLIST

EXHIBIT 10.3 (*continued*)

DEALING WITH THE DECISION OF THE PRIVATE FUNDING SOURCE

Private funding sources generally make their decision and let you know the outcome promptly. You will get a simple yes (accepted) or no (rejected). If the funding source says your proposal is "supportable" but "not fundable," it is a polite no. The easiest way to tell if your grant is funded is by looking for the check.

Review the suggestions outlined in the Private Funding Decision Checklist (exhibit 10.4). If the response is yes—the grant seeker's dream—do the suggestions *immediately*. If it is no—the dreaded response—turn it into a yes for next year by following the suggestions.

EVALUATION

Many grants offices do not see the reviewers' comments and may not even be aware of proposal errors that could have been avoided by a better sign-off system. Besides eliciting feedback from faculty and staff, a procedure for forwarding reviewers' comments to the grants office would assist grants office staff in brainstorming and evaluating what steps could be taken to improve the process.

FOLLOW-UP

Follow-Up with Public Funding Sources

The funding source should view follow-up as an asset rather than a nuisance. Your follow-up activities should position you as an asset in your field of interest, not as a pest.

The Public Funding Source Follow-up Checklist (exhibit 10.5) contains suggestions on how to get to know a funding source better and how to maintain a good relationship. Review this list and determine which suggestions are currently being implemented by members of your organization and which ones should be implemented in the future. If you do not

Two blanks correspond to each suggestion listed. Check the first box if the suggestion is *currently* one of your grants-office procedures. Check the second box if it is *not currently* a procedure but is one which you would like to incorporate in the *future*. At the end of each suggestion, indicate who is now responsible for implementing the suggestion or who will be responsible in the future.

Accepted

_____ _____ 1. Send a thank-you letter. (A foundation reported funding 10% of the proposals submitted to it and receiving very few thank-you letters. An official from the foundation said the funding results created "one ingrate and nine angry, rejected grantees.")

_____ _____ 2. Find out the payment procedures.

_____ _____ 3. Check on any reporting procedures the funding sources may have.

_____ _____ 4. Ask the funding source for an on-site visit by you to them to report on the grant.

_____ _____ 5. Put the funding source on your public relations list so you can send them news releases about you.

_____ _____ 6. IMPORTANT: Ask the funding source for their comments or critique of your proposal. Ask them what they liked and what could have been improved.

Rejected

_____ _____ 1. Send a thank-you letter. Express your appreciation for the time and effort spent reviewing your proposal.

_____ _____ 2. Remind them of your need of them as a source of funds.

_____ _____ 3. Ask them for comments on your proposal.

_____ _____ 4. Ask if they would look favorably on resubmission with certain changes.

_____ _____ 5. Ask if they know of any other funding sources that would be interested in your project.

PRIVATE FUNDING DECISION CHECKLIST

EXHIBIT 10.4

1. Send the funding source notes on special articles or books in your area or field.

2. Invite the funding source to visit you.

3. Ask the funding source to review an article you are writing.

4. Ask the funding source to speak at a conference or seminar, particularly a special grants conference.

5. Ask the funding source what you could do to have an impact on legislation affecting their agency.

6. Watch for meetings announced in the Federal Register and testify at committee hearings that have impact on the agency and its funding level.

7. Send the agency blind carbon copies of your efforts to have an impact on legislation for them (and yourself).

8. Use your association memberships and legislative committees to write and push for changes that benefit the particular agency.

9. Remain on the funding source's mailing list, and review the Federal Register for upcoming opportunities with the funding source.

10. Visit the funding source personally.

Remember, do not wait until next year's deadline to begin thinking about your application—start right after the decision. The aggressive grant seeker does not shelve the project for eleven months. The best way to know what is going on with the funding source is to keep in contact.

PUBLIC FUNDING SOURCE FOLLOW-UP CHECKLIST

EXHIBIT 10.5

currently do so, be sure to disseminate a list of follow-up suggestions to all of the successful and unsuccessful grantees in your organization.

Follow-Up with Private Funding Sources

Keeping your contacts current is the best way to continue success with private funding sources. A system of informing the funders of your activities both by mail and in person is optimum.

Once they have given away their money, many funding sources feel neglected by grantees. You can get on a funding source's list of good grantees through follow-up. See the following Private Funding Source Follow-Up Checklist (exhibit 10.6) for suggestions.

Use the following Checklist for Submission and Follow-Up Procedures (exhibit 10.7) as a starting point for evaluating and improving your existing system or initiating a new system.

Exhibit 10.8 list questions you can use to survey your staff, faculty, and administrators to gather their feedback on tracking proposals, sign-off, submission, and follow-up. Exhibit 10.9 will help you develop your plan.

---

1. Put the funding source on your public relations list, and send them news releases on your agency, organization, program, etc.

2. Send the funding source articles or studies related to your area of concern.

3. Invite the funding source to visit you.

4. Keep your funding-source files updated. Have a staff member or volunteer periodically update lists of new grants awarded to the files.

5. Let the funding source know how successful you are two years after your funding. Commend them for their farsightedness in dealing with the problem, etc.

6. Send thank-you letters to funding sources for both awarded *and* rejected proposals.

PRIVATE FUNDING SOURCE FOLLOW-UP CHECKLIST

EXHIBIT 10.6

---

1. Does your grants office have final sign-off and overall control of the submission procedure?

2. Is there a system in place to identify proposals in their various stages of development?

3. Is there a tracking system that allows you to follow and identify where proposals are at all times?

4. If you have a numbering system, does it allow you to know who wrote the proposal, what kind of funding source the proposal was sent to, how much the request was for, and when the proposal was submitted?

CHECKLIST FOR SUBMISSION AND FOLLOW-UP PROCEDURES

EXHIBIT 10.7

1. Please rate the grant office's assistance in the following areas (if services not used, please leave blank).

	Inadequate	Adequate	More than Adequate
a. Institutional sign-off/approval	_____	_____	_____
b. Transmission/submission of proposal to the funder	_____	_____	_____
c. Responding to the decision of the funder	_____	_____	_____
d. Follow-up with the funder	_____	_____	_____

SURVEY QUESTIONS—THE ROLE OF THE GRANTS OFFICE IN SIGN-OFF, SUBMISSION, AND FOLLOW-UP

EXHIBIT 10.8

For Each Activity/Item listed, Check Status

Activity/Item	Reviewed, Appropriate Part of Grants Office	Reviewed, Appropriate Part of Other Office (List)	Reviewed, Not Applicable Needs Action	Reviewed, Inappropriate Needs	Non-existent, Action
1. Proposal sign-off procedures • Rules, forms, etc. for sign-off • System for recording and monitoring grant proposals 2. System for recording and monitoring matching funds and in-kind contributions					

Complete this Section for Each Activity/Item Needing Action

What Needs to be Accomplished?	By Whom? (Office/ Person)	By When? (Time Frame)	Resources Required— Personnel, Supplies, Equipment, Programming, etc.	Estimated Costs

GRANTS OFFICE INVENTORY—THE ROLE OF THE GRANTS OFFICE IN SIGN-OFF, SUBMISSION, AND FOLLOW-UP

EXHIBIT 10.9

For Each Activity/Item listed, Check Status

Activity/Item	Reviewed, Appropriate Part of Grants Office	Reviewed, Appropriate Part of Other Office (List)	Reviewed, Not Applicable Needs Action	Reviewed, Inappropriate Needs	Non-existent, Action
• Documentation of priority areas in relationship to matching funds' budget 3. Submission and follow-up • Internal identification system for logging each proposal (number identification system, tracking system, etc.					

Complete this Section for Each Activity/Item Needing Action

What Needs to be Accomplished?	By Whom? (Office/ Person)	By When? (Time Frame)	Resources Required— Personnel, Supplies, Equipment, Programming, etc.	Estimated Costs

GRANTS OFFICE INVENTORY—THE ROLE OF THE GRANTS OFFICE IN SIGN-OFF, SUBMISSION, AND FOLLOW-UP

EXHIBIT 10.9 (*continued*)

For Each Activity/Item listed, Check Status

Activity/Item	Reviewed, Appropriate Part of Grants Office	Reviewed, Appropriate Part of Other Office (List)	Reviewed, Not Applicable Needs Action	Reviewed, Inappropriate Needs	Non-existent, Action
• Standardized policy and procedures for: • submission to private and public funding sources • dealing with the funding source's decision • system for receiving reviewers' comments					

Complete this Section for Each Activity/Item Needing Action

What Needs to be Accomplished?	By Whom? (Office/Person)	By When? (Time Frame)	Resources Required—Personnel, Supplies, Equipment, Programming, etc.	Estimated Costs

GRANTS OFFICE INVENTORY—THE ROLE OF THE GRANTS OFFICE IN SIGN-OFF, SUBMISSION, AND FOLLOW-UP

EXHIBIT 10.9 (*continued*)

For Each Activity/Item listed, Check Status

Activity/Item	Reviewed, Appropriate Part of Grants Office	Reviewed, Appropriate Part of Other Office (List)	Reviewed, Not Applicable Needs Action	Reviewed, Inappropriate Needs	Non-existent, Action
• follow-up with private and public funding sources					

Complete this Section for Each Activity/Item Needing Action

What Needs to be Accomplished?	By Whom? (Office/Person)	By When? (Time Frame)	Resources Required—Personnel, Supplies, Equipment, Programming, etc.	Estimated Costs

GRANTS OFFICE INVENTORY—THE ROLE OF THE GRANTS OFFICE IN SIGN-OFF, SUBMISSION, AND FOLLOW-UP

EXHIBIT 10.9 (continued)

CHAPTER 11

The Role of the Grants Office in the Administration of Private Funds

THE NEGOTIATION OF THE FINAL BUDGET

Because only the largest foundations (fewer than 2,000 of the 50,000) have full-time staff who are required to engage in discussions on the final amount of grants or question any line items, negotiation of the final budget is usually a moot question. However, your office should still establish a procedure that addresses this function so you are ready to deal with the larger foundation that does negotiate budgets. Your office should also have an established protocol outlining what to do when a foundation inappropriately sends a check directly to the principal investigator or project director.

To ensure the fiscal integrity of the grant effort of the institution, all budget negotiations and budget-related notifications must include the grants office. Use of personal contact, e-mail, and conference phone calls that include representation by the grants office are strongly advised. Institutions that allow principal investigators/project directors a free hand in budget negotiation are placing the proposed grant recipient and the college or university in a difficult position. In the excitement of actually being awarded the grant, the project director/principal investigator may forget to think of the mission of the institution above self during negotiations, and he or she may be willing to reduce monies in the final budget and forget about indirect costs received. Although some project directors/principal investigators do well in budget negotiations, others make the mistake of thinking that making cuts are no problem and that by doing so, they are demonstrating their desire to accomplish the prescribed work. For example, they may see no difficulty in cutting costs and assuming the institution will pick up travel and telephone costs someplace else, or in providing the same project and scope of work for $20,000 less in support.

It is a problem when your grant seekers concede to a request for the same amount of work for less money. The funding source may feel that if the grant seeker could have accomplished the same thing with $20,000 less, then their original request should have been more accurate and realistic. In short, the grant seeker is viewed as less than honest when he or she agrees to less money without changing the scope of work. The grantor may generalize from the grant seeker to the institution he or she represents, and in the process, you may lose your credibility as well.

To increase respect for your institution, consider following the trustee approach to negotiation. Trustee is defined as one to whom another's property or management is entrusted. One has faith and confidence in a trustee. The grant/contract is an agreement between your institution and the funding source to accomplish tasks that your proposal developer prescribed to meet the outcomes of the grant. Role-playing that you and your principal investigators/project directors are acting as trustees of the grant money helps you view your agreement from the funder's perspective and ensures that the funder receives exactly what it paid for in the most cost-efficient manner possible. This helps your office and your principal investigators/project directors establish a partnership atmosphere for negotiation.

The budget negotiations should center on methods and deal with deleting or reducing protocols and activities while modifying the amount of change called for in meeting the outcomes. Most funding sources will discuss decreases in budget categories as if they had nothing to do with the methods/activities. This is where your project planner or spreadsheet will be very useful. It will remind the funder, as well as the principal investigator/project director, that the expectations of the grant/contract must be reduced in relationship to the reduction of funds. Accurate knowledge of expectations will help to ensure your institution's future relations with the funder, increase trust, and reduce areas of disagreement. By using the project planner to negotiate and manage the budget, you and your grant seeker build confidence and trust.

Usually, elimination of a method or two will still allow your grant seeker to meet his or her objectives. However, when several methods, activities, or protocols are eliminated, the change represented in the objectives or specific aims must be reduced, and in some instances, the anticipated results may also have to be reduced or even eliminated. Remember, the reduction of funding in any area has a direct impact on the ability to complete the activity. For example, if the project director's salary is disputed or the amount allocated for it is reduced, look at the activities he or she must direct. A job description results from the sum of the skills required in accomplishing the methods. Set minimum experience requirements and estimate the cost of hiring a person who meets these standards. Discussion should center not on the project director's salary, or any other personnel costs, but on the qualifications needed to accomplish the prescribed tasks. Of course, you could lower the project director's salary by hiring someone with fewer credentials and less experience, but while this individual might cost less initially, he or she would take longer to accomplish tasks. Likewise, reducing the project's nonpersonnel budget items will also affect your proposal developer's ability to carry out activities and accomplish objectives.

Try to get your grant seekers to approach final budget negotiations as if your institution and the funder were partners in the grant outcome, and have them view the process from the perspective that their proposal uses funders' money to address a mutual concern and that they are actually stewards of the funds. Your institution's image and working relationship with the funding source will be greatly enhanced by reinforcing this cooperative attitude.

OFFICIAL ACCEPTANCE

The grants office should be the point of the official acceptance of the grant. This includes the responsibility of notifying consortium partners and initiating public notification if applicable.

The funding source should be asked about rules or preferences concerning the publicizing of awards. The grants office is responsible for ensuring compliance with the funder's rules and regulations. The office should review any other restrictions the funder may have before the acceptance letter is signed and returned. It is a good idea to review the Official Acceptance Checklist in exhibit 11.1 to ensure that nothing is left out.

The official acceptance letter, whether written by a high-ranking administrator or a grants-office staff member, should reference the appropriate grants administration staff, include their phone numbers, and note your office's willingness to assist in the proper transfer of funds. The letter should also encourage the funder to call the grants office for any reason at all so that the office can stay on top of the funder's concern and/or compliance issues.

---

1. What office or person is in charge of official acceptances?

2. Are the funder's fiscal and report procedures requested in the acceptance letter?

3. Who does the funder call with fiscal questions?

4. Who coordinates or records notification of advocates, politicians, and other helpers in the grants process concerning grant acceptance?

OFFICIAL ACCEPTANCE CHECKLIST

EXHIBIT 11.1

RECORD KEEPING AND REPORTING

When it comes to financial record keeping, most foundations expect their grant recipients to abide by the generally accepted accounting principles established by the Financial Accounting Standards Board (FASB). FASB's accounting standards are compiled and published each year in two sets of bound paperback volumes. These annual resources contain all of the original pronouncements put forth by the FASB and the American Institute of Certified Public Accountants (AICPA). To order annual editions of *FASB Original Pronouncements and Current Text* call John Wiley and Sons, Inc. at (800) 225-5945. The basic business practices outlined in these references are followed by colleges and universities throughout the United States. However, problems can occur when your institution is a partner or subcontractor in a foundation/corporate grant, and you assume that the prime sponsor also abides by these standard business practices. Do not make this assumption. Make sure your partners abide by these standards.

Many of the thousands of smaller foundations do not have sufficient staff to audit grantee records. They merely assume that your college will handle their grant properly. Even so, the grantee institution should submit a completion report to the funding source, including a statement showing income received (grant funds) and the expenditure of this income. A completion report should be submitted to the funding source even if it is not required. While the funder may not review this fiscal report, the fact that you submitted it will enhance your image as a true trustee of their funds.

BUDGET MODIFICATIONS

While private funding sources have different rules on budget modifications, most will allow changes in budget that do not modify the purpose or intent of the grant. Because fewer than 2,000 of the estimated 50,000 active foundations have offices and few have full-time directors and staffs, the private marketplace does not have a large bureaucracy. Private foundations simply do not have a large bureaucracy; they do not want to take the time to develop or institute elaborate forms and rules for budget changes.

Because many foundations meet only once or twice a year and have a limited ability to respond to requests for budget changes, they are usually not concerned with reallocations within budget categories but do not want the approved grant total to be exceeded. Because many of the smaller foundations send a check with the acceptance letter, it is not even possible to exceed the total amount granted. However, it is appropriate to send the funding source a letter stating that you are moving budget amounts and categories as outlined unless they instruct you to the contrary within 30 days.

I once purchased the equipment budgeted for on a foundation grant at a tremendous savings by buying it below wholesale, and as a result, my original equipment budget was left with a considerable balance. When I checked with the funding source for approval to purchase additional equipment with the money I saved, my organization was commended for being a good trustee of funds. The foundation gave us permission to use all of the remaining funds for the purchase of additional equipment related to the grant. Please note that most private funders do not like grantees to return funds. This disturbs their accounting system and affects government rules concerning expenditures and IRS returns. If you are interested in modifying your budget, review the following Checklist for Budget Modification with Private Funds (exhibit 11.2).

---

1. **What office or person in your institution is responsible for obtaining and recording approval to reallocate funds disseminated from private funders?**

2. **Are there any guidelines for requesting changes in private funding allocations?**

CHECKLIST FOR BUDGET MODIFICATION WITH PRIVATE FUNDS

EXHIBIT 11.2

EQUIPMENT AND PURCHASING CONTROLS

All equipment purchased through grants from private funders should have an inventory tag and corresponding number that is recorded in the grants office. The numbering system used should identify

- the grant and the funding source that granted the equipment;
- the location of the equipment (what department, laboratory, building, etc.);
- the investigator, project director, or manager responsible for the equipment; and
- any special rules, regulations, and so on related to the equipment, such as warranties, maintenance requirements, life expectancy (how many years it will be operable), and resale restrictions.

Whether you put this information into a computer or use a manual filing system, it should be readily available. For example, you should be able to quickly produce pertinent lists and reports such as Outdated Equipment for Surplus.

While there are few restrictions on purchase guidelines with private funders, the grantee is expected to follow established business practices. There is usually *no* mandated policy or requirement to go out for a bid on equipment. Foundations assume that you want to get the most for your money, and if you decide to purchase locally so that you receive good maintenance but pay a little more, that's your business. Before you acquire more equipment with foundation funds, take a look at the Checklist for Equipment and Purchasing Controls with Private Funds (exhibit 11.3).

CASH REQUESTS

Unlike federal funding sources, private funders generally do not require that funds be expended by the grantee and then reimbursed. Private funding sources usually operate cash-

1. Does your institution have an equipment-numbering system?

2. If you do have a system, what information does it hold, and is the information filed on computer or manually?

3. What person or office in your institution is responsible for maintaining the system?

CHECKLIST FOR EQUIPMENT AND PURCHASING CONTROLS WITH PRIVATE FUNDS

EXHIBIT 11.3

in-advance systems. The only variable is how much of the granted sum will come in advance. Many small family foundations provide grantees with a lump-sum advance payment for the total amount of the grant. However, most large private funding sources have a sufficient number of staff to operate partial- or installment-payment systems. Because there are few rules in this area, a frank discussion of your cash-flow needs with the funding source will most likely result in an amicable agreement. The use of your time line and project planner will be helpful in this endeavor, as will the Checklist for Cash Requests of Private Funders (exhibit 11.4).

1. Does your institution have written procedures or a policy on who negotiates with private funding sources?

2. Are certain items on each proposed budget identified in advance as "negotiable if necessary?"

3. Does someone or some office in your institution establish the funder's cash policy in advance of the award? If so, who?

CHECKLIST FOR CASH REQUESTS OF PRIVATE FUNDERS

EXHIBIT 11.4

Unlike federal and state grant funds, private funds may be deposited in savings accounts. It has been my experience that any earned interest that accrues ethically and legally belongs to your institution and does not need to be reported to the grantor unless stated by them in their acceptance letter.

PERSONNEL REQUIREMENTS AND PROCEDURES

Private funders will expect you to follow the personnel procedures accepted by the American Institute of Certified Public Accountants. These standard payroll records are usually accepted for both expenditure of the grant funds and documentation of the donation of in-kind services and matching funds.

You will be expected to follow accepted standards and fair employment practices. However, you usually will not be required to sign any assurances or compliances typical of federal grants.

Exhibit 11.5 provides questions you may use to survey your faculty and staff on their opinions and suggestions concerning your office's handling of private funds. Completing exhibit 11.6 will help you improve or establish your office's procedures as related to the administration of private funds.

---

1. Have you received and expended private funds from a foundation, corporation, professional society, or nonprofit organization?
_____ Yes _____ No

If yes, please rate the grants office's handling of your private funds as it relates to the following categories, and answer questions 2 and 3.

	Inadequate	Adequate	More than Adequate
a. Notification of award/acceptance	____	____	____
b. Assistance with negotiations (if any)	____	____	____
c. Establishing project/grant accounts	____	____	____
d. Hiring personnel required on grant	____	____	____
e. Hiring consultants required on grant	____	____	____
f. Purchasing supplies and equipment	____	____	____
g. Maintaining information on expended and unexpended funds	____	____	____
h. Handling budget modifications	____	____	____
i. Processing unexpended funds	____	____	____
j. Inventorying, tracking, and transferring grant-purchased equipment	____	____	____

SURVEY QUESTIONS—THE ROLE OF THE GRANTS OFFICE IN THE ADMINISTRATION OF PRIVATE FUNDS

EXHIBIT 11.5

	Inadequate	Adequate	More than Adequate
k. Documentation of in-kind/matching funds	_____	_____	_____
l. Assistance with reporting requirements	_____	_____	_____

2. What barriers or problems have you encountered in the administration of your private grant funds?

3. What suggestions do you have for improving the grants office's services in this area?

SURVEY QUESTIONS—THE ROLE OF THE GRANTS OFFICE IN THE ADMINISTRATION OF PRIVATE FUNDS

EXHIBIT 11.5 (*continued*)

For Each Activity/Item listed, Check Status

Activity/Item	Reviewed, Appropriate Part of Grants Office	Reviewed, Appropriate Part of Other Office (List)	Reviewed, Not Applicable Needs Action	Reviewed, Inappropriate Needs	Non-existent, Needs Action
1. Budget negotiations • desigination of person or office to handle all budget negotiations • policies and procedures on how to negotiate budgets, center around methods, delete activities,					

Complete this Section for Each Activity/Item Needing Action

What Needs to be Accomplished?	By Whom? (Office/Person)	By When? (Time Frame)	Resources Required—Personnel, Supplies, Equipment, Programming, etc.	Estimated Costs

GRANTS OFFICE INVENTORY—THE ROLE OF THE GRANTS OFFICE IN THE ADMINISTRATION OF PRIVATE FUNDS

EXHIBIT 11.6

For Each Activity/Item listed, Check Status

Activity/Item	Reviewed, Appropriate Part of Grants Office	Reviewed, Appropriate Part of Other Office (List)	Reviewed, Not Applicable Needs Action	Reviewed, Inappropriate Needs	Non-existent, Needs Action
modify amount of change, and identify negotiable items if necessary prior to discussions 2. Official acceptance • designation of person or office in charge of official acceptance					

Complete this Section for Each Activity/Item Needing Action

What Needs to be Accomplished?	By Whom? (Office/ Person)	By When? (Time Frame)	Resources Required— Personnel, Supplies, Equipment, Programming, etc.	Estimated Costs

EXHIBIT 11.6 (*continued*)

For Each Activity/Item listed, Check Status

Activity/Item	Reviewed, Appropriate Part of Grants Office	Reviewed, Appropriate Part of Other Office (List)	Reviewed, Not Applicable Needs Action	Reviewed, Inappropriate Needs	Non-existent, Needs Action
• system to ensure that funding source restrictions are reviewed prior to signature and submittal of acceptance letter • guidelines for what should be included in the acceptance letter					

Complete this Section for Each Activity/Item Needing Action

What Needs to be Accomplished?	By Whom? (Office/Person)	By When? (Time Frame)	Resources Required—Personnel, Supplies, Equipment, Programming, etc.	Estimated Costs

GRANTS OFFICE INVENTORY—THE ROLE OF THE GRANTS OFFICE IN THE ADMINISTRATION OF PRIVATE FUNDS

EXHIBIT 11.6 (*continued*)

For Each Activity/Item listed, Check Status

Activity/Item	Reviewed, Appropriate Part of Grants Office	Reviewed, Appropriate Part of Other Office (List)	Reviewed, Not Applicable Needs Action	Reviewed, Inappropriate Needs	Non-existent, Needs Action
3. Record-keeping and reporting • designation of person in charge of record-keeping and reporting • availability of financial reporting guidelines established by American Institute of Certified Public Accountants					

Complete this Section for Each Activity/Item Needing Action

What Needs to be Accomplished?	By Whom? (Office/ Person)	By When? (Time Frame)	Resources Required— Personnel, Supplies, Equipment, Programming, etc.	Estimated Costs

EXHIBIT 11.6 (continued)

For Each Activity/Item listed, Check Status

Activity/Item	Reviewed, Appropriate Part of Grants Office	Reviewed, Appropriate Part of Other Office (List)	Reviewed, Not Applicable Needs Action	Reviewed, Inappropriate Needs	Non-existent, Needs Action
• retainment of services of professional accountant • submission of completion report to all private funding sources 4. Budget modifications • designation of person or office responsible for obtaining and recording					

Complete this Section for Each Activity/Item Needing Action

What Needs to be Accomplished?	By Whom? (Office/Person)	By When? (Time Frame)	Resources Required—Personnel, Supplies, Equipment, Programming, etc.	Estimated Costs

GRANTS OFFICE INVENTORY—THE ROLE OF THE GRANTS OFFICE IN THE ADMINISTRATION OF PRIVATE FUNDS

EXHIBIT 11.6 (*continued*)

For Each Activity/Item listed, Check Status

Activity/Item	Reviewed, Appropriate Part of Grants Office	Reviewed, Appropriate Part of Other Office (List)	Reviewed, Not Applicable Needs Action	Reviewed, Inappropriate Needs	Non-existent, Needs Action
approval to reallocate funds disseminated by funding source • guidelines for requesting changes in budget allocations such as use of a "letter of notice" 5. Equipment and purchasing controls • computerized or					

Complete this Section for Each Activity/Item Needing Action

What Needs to be Accomplished?	By Whom? (Office/Person)	By When? (Time Frame)	Resources Required—Personnel, Supplies, Equipment, Programming, etc.	Estimated Costs

GRANTS OFFICE INVENTORY—THE ROLE OF THE GRANTS OFFICE IN THE ADMINISTRATION OF PRIVATE FUNDS

EXHIBIT 11.6 (*continued*)

For Each Activity/Item listed, Check Status

Activity/Item	Reviewed, Appropriate Part of Grants Office	Reviewed, Appropriate Part of Other Office (List)	Reviewed, Not Applicable Needs Action	Reviewed, Inappropriate Needs	Non-existent, Needs Action
manual numbering system for all equipment purchased through private grant funds • designation of person or office responsible for maintaining this system 6. Cash requests • designated person or office and written policy					

Complete this Section for Each Activity/Item Needing Action

What Needs to be Accomplished?	By Whom? (Office/ Person)	By When? (Time Frame)	Resources Required— Personnel, Supplies, Equipment, Programming, etc.	Estimated Costs

GRANTS OFFICE INVENTORY—THE ROLE OF THE GRANTS OFFICE IN THE ADMINISTRATION OF PRIVATE FUNDS

EXHIBIT 11.6 (*continued*)

For Each Activity/Item listed, Check Status

Activity/Item	Reviewed, Appropriate Part of Grants Office	Reviewed, Appropriate Part of Other Office (List)	Reviewed, Not Applicable Needs Action	Reviewed, Inappropriate Needs	Non-existent, Needs Action
and procedures for negotiating the type of reimbursement with the funding source 7. Personnel require-ments and procedures • designated person or office to handle personnel issues, pay-roll records, etc.					

Complete this Section for Each Activity/Item Needing Action

What Needs to be Accomplished?	By Whom? (Office/ Person)	By When? (Time Frame)	Resources Required— Personnel, Supplies, Equipment, Programming, etc.	Estimated Costs

GRANTS OFFICE INVENTORY—THE ROLE OF THE GRANTS OFFICE IN THE ADMINISTRATION OF PRIVATE FUNDS

EXHIBIT 11.6 (*continued***)**

For Each Activity/Item listed, Check Status

Activity/Item	Reviewed, Appropriate Part of Grants Office	Reviewed, Appropriate Part of Other Office (List)	Reviewed, Not Applicable Needs Action	Reviewed, Inappropriate Needs	Non-existent, Needs Action
• availability of personnel procedures accepted by the American Institute of Certified Public Accountants • use of standard pay-roll records for the ex-penditure of funds and the documentation of					

Complete this Section for Each Activity/Item Needing Action

What Needs to be Accomplished?	By Whom? (Office/ Person)	By When? (Time Frame)	Resources Required— Personnel, Supplies, Equipment, Programming, etc.	Estimated Costs

EXHIBIT 11.6 (*continued*)

For Each Activity/Item listed, Check Status					
Activity/Item	Reviewed, Appropriate Part of Grants Office	Reviewed, Appropriate Part of Other Office (List)	Reviewed, Not Applicable Needs Action	Reviewed, Inappropriate Needs	Non-existent, Needs Action
in-kind services and matching funds • written policy and procedures outlining fair employment practices					

Complete this Section for Each Activity/Item Needing Action

What Needs to be Accomplished?	By Whom? (Office/ Person)	By When? (Time Frame)	Resources Required— Personnel, Supplies, Equipment, Programming, etc.	Estimated Costs

EXHIBIT 11.6 (*continued*)

CHAPTER 12

The Role of the Grants Office in the Administration of Federal Funds

When an application is approved for funding, the grants-management officer will prepare a Notice of Grant Award. Most negotiations of budget amounts will be done with the federal program officer in conjunction with the principal investigator or proposal developer before the Notice of Grant Award is issued.

NEGOTIATING GRANT AWARDS

Arguing against reductions in your original proposed budget without referencing the impact of reductions on your project is futile. You must relate changes in the final budget to the reduction or elimination of methods/activities and the effect of these reductions on the hypothesis, specific aims, and/or the attainment of proposed objectives. Your project planner (chapter 8) will provide the necessary linkage between activities and budget categories and amounts. Therefore, include a project planner with your proposal as an attachment, or send one to the program officer when the negotiation process begins.

Because federal government applications request information on project directors (e.g., name, phone number), the funding source may contact the project director or principal investigator directly to negotiate the budget. Some project directors have the skills necessary to negotiate a budget, but mistakes are more likely if the grants office is not involved in the process. To ensure fiscal integrity, it is imperative that your grants system mandate the inclusion of the grants office in all budget negotiations. Because the federal cover sheet includes the names of the fiscal agents, agents are usually included in the award process. The fiscal agent may be the business office rather than the grants office. Both need to be informed.

In many cases, the program officer who has been the main contact in the grants process up to this point appoints a member of his or her fiscal team to complete the budget. The federal fiscal representative is not concerned with objectives, protocol, or degrees of change in measurement indicators. He or she simply wants all of the columns to add up so the process of distributing the funds can begin. You may be successful in transferring funds by category, but the total amount of the award will be changed only with the intervention of the program officer.

The federal fiscal agent can answer your questions on allowable expenses (e.g., rental/ purchase of equipment). In one grant I was involved with, the federal fiscal agent acted as the fiscal officer for both grants and contracts. When confronted with a question on how best to handle an equipment lease/rental agreement, the officer suggested we change our grant to a contract to allow the rent to apply toward the purchase of equipment. By starting out as a contract, we would not have to make changes later.

The best time to talk with a federal funding official is before the final award amount is determined, categories of funding are designated, and forms are signed. In some cases, the amount that the federal official announces as the total is fixed and nonnegotiable. In these instances, your project planner should be adjusted to reflect a realistic scope of work based on the size of the award.

Once the final award amount and categories of funding are agreed upon, the type of payment must be decided.

TYPE OF PAYMENT

Payments are made on either a cash-in-advance-of-expenditures or reimbursement basis. The advance payment method is preferable to the reimbursement method because the former does not require an organization to expend its own funds for items or services that will be reimbursed at a later date, or force it to borrow interest-laden cash to meet project expenses.

Recipients can be paid in advance, provided they maintain or demonstrate a willingness to maintain (1) written procedures that minimize the time elapsing between the transfer of funds and disbursement by the recipient, and (2) financial management systems that meet the standards for fund control and accountability as established in the appropriate OMB circular (see the following section). Advance payment mechanisms include, but are not limited to, Treasury check and electronic funds transfer, and they are subject to the procedures codified in Title 31 Code of Federal Regulations (CFR) Part 205. Subparts A and B of this part implement the Cash Management Improvement Act and prescribe rules and procedures for the transfer of funds. Subparts A and B of 31 CFR Part 205 can be retrieved online by visiting http://www.access.gpo.gov/nara/cfr.

When paid by the cash-in-advance system, you need to monitor your cash needs carefully. Among other things, you should

- limit the amount requested to the minimum required to accomplish your objective(s),
- refrain from building up extra cash,
- move the cash through your books swiftly, and
- deposit federal funds in minority banks.

Your project planner and grants time line will help you develop monthly cash forecasts and estimates of your expenditure rate, which will assist you in accomplishing the above and meeting the federal regulations outlined in 31 CFR Part 205.

Obviously, reimbursement is the preferred method when the requirements for payment in advance cannot be met.

As a result of the Paperwork Reduction Act Notice and the advances brought about by computers, the grants payment process has been simplified, and the time involved in mailing forms and checks has been greatly reduced. For a deeper understanding of this area and information on subjects such as letters of credit, monthly cash request (Treasury check), reimbursement by Treasury check, secondary recipient advances, and assignment of payments, review the Public Health Service Grants Policy Statement on payments at http://grants.nih.gov/grants/policy/gps/5award.htm.

OMB CIRCULARS

Once an application is approved for funding, your financial management system must meet or exceed the accountability standards outlined in grants management circulars produced by the federal Office of Management and Budget (OMB). Known as OMB Circulars, these publications outline uniform standards for financial dealings with government granting agencies. These highly regulated, detailed standards are probably the most imposing characteristic of federal grants. However, once you and your fiscal staff have reviewed and become familiar with the appropriate grants management circulars, your fears about your institution's ability to comply with federal grants requirements specifying allowable costs, indirect-cost rates, accounting requirements, procurement, and the like, will gradually diminish. From purchasing to personnel, your organization must have necessary safeguards in place. Those areas that look as if they will pose a problem can be addressed in a general manner, for all federal grants, or handled separately, case by case, to avoid any difficulties. The circulars can be ordered from the Superintendent of Documents, Government Printing Office, Washington, DC 20402-9238, (202)512-1800. They can also be obtained from the Internet at http://www.doleta.gov/regs/omb/index.htm or http://www.whitehouse.gov/OMB/circulars/index.html. To obtain circulars available in hard copy only, you may also call the Office of Administration, Publications Office at (202) 395-7332.

Colleges and Universities will be most interested in OMB Circular A-110, Uniform Administrative Requirements for Grants and Agreements with Institutions of Higher Education, Hospitals, and Other Non-Profit Organizations (11/19/93, amended 9/30/99), OMB Circular A-21, Cost Principles for Educational Institutions (10/27/98), and OMB Circular A-133, Audits of States, Local Governments, and Non-Profit Organizations (6/24/97).

OMB Circular A-110

OMB Circular A-110 is a guide to the rules regarding federal grants. Among other things, it sets forth standards for the pre-award and post-award administration of grants to and agreements with institutions of higher education and includes provisions related to property, procurement standards, reports, and records. Broken into four subparts and an appendix, the circular covers the following areas:

Subpart A—General
- Purpose
- Definitions
- Effect on other issuances
- Deviations
- Subawards

Subpart B—Pre-Award Requirements
- Purpose
- Pre-award policies
- Forms for applying for federal assistance
- Debarment and suspension
- Special award conditions
- Metric system of measurement
- Resource Conservation and Recovery Act
- Certifications and representations

Subpart C—Post-Award Requirements
Financial and Program Management
- Purpose of financial and program management
- Standards for financial management systems
- Payment
- Cost sharing or matching
- Program income
- Revision of budget and program plans
- Non-federal audits
- Allowable costs
- Period of availability of funds
- Conditional exemptions

Property Standards
- Purpose of property standards
- Insurance coverage
- Real property
- Federally-owned and exempt property
- Equipment
- Supplies and other expendable property
- Intangible property
- Property trust relationship

Procurement Standards
- Purpose of procurement standards
- Recipient responsibilities
- Codes of conduct
- Competition
- Procurement procedures
- Cost and price analysis
- Procurement records

- Contract administration
- Contract provisions
- Reports and Records
- Purpose of reports and records
- Monitoring and reporting program performance
- Financial reporting
- Retention and access requirements for records

Termination and Enforcement
- Purpose of termination and enforcement
- Termination
- Enforcement

Subpart D—After-the-Award Requirements
- Purpose
- Closeout procedures
- Subsequent adjustments and continuing responsibilities
- Collection of amounts due

Appendix A—Contract Provisions

OMB Circular A-21

Colleges and universities will also be interested in OMB Circular A-21, which defines cost principles for federal research and development grants to educational institutions, and governs direct and indirect charges made by educational institutions to the federal government. The circular covers the following areas:

A. Purpose and Scope
- Objectives
- Policy guides
- Application
- Inquiries

B. Definition of terms
- Major functions of an institution
- Sponsored agreement
- Allocation
- Facilities and administrative (F&A) costs

C. Basic considerations
- Composition of total costs
- Factors affecting allowability of costs
- Reasonable costs
- Allocable costs
- Applicable credits
- Costs incurred by state and local governments
- Limitations on allowance of costs
- Collection of unallowable costs
- Adjustment of previously negotiated F&A cost rates containing unallowable costs
- Consistency in estimating, accumulating, and reporting costs

- Consistency in allocating costs incurred for the same purpose
- Accounting for unallowable costs
- Cost accounting period
- Disclosure statement

D. Direct costs
- General
- Application to sponsored agreements

E. F&A costs
- General
- Criteria for distribution

F. Identification and assignment of F&A costs
- Definition of Facilities and Administration
- Depreciation and use allowances
- Interest
- Operation and maintenance expenses
- General administration and general expenses
- Departmental administration expenses
- Sponsored projects administration
- Library expenses
- Student administration and services
- Offset for F&A expenses otherwise provided for by the federal government

G. Determination and application of F&A cost rate or rates
- F&A cost pools
- The distribution basis
- Negotiated lump sum for F&A costs
- Predetermined rates for F&A costs
- Negotiated fixed rates and carry-forward provisions
- Provisional and final rates for F&A costs
- Fixed rates for the life of the sponsored agreement
- Limitation on reimbursement of administrative costs
- Alternative method for administrative costs
- Individual rate components
- Negotiation and approval of F&A rate

H. Simplified method for small institutions
- General
- Simplified procedure

I. Reserved

J. General provisions for selected items of cost
- Advertising and public relations costs
- Alcoholic beverages
- Alumni/ae activities
- Bad debts
- Civil defense costs
- Commencement and convocation costs
- Communication costs

- Compensation for personal services
- Contingency provisions
- Deans of faculty and graduate schools
- Defense and prosecution of criminal and civil proceedings, claims, appeals, and patent infringement
- Depreciation and use allowances
- Donations and contributions
- Employee morale, health, and welfare costs and credits
- Entertainment costs
- Equipment and other capital expenditures
- Executive lobbying costs
- Fines and penalties
- Goods or services for personal use
- Housing and personal living expenses
- Insurance and indemnification
- Interest, fund raising, and investment management costs
- Labor relations costs
- Lobbying
- Losses on other sponsored agreements or contracts
- Maintenance and repair costs
- Material costs
- Memberships, subscriptions, and professional activity costs
- Patent costs
- Plant security costs
- Preagreement costs
- Professional service costs
- Profits and losses on disposition of plant equipment or other capital assets
- Proposal costs
- Rearrangement and alteration costs
- Reconversion costs
- Recruiting costs
- Rental cost of buildings and equipment
- Royalties and other costs for use of patents
- Sabbatical leave costs
- Scholarship and student aid costs
- Selling and marketing
- Severance pay
- Specialized service facilities
- Student activity costs
- Taxes
- Transportation costs
- Travel costs
- Termination costs applicable to sponsored agreements
- Trustees

K.   Certification of charges
Exhibit A—List of Colleges and Universities Subject of Section J.12.f of Circular-21
Exhibit B—Listing of Institutions that are eligible for the utility cost adjustment
Exhibit C—Examples of "major project" where direct charging of administrative or clerical staff salaries may be appropriate
Appendix A—CASB's Cost Accounting Standards (CAS)
Appendix B—CASB's Disclosure Statement (DS-2)

OMB Circular A-133

OMB Circular A-133 sets forth standards for obtaining consistency and uniformity among federal agencies for the audits of states, local governments, and nonprofit organizations expending federal awards. A-133 requires a single annual compliance audit of educational institutions receiving federal funding.

Additional OMB Circulars

All nonprofit organizations should familiarize themselves with OMB Circular A-122, "Cost Principles for Non-Profit Organizations," and state and local governments must also review OMB Circular A-87, "Cost Principles for State, Local, and Indian Tribal Governments" and OMB Circular A-102, "Grants and Cooperative Agreements with State and Local Governments." Please be advised that you should always refer to the most current circular for the specific rules and regulations in your area. Exhibit 12.1 lists all available OMB Circulars in numerical sequence.

EMPLOYMENT ISSUES RELATED TO GRANTS

As mentioned in chapter 9, the acceptance of federal funds requires the signature of assurances relating to federal nondiscrimination laws. However, most grantees are so elated when their proposals are accepted that they do not think about the nondiscrimination assurances they signed months ago when they submitted the proposal. It is the responsibility of the grants office to ensure that these rules and regulations are adhered to in the administration of the federal funds and that the institution's personnel office is aware of them. See chapter 9 for a review of the more common federal nondiscrimination laws governing this area.

Many smaller institutions use their personnel departments to handle grant-related employees as well as those on their regular payroll. There are issues with grant-related staff that are different from those of regular staff, and the personnel department needs to be aware of them.

1.   Compliance with grantor regulations. Read over the guidelines and circulars that relate to personnel policy and decisions and forward them to the personnel director.
2.   Grant-funded employees must face the fact that the grant will eventually end. Their performance on the grant may have little relationship to the continuation of the grant. Even if they work particularly hard, efficiently, and loyally, the grant will end, and they will have to face locating another job.
3.   The grants area has always been weak in the employee-evaluation area. Performance measures and evaluations are rarely outlined in advance. However, assurance is

OMB Circular A-1, dated 08/07/52
  System of Circulars and Bulletins to Executive Departments and Establishments

OMB Circular A-11, Transmittal Memorandum #72, dated 07/12/99; revised 11/10/99
  Part 1—Preparation and Submission of Budget Estimates
  Part 2—Preparation and Submission of Strategic Plans and Annual Performance
        Plans and Annual Program Performance Reports
  Part 3—Planning, Budgeting, and Acquisition of Capital Assets
  Supplement to Part 3, Capital Programming Guide

OMB Circular A-16, dated 10/19/90
  Coordination of Surveying, Mapping, and Related Spatial Data Activities

OMB Circular A-19, dated 09/20/79
  Legislative Coordination and Clearance

OMB Circular A-21, dated 10/27/98
  Cost Principles for Educational Institutions

OMB Circular A-25, Transmittal Memorandum #1, dated 07/08/93
  User Charges

OMB Circular A-34, Transmittal Memorandum #15, dated 10/19/99
  Instructions on Budget Execution

OMB Circular A-45, dated 10/20/93
  Rental and Construction of Government Quarters

OMB Circular A-50, dated 09/29/82
  Audit Followup

OMB Circular A-76, Performance of Commercial Activities
  Circular A-76 in HTML, WPD or PDF format, dated 08/04/83; revised 06/14/99
  Supplemental Handbook in HTML, WPD, PDF format, dated 04/01/96; revised 06/
      14/99
  Transmittal Memorandum #19 in HTML format, dated 03/24/99
  Performance of Commercial Activities
  Transmittal Memorandum #20 in HTML, WPD or PDF format, dated 06/14/99
  Implementing the FAIR Act
  OMB's Fair Act Inventory in HTML or WPD format, dated 09/27/99
  1999 Inventory of Commercial Activities Under the Federal Activities Inventory
      Reform Act (P.L. 105-260)

OMB Circular A-87, dated 05/04/95, further amended 08/29/97
  Cost Principles for State, Local and Indian Tribal Governments

OMB Circular A-89, dated 08/17/84
  Catalog of Federal Domestic Assistance

OMB CIRCULARS

EXHIBIT 12.1

OMB Circular A-94, dated 10/29/92
  Discount Rates to be Used in Evaluating Time-Distributed Costs and Benefits

OMB Circular A-97, dated 08/29/69
  Transmittal Memorandum #1, dated 03/27/81
  Specialized or Technical Services for State and Local Governments

OMB Circular A-102, dated 10/07/94, further amended 08/29/97
Grants and Cooperative Agreements with State and Local Governments

OMB Circular A-109, dated 04/05/76 (available in hard copy only)
Major Systems Acquisitions

OMB Circular A-110, dated 11/19/93, further amended 09/30/99
Uniform Administrative Requirements for Grants and Other Agreements with Institutions
of Higher Education, Hospitals and Other Non-Profit Organizations

OMB Circular A-119, Transmittal Memorandum dated 02/10/98
Federal Participation in the Development and Use of Voluntary Standards

OMB Circular A-122, dated 06/01/98
Cost Principles for Non-Profit Organizations

OMB Circular A-123, dated 06/21/95
Management Accountability and Control

OMB Circular A-125, was rescinded and replaced by the Prompt Pay
regulations at 5 CFR Part 1315

OMB Circular A-126, dated 05/22/92
Improving the Management and Use of Government Aircraft
Attachment A
Attachment B

OMB Circular A-127, dated 07/23/93
Financial Management Systems
Transmittal Memorandum #2, dated 06/10/99

OMB Circular A-129, dated 01/11/93
Managing Federal Credit Programs

OMB Circular A-130, Transmittal Memorandum #3, dated 02/08/96
Management of Federal Information Resources

OMB Circular A-131, dated 05/21/93
Value Engineering

OMB Circular A-133, dated 06/24/97
Audits of States, Local Governments, and Non-Profit Organizations
Appendix A: Data Collection Form (Form SF-SAC), PDF format
Appendix B: April 1999 Compliance Supplement

OMB CIRCULARS

EXHIBIT 12.1 (*continued*)

OMB Circular A-134, dated 05/20/93
Financial Accounting Principles and Standards

OMB Circular A-135, dated 10/05/94
Management of Federal Advisory Committees

OMB CIRCULARS

EXHIBIT 12.1 (*continued*)

given that grant-related employees will be treated the same as the regular staff, and therefore, if the regular employees undergo evaluation, so must the grant employees.

4. High job turnover is common in the grants area. It is natural for individuals to want job security, and the anxiety of grant renewals and so on takes it toll.

Many of the same techniques in chapter 5 for increasing interest in proposal development and grant involvement will produce great benefits with grant staff. Review that chapter and you may find ways to avoid problems that arise when grant employees are not treated the same as nongrant-funded staff. In addition, your efforts in developing a good work atmosphere will decrease your chances of grievances and lawsuits. Just remember, the most important personnel/employment rules to obey are those of the grantor.

PROCUREMENT AND CONTROL

The basic requirements for procurement are outlined in OMB Circulars A-110 and A-102. In addition to the appropriate OMB circulars, review the NIH Grants Policy Statement (http://grants.nih.gov/grants/policy/nihgps/), and the Federal Acquisition Regulation (http://www.arnet.gov/far/) for a deeper understanding of the area.

TRAM

For quick access to post-award regulations regarding federal grants, visit TRAM at http://tram.east.asu.edu/index.html. TRAM is a service initially developed by the Texas Research Administrators Group. Besides providing links to servers related to research funding and administration, it also contains a search engine for locating funding opportunities from many different agencies, and provides grant application forms collected from various sources, as well as standard agreements for subcontracts, nondisclosures, and licenses.

Exhibit 12.2 provides a list of suggested questions for surveying your institution's faculty and staff concerning their perceptions of your office's role in the administration of federal funds. Complete exhibit 12.3 to help you develop your overall plan.

1. Have you received and expended public funds from the state or federal government?

_____Yes _____ No

If yes, please rate the grants office's handling of your public funds as it relates to the following categories, and answer questions 2 and 3.

	Inadequate	Adequate	More than Adequate
a. Assistance in negotiating the final grant award	_____	_____	_____
b. Assistance in establishing accounts and explaining your institution's post-award system	_____	_____	_____
c. Handling cash requests	_____	_____	_____
d. Handling grant-related employment issues including the hiring of personnel and consultants called for in the grant	_____	_____	_____
e. Purchasing supplies and equipment	_____	_____	_____
f. Ensuring the basic procurement requirements are adhered to	_____	_____	_____
g. Maintaining information on expended funds	_____	_____	_____
h. Handling budget modifications	_____	_____	_____
i. Processing unexpended funds	_____	_____	_____
j. Inventorying, tracking, and transferring grant-purchased equipment	_____	_____	_____
k. Documentation of in-kind/matching funds	_____	_____	_____
l. Assistance with reporting requirements	_____	_____	_____
m. Making appropriate OMB circulars, policy statements, etc. available	_____	_____	_____

2. What barriers or problems have you encountered in the administration of your public grant funds?

SURVEY QUESTIONS—THE ROLE OF THE GRANTS OFFICE IN THE ADMINISTRATION OF FEDERAL FUNDS

EXHIBIT 12.2

3. What suggestions do you have for improving the grants office's services in this area?

SURVEY QUESTIONS—THE ROLE OF THE GRANTS OFFICE IN THE ADMINISTRATION OF FEDERAL FUNDS

EXHIBIT 12.2 (*continued*)

For Each Activity/Item listed, Check Status

Activity/Item	Reviewed, Appropriate Part of Grants Office	Reviewed, Appropriate Part of Other Office (List)	Reviewed, Not Applicable	Reviewed, Inappropriate Needs Action	Non-existent, Needs Action
1. Negotiating grant awards • designation of person to handle all budget negotiation • policy to relate all changes in the budget to the reduction of elimin-ation of methods/activities and the outcomes					

Complete this Section for Each Activity/Item Needing Action

What Needs to be Accomplished?	By Whom? (Office/ Person)	By When? (Time Frame)	Resources Required— Personnel, Supplies, Equipment, Programming, etc.	Estimated Costs

GRANTS OFFICE INVENTORY—THE ROLE OF THE GRANTS OFFICE IN THE ADMINISTRATION OF FEDERAL FUNDS

EXHIBIT 12.3

For Each Activity/Item listed, Check Status

Activity/Item	Reviewed, Appropriate Part of Grants Office	Reviewed, Appropriate Part of Other Office (List)	Reviewed, Not Applicable	Reviewed, Inappropriate Needs Action	Non-existent, Needs Action
2. Cash requests • designation of person or office to handle all cash requests • existence of financial management system that meets or exceeds the accountability standards outlined in the appropriate OMB circulars					

Complete this Section for Each Activity/Item Needing Action

What Needs to be Accomplished?	By Whom? (Office/Person)	By When? (Time Frame)	Resources Required—Personnel, Supplies, Equipment, Programming, etc.	Estimated Costs

GRANTS OFFICE INVENTORY—THE ROLE OF THE GRANTS OFFICE IN THE ADMINISTRATION OF FEDERAL FUNDS

EXHIBIT 12.3 (*continued*)

For Each Activity/Item listed, Check Status

Activity/Item	Reviewed, Appropriate Part of Grants Office	Reviewed, Appropriate Part of Other Office (List)	Reviewed, Not Applicable	Reviewed, Inappropriate Needs Action	Non-existent, Needs Action
• reviewing the appropriate OMB circulars 3. Availability of appropriate OMB circulars, Public Health Service Grants Policy Statements, and Federal Acquisition Regulations					

Complete this Section for Each Activity/Item Needing Action

What Needs to be Accomplished?	By Whom? (Office/ Person)	By When? (Time Frame)	Resources Required— Personnel, Supplies, Equipment, Programming, etc.	Estimated Costs

Grants Office Inventory—The Role of the Grants Office in the Administration of Federal Funds

EXHIBIT 12.3 (*continued*)

For Each Activity/Item listed, Check Status

Activity/Item	Reviewed, Appropriate Part of Grants Office	Reviewed, Appropriate Part of Other Office (List)	Reviewed, Not Applicable	Reviewed, Inappropriate Needs Action	Non-existent, Needs Action
4. Employment issues • designation of person or office to handle grant-related employees 5. Procurement and control • designated person or office to ensure that the basic requirements for procurement are followed					

Complete this Section for Each Activity/Item Needing Action

What Needs to be Accomplished?	By Whom? (Office/Person)	By When? (Time Frame)	Resources Required—Personnel, Supplies, Equipment, Programming, etc.	Estimated Costs

GRANTS OFFICE INVENTORY—THE ROLE OF THE GRANTS OFFICE IN THE ADMINISTRATION OF FEDERAL FUNDS

EXHIBIT 12.3 (*continued*)

CHAPTER 13

Indirect Cost Recovery and Disbursement

Costs involved in conducting sponsored projects are divided into two categories: direct costs and indirect costs. In some colleges and universities, the indirect-cost calculations and negotiations are the responsibility of the grants office, and in others they are done by the business office. Even if your office is not directly involved in the negotiation, your grants office staff must be familiar with the process for determining indirect costs and must understand its purpose. Grants administrators are often called upon to provide information on direct and indirect costs to faculty, other administrators, and representatives from the community who may have little understanding of the basic concepts that underlie indirect costs.

Direct costs are those that can be identified specifically with a particular project, and these are itemized in the proposal budget with a justification for each line item. Common direct costs include project salaries, student stipends, equipment, materials, supplies and service costs, postage or delivery costs, printing and publications, remodeling costs, subscriptions, long-distance toll charges, travel, off-campus custodial and laundry costs, data processing, payment to study subjects, subcontracts, and consortium agreements. To be charged to a federally sponsored project, direct costs must be

- allowable—as described by federal cost principles;
- reasonable—what a prudent person would spend;
- allocable—limited to that portion of expenses directly benefitting the project; and
- consistently treated as direct charges.

Indirect costs are defined as those that are incurred for common or joint objectives. Unlike direct costs, they cannot be specifically attributed to an individual project. Instead, they should be thought of as costs for services that create an environment in which individual projects can exist. Some of the resources considered as indirect costs by many colleges and universities include laboratory space, office space, utilities, insurance, research accounting, human resources, purchasing, legal counsel, security services, custodial services, building maintenance, office supplies, libraries, health and safety, animal and human subjects protection, departmental administrative assistants, telecommunications, infrastructure, college research offices, sponsored programs, deans, and department chairs. In some instances, costs ordinarily claimed as indirect may be considered direct due to the size, nature, and/or complexity of the sponsored project and/or the fact that they are being used in significantly greater proportions than a routine level of support would require. For example, envelopes, postage, and normal reproduction and printing would be covered under indirect costs, but printing and mailing 5,000 surveys that require an envelope to send and one postage-paid envelope to return would fall under the category of direct costs.

The federal government officially refers to indirect costs as Facilities and Administrative (F&A) costs and reimburses colleges and universities for these costs. In fact, nearly one-third of the federal support for academic research takes the form of indirect-cost recovery that goes to the institution and is disbursed in whatever way the institution feels appropriate. This reimbursement is in addition to the awarded amount unless it is stated by the funding source that the grant award cannot exceed a certain dollar limit and must include the indirect costs. The reimbursement is based on a negotiated rate that is an *average* of the costs of providing support to various projects. Hence, the rate is the same for all projects, even though some projects may use more resources than others. This is an important concept for the grants administrator to be able to explain to faculty and staff because some principal investigators and project directors mistakenly believe they are being taken advantage of. Some claim that their projects use more resources than others and therefore should recover a greater percentage of the indirect costs; others claim that their projects use less resources than others and because of this, are not receiving their fair share of the indirect costs recovered.

In order to receive indirect-cost reimbursement, an institution must have an approved permanent rate. Although indirect costs will be awarded by funding agencies to institutions with provisional or past permanent rates, the payment will be disallowed if the institution fails to establish an effective permanent rate.

Through the indirect-cost process colleges and universities can recover a portion of their actual costs associated with supporting externally funded projects. Unfortunately, some faculty operate under the misconception that the indirect-cost portion of their grant constitutes a profit to the institution. In truth, colleges and universities never recover all of the costs related to research. However, this is acceptable to them because most have a commitment to providing a scholarly environment that supports research.

Office of Management and Budget (OMB) Circular A-21 establishes accounting principles upon which an indirect-cost rate can be negotiated. (OMB Circular A-21 can be found on the Web at http://www.doleta.gov/regs/omb/index.htm or http://www.whitehouse.gov/OMB/circulars/index.html.) The indirect-cost calculation begins with the categorization of expenditures of indirect costs into eight general groups or homogeneous cost pools: departmental administration, operations and maintenance of plant, general and administrative expenses, building and equipment costs, sponsored projects administration, library, student administration and services, and interest on debt. OMB regulations require that a base is established for each of these cost pools. The base cost is then apportioned to reasonably represent its benefit to major institutional activities such as research and instruction. These costs are converted into a rate that is applied to each grant and contract awarded to the institution.

The final indirect-cost rate is negotiated between the Department of Health and Human Services (DHHS) or the Office of Naval Research (ONR) and the institution. Once the agreement is reached, the institution receives an indirect-cost rate agreement stating the negotiated indirect cost for its research and instruction. The indirect-cost reimbursement agreement is issued for a specified period of time. Rate agreements are usually for a period of one to five years and may contain different rates during that period.

The indirect-cost study must be submitted promptly to avoid penalties from funding agencies. If a funding agency declares that an institution is unreasonably delinquent in submitting its indirect-cost proposal for review, the agency may elect not to reimburse indirect costs during the period of delinquency.

Sometimes the physical and/or administrative environment in which certain activities are performed require the establishment of an off-campus rate for the institution. The on-campus rate applies to projects conducted entirely on campus; the off-campus rate applies to projects conducted entirely off campus. The off-campus rate can be established for a specific location or it can be one rate that applies to all off-campus sites. When an off-campus location is identified with a specific rate, the rate applies only to those activities conducted at that site. The indirect-cost rate agreement specifies the circumstances under which activities are eligible for an off-campus rate.

A project that takes place both off and on campus is usually designated as either an on-campus or off-campus project according to where the majority of the work will be done. The use of both on- and off-campus rates for a given project may be justified if both rates can be clearly identified with a significant portion of salaries and wages of the project.

The reimbursement of indirect costs on training grants is limited to 8 percent of the total direct cost unless the institution agrees to a lower rate. Training grants are any grants that provide support for educational services and training, such as summer institutes, the development and introduction of new courses, community workshops, and research training programs. The 8 percent training rate applies to any proposed training program that requests federal support.

The federal agency may refer to modified total direct costs. In this case, certain direct costs may be subtracted from the total, which would result in a modified total. For example, indirect costs generally are not reimbursed on awards for equipment, construction, and conferences. Fellowship or tuition awards to faculty or students are usually made for a fixed amount or to cover the actual cost and do not reimburse direct costs.

Funding agencies set an award amount for each project, including direct and indirect cost figures. This total dollar figure then constitutes the ceiling on the amount available for the project. The investigator and the institution may request increased funds, but the agency is not obligated to make supplemental awards. After an award is made, most agencies will adjust the indirect-cost allocation to an institution as soon as its indirect-cost rate is established. Adjustments are likely if the institution is in the process of negotiating its indirect-cost rate when the project proposal is submitted to the agency. Funds to cover indirect costs associated with an additional direct-cost award for expansion, extension, or other reasons may be given at the discretion of the agency.

Institutions may transfer funds meant for direct costs to indirect costs and vice versa without prior approval from a federal funding agency as long as the objectives of the project remain the same. If a principal investigator, project director, or the institution desires to change the objectives or scope of the project, approval is required. Agency approval is also required under other prior-approval requirements, such as the purchase of equipment costing more than $25,000.

If an institution has never established an indirect-cost rate, it must submit an indirect-cost proposal to the regional Division of Cost Allocation (DCA). The rate negotiator works with the institutional representative to negotiate a reimbursement rate. The proposal for an indirect-cost reimbursement rate should be submitted and approved prior to the submission of grant proposals to federal agencies. However, it is possible to submit the indirect-cost and grant proposals at the same time or even to submit the indirect proposal after the grant proposal. If an indirect-cost rate is not established prior to the grant award, a provisional award will be included for one-half the requested rate up to the maximum allowable percentage of direct salaries and wages supported by the agency. The funding agency reserves the balance of the requested indirect-cost rate. If a rate is established, the additional funds for the difference will be awarded based on the approval rate.

Faculty tend to have a negative attitude toward indirect-cost recovery. As previously mentioned, some think the indirect-cost portion of their grant constitutes a profit to the institution. Others feels they are not getting their fair share of the recovery. And still others believe that the indirect-cost rate interferes with their competitive position in seeking external funds. The truth of the matter is that, although federal agencies handle indirect-cost recovery in a variety of ways, all federal agencies are familiar with indirect-cost recovery requirements and thus faculty are not disadvantaged by the institution's indirect-cost rate. On the other hand, private funding sources and state agencies have different rules governing the payment of indirect costs. For example, some foundations refuse to fund any indirect costs, and some corporations refund 100 percent of the indirect costs related to projects funded by them. Therefore, the grants office must be familiar with each individual sponsor's guidelines on indirect costs.

One problem that continually surfaces from federal sponsors is why colleges and universities charge them indirect costs, while allowing corporations and foundations to avoid such costs even though they (the private sponsors) also take advantage of the institution's infrastructure to carry out their research. This issue and disclosures of misrepresenting costs will continue to affect your grants office.

It is crucial for grants administrators to understand the purpose of indirect-cost allocations and how they are used to support university research and academic projects. The National Association of College and University Business Officers (NACUBO) offers publications that explain the preparation of indirect-cost studies and rate proposals. NACUBO also hosts workshops on facilities and administrative (F&A) costs. A grants administrator, whether or not directly involved in the post-award administration and indirect-cost calculation, should attend one of these workshops every few years to remain knowledgeable about the guidelines for indirect costs. For more information on NACUBO's publications and seminars, visit them on the Web at http://www.nacubo.org.

Use the questions in exhibit 13.1 to survey your faculty on their knowledge of and beliefs about indirect-cost recovery. The feedback you gather will help you determine how to better educate your faculty and staff on indirect costs. Completing the inventory in exhibit 13.2 will help you identify the areas of indirect recovery that need attention at your institution.

---

1. How knowledgeable do you feel you are concerning indirect cost recovery?
   _____ no knowledge
   _____ little knowledge
   _____ somewhat knowledgeable
   _____ very knowledgeable

2. Do you understand the difference between indirect costs and direct costs?
   _____ Yes _____ No

3. Do you understand why indirect costs are charged to your projects?
   _____ Yes _____ No

4. Do you know how our institution's indirect cost rate is calculated?
   _____ Yes _____ No

5. Do you feel you are receiving your fair share of the indirect costs recovered by the institution?
   _____ Yes _____ No

6. Do you feel you need to know more about indirect cost recovery?
   _____ Yes _____ No

7. Has our institution's cost rate agreement ever been made available to you?
   _____ Yes _____ No

If yes,

a) who made it available to you? _____
b) have you read it? _____ Yes _____ No

SURVEY QUESTIONS—INDIRECT-COST RECOVERY AND DISBURSEMENT

EXHIBIT 13.1

For Each Activity/Item listed, Check Status

Activity/Item	Reviewed, Appropriate Part of Grants Office	Reviewed, Appropriate Part of Other Office (List)	Reviewed, Not Applicable	Reviewed, Inappropriate Needs Action	Non-existent, Needs Action
1. Institution has approved indirect cost rate. 2. Copy of the indirect-cost rate agreement is made available to principal investigators, project directors, research administrators, grant writers, etc.					

Complete this Section for Each Activity/Item Needing Action

What Needs to be Accomplished?	By Whom? (Office/ Person)	By When? (Time Frame)	Resources Required— Personnel, Supplies, Equipment, Programming, etc.	Estimated Costs

GRANTS OFFICE INVENTORY—INDIRECT-COST RECOVERY AND DISBURSEMENT

EXHIBIT 13.2

For Each Activity/Item listed, Check Status

Activity/Item	Reviewed, Appropriate Part of Grants Office	Reviewed, Appropriate Part of Other Office (List)	Reviewed, Not Applicable	Reviewed, Inappropriate Needs Action	Non-existent, Needs Action
3. Designated person or office to ensure that the indirect cost rate is utilized in all applicable proposals					
4. Designated person or office to negotiate the indirect cost rate					
5. Policy and procedures outlining who has a say					

Complete this Section for Each Activity/Item Needing Action

What Needs to be Accomplished?	By Whom? (Office/ Person)	By When? (Time Frame)	Resources Required— Personnel, Supplies, Equipment, Programming, etc.	Estimated Costs

GRANTS OFFICE INVENTORY—INDIRECT-COST RECOVERY AND DISBURSEMENT

EXHIBIT 13.2 (*continued*)

For Each Activity/Item listed, Check Status

Activity/Item	Reviewed, Appropriate Part of Grants Office	Reviewed, Appropriate Part of Other Office (List)	Reviewed, Not Applicable	Reviewed, Inappropriate Needs Action	Non-existent, Needs Action
in what is included in the institution's cost pools 6. Designated person or office to explain to faculty/staff about the purpose of indirect-cost reimbursement (provision of fact sheet, etc.)					

Complete this Section for Each Activity/Item Needing Action

What Needs to be Accomplished?	By Whom? (Office/Person)	By When? (Time Frame)	Resources Required—Personnel, Supplies, Equipment, Programming, etc.	Estimated Costs

GRANTS OFFICE INVENTORY—INDIRECT-COST RECOVERY AND DISBURSEMENT

EXHIBIT 13.2 (continued)

CHAPTER 14

The Role of the Grants Office in the Politics of the Funding Process

PUBLIC FUNDS—KEEPING THE DOOR OPEN—THE ROLE A RESPONSIBLE GRANTS ADMINISTRATOR PLAYS IN PROMOTING THE GRANTS MARKETPLACE

Many college and university grants offices perform valuable functions that center on protecting the funding opportunities currently available to their institution and promoting new opportunities. Higher education associations such as the American Council on Education, the American Association of State Colleges and Universities, and associations for private colleges and community colleges collectively seek to make legislators aware of the impact that grant funding plays in educational programming and research.

According to our legislative process, bills are introduced and voted upon, and some become law. There is no guarantee that a newly established law will be funded and, if funded, there is no guarantee that its appropriation for funding will continue. Legislation and pressure for funding and continued funding on the state and federal levels is introduced through state and federal elected officials, with additional pressure applied by concerned groups, associations, and lobbyists.

The groups that seek to influence legislation and appropriations through lobbying are required to register with the federal government and forfeit any advantageous tax status they may have. Therefore, it is important that your efforts as a college or university official are intended only to educate and provide accurate information to elected representatives on which to base their actions.

To have an impact on the system, you must educate the key individuals who influence the legislation. Most colleges and universities rely extensively on associations or membership groups to provide this legislative function. However, problems can occur if the legislative staff person for the association is not a grants person. The process of appropriation of funds and the rules that govern who are eligible recipients of the funds may be altered in such a way that your college or university may not be allowed to compete.

After laws are passed, the state or federal bill must go through a committee process that designates which program will be appropriated funds and under which agency's budget. Tracking the progress of your program through this process is complex and tedious. Many reports, hearings, and compromises occur along the way.

What might seem a trivial change may result in disastrous effects on your favorite grant program. Consider what happened recently in a program for colleges and universities. Through this program, millions of dollars were appropriated annually to fund both two-year and four-year institutions. Originally, two-year colleges were designated to receive a percentage of the funds so that the larger four-year institutions did not take it all. However, a small change was made that no one noticed—a dollar figure was substituted for the percentage. At first glance the dollar figure looked commensurate with the past years' percentages. But the appropriation to the program ended up being significantly less than it had been in previous years. Because the dollar figure, and not the percentage, for two-year colleges was in the bill, two-year colleges received the dollar amount, which left the four-year colleges with almost nothing.

Understanding the system, and how bills and appropriations result in grants that your institution depends upon, is critically important to the "health" of your grants system.

SUBVERSION OF THE GRANTS SYSTEM

Unfortunately, it has become increasingly common to subvert the grants system through the political process. While publicity concerning this subversion occasionally receives attention, this abuse has been around for a long time. At the risk of further publicizing the abuse and hence increasing it, I have chosen to include this section with the hope that the astute grants administrator will see that such abuse puts the entire grants system in jeopardy.

I first became aware of the subversion of the grants-award process in the early 1970s. One of my institution's proposals was rejected but placed as the highest priority for the next competition. The president of the institution instructed me to pursue funding. The federal agency told me to apply again next year and that they would actually hold my rejected proposal for another year. Then I read that the same federal agency had just awarded another institution a grant for $1 million! I flew to Washington, D.C., went directly to the agency director, and was told that the funded institution had not been on the list of prospective grantees and had not even undergone peer review. What the institution did was convince its congressperson and senators to add a provision or rider to a popular bill that earmarked, or designated, $1 million to be awarded to the institution to fund their project. This process of legislating grant awards not only sidesteps the peer review process but also has the potential of dismantling the entire grant award system.

While the entrepreneurial grant seeker who espouses survival of the fittest may say that all is fair in developing resources for his or her program and college or university, the practice of adding grants to every congressperson's and senator's bills causes chaos. Fortunately, many college and university presidents have refused to accept grants acquired through a noncompetitive system that subverts peer review.

Will the process of earmarking state and federal bills continue to cloud the competitive grants scene? Yes! Should grants professionals support it? No! Should grants professionals speak out against it? Yes!

I encourage you, the director of the grants effort, to take steps to identify the grant funds for the programs and research that are critical to your institution and develop a plan and educational materials, which you can then provide to the responsible official. A knowledge of the federal funding mechanism will assist you in the task of promoting an educated decision.

GRANT-RELATED RULES

The Federal Register and various agency bulletins print announcements publicizing opportunities to comment on the rules that govern what types of organizations are eligible to apply for and receive federal funds, the review system, priorities, and so on. Newly created funding programs must by law offer opportunities to participate in the development of the rules governing the program. Older, existing programs must announce opportunities to comment on last year's rules, rule changes, and the issuing of final rules.

Action: Alert appropriate administrators, associations, and agencies of the necessity to submit favorable and unfavorable comments on the rules. Because few people actively track the grants system at this level, federal officials receive very few comments. When they receive a few, they assume that there are many more individuals who feel the same but did not respond. Remember, rules that affect you dramatically may be changed based on the comments of a few.

FEDERAL REVENUE SHARING AND FORMULA GRANTS DESIGNED TO DISTRIBUTE FUNDS TO INDIVIDUAL STATES

States are required to sponsor hearings on the expenditure of federal funds that pass through the state to nonprofit organizations and colleges and universities.

Action: Review your institution's current grants to determine what monies are now derived under this federal revenue sharing through the state's funding mechanism and designate an individual to track the rules process and testify at the appropriate hearings.

PUBLIC HEARINGS (STATE AND FEDERAL)

The Federal Register announces public hearings on federal funding programs. Testifying at and/or attending these hearings may result in several advantages for your institution, including more appropriations. Many state priorities are developed from testimony and comments made at state hearings.

Action: The grants office could schedule a trip to your state capitol or to Washington, D.C. Alert the appropriate staff to the hearing dates, and ask them to attend and to testify on the importance and affect of past funding.

CONTACTING ELECTED OFFICIALS

It is a wise idea to designate one office at your college or university to track all contact with federal officials to avoid confusion. The grants office provides a unique clearinghouse that monitors all contact with funding sources to exert influence and increase elected officials' knowledge of

- the institution's "official" position on a particular area, and
- the need for more funding (letters from administrators, advisory committee members, etc.).

Action: This may entail more than monitoring contact. The grants administrator may track legislation and appropriations and *initiate* the appropriate response. This may include drafting letters from your institution's administrators to sending telegrams and even visiting federal and state officials.

This contact with elected officials and suggested action should always be predicated on providing information on the need to fund the area in question. You are not suggesting the earmarking of federal funds or any illegal action. Several federal officials have gone to jail over their approval of grants before the applicant wrote the proposal.

WEBBING AND LINKAGES TO ELECTED OFFICIALS

The advantage of a system of developing and recording linkages to funding sources has been discussed in chapter 7. Expansion of that system to include state and federal elected officials provides a unique resource when there is an attempt to introduce grant-related legislation favorable to your institution.

It is recommended that your linkages system with elected officials be carried out separately from your linkages system with grant officials.

Review with your staff, faculty members, advisory committees, and volunteers the importance of discussing with elected officials the concerns and needs of your institution. After review of the purpose of the activity and reassurance that *you will not contact any of their linkages* without their permission, you are ready to distribute the Elected Officials Worksheet in exhibit 14.1.

You may decide to leave the elected officials section of the worksheet blank for the respondent to complete, or you may list the names of those officials in which you are particularly interested.

Record the information collected from the worksheets in a special data-retrieval system that can be secured to restrict access of usage. When the occasion to act on a legislative issue arises, the information contained in your system will help you design your political strategy quickly. Whom do you know who can reach the official? Linkages, including names, addresses, phone numbers, fax numbers, and e-mails should be easily retrievable for your action plans.

Remember, you are not lobbying for your institution. The purpose of this system is to provide information that will educate the elected officials so they may act wisely in their decisions related to programs affecting higher education.

Your Name _____   **STATE LEGISLATORS**
Your Address _____
Your Phone Number _____   _____
Your Fax Number _____   _____
Your E-Mail _____   _____
                                                    _____

1. To what political party do you belong?   **FEDERAL**
    _____   **CONGRESSPERSONS**

2. Have you worked on an elected official's
    campaign? _____ Yes _____ No   _____
    If yes, whose? _____   _____

3. Did you make campaign contributions   **SENATORS**
    to any of the candidates currently in office?   _____
    _____Yes _____No   _____

    If yes, please put "$" next to name(s) on list

4. Do you know any of the current office   **STAFF (ADMIN. ASSTS.)**
    holders? _____ Yes _____ No   _____
                                                    _____
                                                    _____
    If yes, put an * next to name(s) on list   _____

5. Do you know anyone who knows any of the   **COUNTY OFFICIALS**
    current office holders? ___ Yes ___ No   _____
                                                    _____
    If yes, please list   _____
           Name   Official Known   _____

    _____   _____   _____

    _____   _____

    _____   _____

6. Please list any other information you may   **CITY OFFICIALS**
    know about an elected official(s), such as   _____
    educational background, military background,   _____
    service club/association memberships, etc.   _____

    _____   _____

ELECTED OFFICIALS LINKAGE WORKSHEET

EXHIBIT 14.1

POLITICS OF CORPORATIONS

In addition to setting up a webbing and linkage system with political officials and funding officials of foundations, corporations, and government programs, you must take into consideration local corporate politics. Your webbing system, discussed in chapter 7, will yield contact people to assist in approaching corporations, but it's also important to be aware of the politics of corporate commitment to your community and your institution.

You gain this knowledge by

- buying shares of corporate stock;
- tracking corporate officials;
- logging financial reports, Dunn and Bradstreet reports, etc.;
- cataloging annual reports; and
- contracting with a clipping service to collect news articles on the corporation.

In some cases, the development office may record this information. However, in most colleges and universities the information is scattered throughout the institution in a variety of offices. It is useful for the grants office to know

- what banks handle your institution's checking and savings accounts;
- what companies handle your endowments/investments; and
- who your institution's major suppliers are for materials, equipment, etc.

Remember that your business office and purchasing departments are probably asking your major suppliers for their best price, thereby lowering their profits. Therefore, you must show a little discretion when requesting contributions from them. After all, they always have the option of declining your request.

Use the questions in exhibit 14.2 to gather feedback on the politics of the funding process from your faculty and staff. Complete exhibit 14.3 to help you develop a plan of action for this area.

---

1. Are you aware of the grants office's activities to educate elected officials about the importance of funding in your field of interest?
   _____Yes   _____ No

2. Have you ever notified the grants office of your concerns related to the public funding of your field of interest? _____Yes _____No

   a. If yes, please rate the action(s) that your grants office took to impact funding?

   _____nonexistent
   _____inadequate
   _____adequate
   _____more than adequate
   _____don't know

SURVEY QUESTIONS—THE ROLE OF THE GRANTS OFFICE IN THE POLITICS OF THE FUNDING PROCESS

EXHIBIT 14.2

For Each Activity/Item listed, Check Status

Activity/Item	Reviewed, Appropriate Part of Grants Office	Reviewed, Appropriate Part of Other Office (List)	Reviewed, Not Applicable	Reviewed, Inappropriate Needs Action	Non-existent, Needs Action
1. Availability of written materials explaining how bills and appropriations result in grants for which your institution is eligible to apply for 2. Designation of individual or office to:					

Complete this Section for Each Activity/Item Needing Action

What Needs to be Accomplished?	By Whom? (Office/ Person)	By When? (Time Frame)	Resources Required— Personnel, Supplies, Equipment, Programming, etc.	Estimated Costs

GRANTS OFFICE INVENTORY—THE ROLE OF THE GRANTS OFFICE IN THE POLITICS OF THE FUNDING PROCESS

EXHIBIT 14.3

For Each Activity/Item listed, Check Status

Activity/Item	Reviewed, Appropriate Part of Grants Office	Reviewed, Appropriate Part of Other Office (List)	Reviewed, Not Applicable	Reviewed, Inappropriate Needs Action	Non-existent, Needs Action
• track legislation • facilitate the appropriation of grant funds • monitor possible attempts to subvert the grants system through the political process • monitor announcements concerning					

Complete this Section for Each Activity/Item Needing Action

What Needs to be Accomplished?	By Whom? (Office/Person)	By When? (Time Frame)	Resources Required—Personnel, Supplies, Equipment, Programming, etc.	Estimated Costs	

EXHIBIT 14.3 (*continued*)

For Each Activity/Item listed, Check Status

Activity/Item	Reviewed, Appropriate Part of Grants Office	Reviewed, Appropriate Part of Other Office (List)	Reviewed, Not Applicable	Reviewed, Inappropriate Needs Action	Non-existent, Needs Action
opportunities to comment on grant-related rules • alert appropriate individuals, group, etc. of the necessity to submit comments on grant-related rules • attend and testify at hearings on federal					

Complete this Section for Each Activity/Item Needing Action

What Needs to be Accomplished?	By Whom? (Office/Person)	By When? (Time Frame)	Resources Required—Personnel, Supplies, Equipment, Programming, etc.	Estimated Costs

GRANTS OFFICE INVENTORY—THE ROLE OF THE GRANTS OFFICE IN THE POLITICS OF THE FUNDING PROCESS

EXHIBIT 14.3 (continued)

For Each Activity/Item listed, Check Status

Activity/Item	Reviewed, Appropriate Part of Grants Office	Reviewed, Appropriate Part of Other Office (List)	Reviewed, Not Applicable	Reviewed, Inappropriate Needs Action	Non-existent, Needs Action
funding programs • monitor all contact with elected officials 3. System to record and monitor linkages to state and federal elected officials • availability of data retrieval system that restricts access of usage					

Complete this Section for Each Activity/Item Needing Action

What Needs to be Accomplished?	By Whom? (Office/Person)	By When? (Time Frame)	Resources Required—Personnel, Supplies, Equipment, Programming, etc.	Estimated Costs

GRANTS OFFICE INVENTORY—THE ROLE OF THE GRANTS OFFICE IN THE POLITICS OF THE FUNDING PROCESS

EXHIBIT 14.3 (*continued*)

For Each Activity/Item listed, Check Status

Activity/Item	Reviewed, Appropriate Part of Grants Office	Reviewed, Appropriate Part of Other Office (List)	Reviewed, Not Applicable	Reviewed, Inappropriate Needs Action	Non-existent, Needs Action
4. Designated individual or office to coordinate, record, and monitor corporate research					

Complete this Section for Each Activity/Item Needing Action

What Needs to be Accomplished?	By Whom? (Office/Person)	By When? (Time Frame)	Resources Required— Personnel, Supplies, Equipment, Programming, etc.	Estimated Costs

GRANTS OFFICE INVENTORY—THE ROLE OF THE GRANTS OFFICE IN THE POLITICS OF THE FUNDING PROCESS

EXHIBIT 14.3 (continued)

CHAPTER 15

Developing and Evaluating Your Grants Office Web Site

In the rush to legitimize grants efforts and to demonstrate that the grants area of higher education is keeping pace with technology, most colleges and universities have created a grants office Web site. In creating this book, I visited many sites to observe how they dealt with issues related to the grants office functions, services, etc. However, it was difficult for me to evaluate the Web sites I visited because I did not know the purposes for the construction of the sites, or who their target populations were. While it was very clear that some sites appeared to be better organized, easier to use, and more informational than others, it was also clear that most of the sites were not designed with the thirty-year grants veteran in mind.

Whether you want to evaluate an existing Web site, or develop a new one, ask yourself and your staff what the purposes of the site are or should be. What is it supposed to accomplish? Possibilities include, but are not limited to

- increasing motivation to get involved in grant seeking;
- improving knowledge of grant-seeking techniques;
- expanding access to information on sources of grants and new grantors (searching systems, links to grantor databases, etc.);
- encouraging grant seekers to take responsibility for initiating and implementing the steps necessary in the grants process;
- increasing access to other researchers in the same fields and promoting consortia;
- assisting successful grant seekers with the administration and expenditure of their grant funds;
- encouraging feedback on the functions and services of the grants office;
- providing immediate e-mail assistance in the form of links, phone numbers, etc. to principal investigators (PIs) and project directors (PDs) who are unable to obtain

the grant-related services and/or information they need by going through the regular channels; and

- fostering the understanding of the grants system/process at your institution and the grants office staff's responsibilities.

Also ask whom the Web site is or should be aimed at. In other words, who are the target populations? Target populations could include

- new and beginning grant seekers who have never received funding,
- grant seekers who have been funded in the past but are not currently funded, and
- currently funded grant seekers.

One of the problems in developing a Web site is that you and your staff may not be the correct people to design the site. Why? Because you know too much! You may not be able to rid yourself of your experience and knowledge and look at the site from the perspective of faculty and staff who are new to grants and contracts. The development and implementation of a user committee might help ensure that your Web site covers the concerns of the populations at which it is aimed.

How well does your Web site meet your intended purposes? By rating or scoring your site by how well it provides the functions it was designed to provide, you will be able to evaluate its effectiveness and determine ways to improve it. Grants offices with effective Web sites test them periodically to determine if they meet the needs of the target groups and support their (the office's) defined purposes.

Few of the institutions I have met with have gone through this process. Many have visited Web sites of other institutions they felt were similar to theirs and copied what they have done. But even when evaluating other Web sites, you must take into consideration your own specific target populations and purposes. Visit some of your colleagues' Web sites, but be sure to view them from the target population groups you are seeking to serve. (You can start your search of Web sites by visiting the National Council of University Research Administrator's (NCURA's) list of institutional sponsored research offices at http://www.ncura.edu/resources/sponsored.htm.) Are the sites user-friendly? Do they require advanced knowledge to utilize? What level of computer vocabulary or jargon is used?

When reviewing the results of your site evaluations, be careful about drawing conclusions from the data. For example, when discovering that a significant portion of their *veteran* faculty had visited their Web site but had not placed their keywords and interest profiles in the search database, the grants office I was working with assumed that the problem was due in some way to the difficulty level of adding this information to the database. So, I asked several *new* faculty whom I introduced to the database to help me pinpoint the difficulties by placing their keywords and interest profiles on line. They had no problem at all! It seemed that the problem lay with the motivation to initiate the grant searching activity, and not the user-friendliness of the site. To make sure this doesn't develop into a continuing problem, the grants office diagramed the forces acting on the new faculty members to find the appropriate point in their orientation that the building of a search profile and placing it on the institution's Web site would be most effective. In addition, the office is currently working on ways to get the veteran faculty to motivate themselves to place their keywords and interest profiles in the system.

Exhibit 15.1 provides questions you can use to initiate feedback from your faculty and staff that may help you improve your existing Web site or develop a new one. By completing the inventory in exhibit 15.2 you can ensure that this valuable aspect of your grants office will not be overlooked.

1. Are you aware of the grants office's Web page? _____Yes _____No

    a. If you are aware of it, have you used it in the past year?
       _____Yes _____No

    If you have used it in the past year, please answer the following:

	Yes	No
b. Did it provide the information you were seeking?	_____	_____
c. Could you easily find the information you needed?	_____	_____
d. Did it contain the information you expected?	_____	_____
e. Did it add to your motivation to become more involved in grant seeking?	_____	_____
f. What additional information should be included?		

    SURVEY QUESTIONS—DEVELOPING AND EVALUATING YOUR GRANTS OFFICE WEB SITE

    EXHIBIT 15.1

For Each Activity/Item listed, Check Status

Activity/Item	Reviewed, Appropriate Part of Grants Office	Reviewed, Appropriate Part of Other Office (List)	Reviewed, Not Applicable	Reviewed, Inappropriate Needs Action	Non-existent, Needs Action
1. Identify purpose(s) of Web site 2. Identify target population(s) 3. Setup user committee 4. Develop & implement test to determine if needs of target population & purposes are adequately addressed					

Complete this Section for Each Activity/Item Needing Action

What Needs to be Accomplished?	By Whom? (Office/ Person)	By When? (Time Frame)	Resources Required—Personnel, Supplies, Equipment, Programming, etc.	Estimated Costs

CHAPTER 16

The Grants Office Personnel—Past, Present, and Future

After performing audits of grants offices and conducting seminars with hundreds of participants who administer grants programs in higher education, I have found that there are no two grants administrator jobs or job descriptions that are exactly alike. From community college grants offices to the largest Carnegie 1 research institutions and the 3,000 colleges and universities in between, how grant seeking evolved, the name of the grants office, the reporting structure, the staffing, and the budget are all unique to the institution and dependent on the duties that the office carries out. The preceding chapters are designed to provide you with a review of the functions found in many grants offices. The book's worksheets, survey questions, and inventories provide a vehicle to compare your existing goals, objectives and services (what is) with the role your office could play (what could be).

By providing your supervisor(s) with challenging and changing views of what your office could become, you will shape your job, your staff's expectations, and your institution. Unfortunately, this book is only written and based upon what the author and the book's contributors have experienced. The future will create many more challenges, opportunities, and problems for those in the grants field. While this chapter provides sample job descriptions for grants office personnel, you must strive to be sensitive to the subtleties and pressures of the changing marketplace when creating your own tailored job descriptions.

A. TRENDS IN THE GRANTS ADMINISTRATION MARKETPLACE

1. *Decentralization*—After the centralization theme of the 1970s and 1980s, the 1990s witnessed an increased attention and expansion of the concept of the decentralized grants office. The movement usually occurred at the preproposal stages of grant seeking, and was

the result of initiatives aimed at getting the principal investigator/project director involved with the grants office early in the grants process.

Pre-Award—Some institutions sought to develop a relationship between their grants office staff and their faculty by assigning grants office staff to specific colleges, schools, institutes, and centers. Even though there were technology advances that could link the grants staff to the grant seeker (e.g., e-mail, etc.), several institutions chose to physically move the grants staff person out of the central office and relocated to the areas for which they were responsible. In today's decentralized system, the grants staff person is physically located in the area assigned to him or her to assist in idea generation and the development of keywords and interest profiles, and to attend department and dean's meetings to increase the faculty and staff's awareness of the role grant seeking plays and the availability of services to increase grant opportunities to meet their institution's mission. They only return to the central grants office for meetings and assistance with their constituents' grants needs.

This movement is designed to increase the accountability of the grants staff to the institution and improve the performance of the grants system. The performance indicators and the evaluation of the grants staff are dramatically altered under this system. Instead of the grant seeker coming to the grants staffer, the grants staffer is now responsible for taking a proactive role that is based on encouraging and serving the grant seeker. This is much different from the traditional, more reactive role of providing services from a central office to only those grant seekers who take the initiative to seek assistance.

One challenge of the decentralized system is to adequately adjust the grant staffer's job description and performance standards to fairly reflect his or her new role and the changed expectations of the grants effort. For example, the measurement indicators for job performance should now include the number of new proposal ideas that get generated or assisted by the grants staff person. Incorporation of a system that records the ideas generated, the searches carried out, and the work of brainstorming and redefining proposal concepts also need to be measured. This new grants person must be detail-oriented and be able to conduct follow-up in the same manner as a centralized grants person, but must be more of an initiator. The necessary changes in the job description are centered around the need for different or more intensive skills and perhaps even different personality types. Review the survey questions at the end of each chapter and the services you have selected to offer your clients to help you develop an appropriate job description and measurement indicators. Exhibit 16.1 provides a sample job description for the grants office staff person entitled Research and Program Officer. It includes suggested performance measurements that could be used in the decentralized system. These performance measurements can be further defined once the baseline of current activity is known (i.e., number of grant ideas, number of faculty with profiles in the grants database, number of submissions, number of awarded projects, etc.).

Post-Award—When you consider that getting more funded proposals for your institution is directly related to the post-award experiences of your successful grant seekers, it makes sense to extend the decentralization process one step further to include post-award functions. If you have carried out a survey of your institution's post-award process, you probably already have the data that reinforces the need to place the accountability for the post-award services closer to where the problems start. If you have not administered a post-award feedback survey, it is still reasonable to assume that if you did, your results would substanti-

POSITION PURPOSE:

To advise and assist faculty and staff in obtaining external funding for research and sponsored projects and to formulate and monitor research policies and procedures.

NATURE AND SCOPE:

Location:

The incumbent reports to the Associate to the Vice President for Research, as do one (1) Project Specialist; one (1) Senior Research and Program Officer; one (1) other Research and Program Officer; one (1) Executive Secretary II; one (1) Executive Secretary I; one (1) Secretary I; and four (4) student employees. The Associate to the Vice President for Research, in turn, reports to the Vice President for Research. This position does not supervise.

Environment:

The Office of the Vice President for Research is responsible for the development and articulation of the University's research mission and provides energetic leadership in conveying the research vision to internal and external constituencies. Its administrative units, Research and Sponsored Programs, and Grants and Contracts, monitor research-related state and federal policies and public and private funding opportunities and support externally funded activities in the University. This office establishes and administers policies which foster research and creative activities among faculty and ensure compliance with state and federal regulations governing research, as well as contract specifications for each project, in order to safeguard the integrity of the research enterprise. A number of programs administered in this Office (e.g., Centers for Excellence, University Research Fellows, New Faculty Research Support Program, Research Equipment) are supported by institutional funds, and are used to encourage and support applications for externally funded projects and to increase the number and variety of these activities. Other programs administered in this office are themselves centers of interdisciplinary research (e.g., Institute for Water Sciences, Service Quality Institute). The University's liaison functions for federally mandated regulatory boards is also housed in the Office of the Vice President for Research. Additional responsibilities of this office include patent proposals, publications, including a regular newsletter describing available funding and new grant awards, and training appropriate to University-wide audiences.

Research and Sponsored Programs provides assistance with the preparation and submission of proposals for external funding; the identification of funding sources; the development of budgets; and the review and duplication of proposals. The department reviews copyright for University faculty and staff and administers a number of University-funded programs designed to provide financial support to faculty in their research and creative activities, such as the Faculty Research and Creative Activities Support Fund and the Faculty Research Travel Fund.

The Office of Grants and Contracts provides assistance to project directors and the institution in following the requirements of sponsoring agencies. Safeguarding the

JOB DESCRIPTION: RESEARCH AND PROGRAM OFFICER

EXHIBIT 16.1

integrity of the research enterprise, Grants and Contracts support services for project directors and assist in the administration of various fiscal activities (e.g., assigning cost centers, setting up budgets, monitoring expenditures against the budget, requesting cash, and preparing and submitting interim and final financial reports). Staff are fiscally accountable for 300 to 400 separate grants and contracts representing $35,000,000 to $40,000,000 in cash accountability; half of these funds are contracts. Staff administer sponsor dollars according to the award document, protect the University against liability, and facilitate cooperation between project directors and their agencies.

Deadlines are established by external funding agencies. Energetic leadership and articulate representation of the University, its research mission, and resources are essential to advocating for the institution and the research enterprise to internal and external constituencies.

Functions:

This position is responsible for encouraging project development and overseeing proposal preparation. The position works with associate deans for research and chairs on developing long-term research and sponsored project efforts and assists faculty researchers in identifying potential funding and developing, preparing, and submitting proposals for external support of research and/or service activities. This is accomplished through informal contacts or formal contacts such as meetings, letters, telephone calls, information dissemination, grant writing workshops, and actual proposal preparation, including assisting in developing research designs and budgets.

The incumbent serves as a resource person for members of the University community, identifying external sponsors and advising them about grant seeking. The incumbent reads, synthesizes, and disseminates information concerned with funding patterns, agency priorities, federal and state regulations, and research policies. The incumbent develops, prepares, and submits applications to external support of research and/or other projects by discussing the project concept with faculty; identifying potential sponsors; providing technical assistance with the writing of the proposal, cost estimates, and technical preparation of the proposal or related forms; submitting the proposal in a timely manner to the potential sponsor; and following up as necessary. The incumbent provides advice and assistance as necessary for proposal preparation, negotiation, revision, and conflict resolution within the University and with sponsoring agencies.

The incumbent ensures that the preparation and submission of grant and/or contract proposals is in accordance with University policies and procedures and sponsor requirements for support of research and program development projects. The position also ensures that all University commitments are approved and appropriate signatures secured prior to proposal submission. Further, the position ensures that all necessary assurance forms are prepared and sent to sponsors.

The incumbent maintains contact with sponsors and funding agencies to monitor the status of submitted proposals, to promote the University's research expertise, and to obtain information on any changes in policies, protocols, or the agencies' research interests. This position hosts visits by sponsors to the University campus. The incumbent also prepares subcontracts as required and conducts the negotiation of

JOB DESCRIPTION: RESEARCH AND PROGRAM OFFICER

EXHIBIT 16.1 (*continued*)

terms and conditions of project awards and contracts (e.g., budget, contract review and revision). The incumbent monitors post-award activities to ensure that appropriate technical reports are submitted and that researchers are informed of changes in protocols or University research policies. In collaboration with principal investigators and associate deans for research, the incumbent monitors the progress of research activities to ensure their compliance with protocols specified in the award document.

This position is responsible for expanding externally funded activities within assigned areas of the University in cooperation with the Vice President for Research, deans, associate deans, and chairs; the incumbent develops an annual action plan of support for college and unit research and sponsored projects goals and activities. The incumbent identifies research expertise in assigned colleges and informs those faculty members of available funds, encouraging them to prepare and submit proposals. In collaboration with the vice president, the incumbent develops competitive bidding proposals for contract research.

The incumbent serves as a facilitator in workshops and seminars, instructing faculty in procedures to be used in preparing and submitting research proposals. The incumbent is expected to conduct and/or coordinate one or two workshops for constituent areas each fiscal year. The incumbent may also conduct grantsmanship workshops for external organizations.

This position participates in the development and evaluation of research policies. The incumbent reviews changes in state or federal regulations governing research activities, and changes in sponsors' policies, and informs the Vice President of these changes and their impact on University research policies and procedures. The incumbent may draft policy statements for review and/or signature by the Vice President for Research and represent the Vice President to policy groups, within and outside of the University, and research constituencies as necessary.

This position fulfills all duties associated with membership on and/or representation at meetings of University regulatory bodies (i.e., Human Subjects Institutional Review Board, Institutional Animal Care and Use Committee, and Institutional Biosafety Committee). The incumbent ensures compliance with regulations and protocols governing research activities by assisting in the development and evaluation of institutional research policies. The incumbent also represents the University's research interests and expertise in various professional forums (e.g., SRA and NCURA) regionally and nationally.

The position provides assistance to other research officers during peak periods and in their absence. The incumbent may also assist in the coordination of the Faculty Research and Creative Activities Support Fund (FRCASF) or other internal programs and may assist faculty and staff in matters related to requirements for copyright. S/he also performs tasks outside the constituent areas as tasks assigned by the Vice President for Research or his/her designee.

Subordinate Organization:

This position does not supervise.

JOB DESCRIPTION: RESEARCH AND PROGRAM OFFICER

EXHIBIT 16.1 (continued)

Major Challenge:

The incumbent finds the major challenge of this position as initiating activities that take advantage of funding opportunities and obtaining as many funded projects and/or awards as possible. Related challenges include effectively identifying research expertise within the institution and developing funding sources for that research; developing supportive working relationships with faculty researchers; motivating faculty and staff to seek external funds and to submit high-quality proposals pertinent to the sponsors' funding priorities; keeping abreast of changing funding opportunities and faculty research interests and communicating this successfully to the researcher; and working on several complex tasks simultaneously, attending to the details of each under the pressure of externally imposed deadlines.

Latitude:

The incumbent works in collaboration with associate deans for research and other administrators in the preparation of annual action plans. This position works without direct supervision in developing and implementing plans to expand sponsored funding in assigned areas. The incumbent works directly with faculty, initiating contacts, developing proposals, and resolving problems in the application process. The incumbent works independently with faculty, department staff, and sponsors to address questions and resolve problems. This position complies with policies, protocols, and deadlines established by prospective funding agencies. The incumbent participates in developing and evaluating departmental and institutional policies and procedures. Issues relating to implementation of an award according to sponsor guidelines are referred to the appropriate University area. Issues which must be referred to the supervisor include clarifying roles and/or relationships between this office and college research offices and those centering on fiscal policy as it relates to grant monies, general University policy, and personnel policies.

Performance Measurements:

The incumbent suggests that the following factors might be used as indicators of competence in carrying out this position's accountabilities:

1. Effective liaison with potential funding sources is maintained; funding information is disseminated to faculty and staff in a timely and effective manner.

2. Contacts are made with faculty and staff to determine areas of interest and expertise; a thorough and effective action plan is developed for encouraging proposal submission by assigned constituents.

3. High-quality proposals are developed and submitted in a timely manner to appropriate funding sources.

4. Post-award follow-up is provided to resolve fiscal and administrative questions associated with funded projects and to ensure the University's good standing with funding entities.

5. Effective membership and/or representation is provided at meetings of University regulatory bodies; all unit policies adhere to regulations and protocols governing research activities.

JOB DESCRIPTION: RESEARCH AND PROGRAM OFFICER

EXHIBIT 16.1 (*continued*)

6. Effective training activities regarding grantsmanship are developed and implemented.

7. Effective research policies and procedures are developed and implemented.

<u>Contacts:</u>

This position has extensive contact with faculty members in a wide variety of disciplines, to assist in identifying and obtaining external funding. The incumbent has frequent and extensive contact with associate deans for research to provide information on protocols and to assist in developing institutional policies. The incumbent also has frequent contact with deans, department chairs, and unit directors in matters related to approval of proposals or contract negotiation. The incumbent also has contact with human resources, Grants and Contracts, Vice Presidents, and the President in seeking advice and providing information in applying and conducting projects. The incumbent may serve on numerous institutional committees, either as a consultant, staff support, or a participant in the decision-making process. The incumbent has frequent contact with representatives of external public and private funding agencies including community businesses and municipal offices, to discuss funding opportunities, to advocate for proposals submitted by University researchers, and to obtain and provide information as needed.

<u>Knowledge and Skills:</u>

To be successful in this position, the incumbent must have a familiarity with academic disciplines in order to accommodate the needs of faculty constituents. Knowledge of funding sources and grant administration is necessary. Excellent research and analytical skills or background in research methods, including the ability to track, analyze, and synthesize a great deal of information, are required. Prior experience in project planning and budget development and an understanding of research budgeting principles and processes are required. An understanding of contract language and terminology is required, as is familiarity with research in higher education. A thorough understanding of research protocols, ethical and professional practice standards in the conduct of research, and legislation governing research and sponsored activities is necessary. Excellent human relations, oral communication, technical writing, and problem solving skills are necessary. The incumbent must be able to work independently; prioritize and meet sponsor deadlines; and follow complex sets of guidelines for federal, state, and other sponsors. Knowledge of word processing and spreadsheet applications is necessary. Advanced formal education in a field related to the administration of research in higher education or in a field requiring individual research experience, combined with progressively responsible experience in the development and administration of sponsored activities, or an equivalent combination of education and experience are necessary.

<u>PRINCIPAL ACCOUNTABILITIES:</u>

A partial list of accountabilities for this position might include:

Maintain and increase the acquisition of external monies for projects through proposal submission to ensure continued support for faculty research activities.

JOB DESCRIPTION: RESEARCH AND PROGRAM OFFICER

EXHIBIT 16.1 (*continued*)

Communicate with agencies, foundations, public offices, and other potential grant sources to gather information pertinent to campus research activities; encourage improved faculty/staff participation in research and sponsored program activity through information dissemination and liaison activities.

Identify faculty interests and expertise to develop sponsored research plan for assigned areas.

Coordinate proposal preparation to facilitate timely submission of quality proposals to appropriate funding sources.

Assist in the development and implementation of University research policies to facilitate research activities and protect the reputation of the University; advise faculty; chairs, and staff in order to ensure consistent administration of research activities; and carry out appropriate post-award activities.

Make presentations before campus and community groups regarding grantsmanship.

Coordinate and administer the operation of the University regulatory bodies to ensure compliance with regulations.

JOB DESCRIPTION: RESEARCH AND PROGRAM OFFICER

EXHIBIT 16.1 (*continued*)

ate the need to place the post-award grants administration functions at the unit level. By placing post-award grants administration functions at the unit level (college, department, etc.), your grants staff have the opportunity to

- help grant seekers create logical budgets;
- keep grant seekers happy when they become successful grantees;
- initiate all personnel requests;
- assist with the inputting of purchasing requisitions; and
- troubleshoot problems and interface in interactions between grantees and institutional compliances.

The accountability and sense of control that a decentralized pre- and post-award system provides for the grants office staff person are welcome additions in your quest to reduce bureaucracy and avoid problems with aloof or unconcerned personnel. I was involved in initiating a decentralized pre- and post-award system at the University of Alabama at Birmingham (UAB) School of Education. I was pleasantly surprised at how it almost instantly cleaned up disputes surrounding the payment of personnel and stipends that had been going back and forth between various university offices and project directors for over one year! Accountability was established, and as morale increased, so did the faculty and staff's willingness to become involved in grant seeking.

2. Resource Development—The future will bring even more changes than decentralization to the grants office. Many progressive college and university administrators have begun questioning the logic and effectiveness of the traditional separation between development (i.e., institutional development/fund raising) and grant seeking. This separation is now being evaluated and viewed by some as counterproductive to *everyone* being accountable for developing resources at the institution. The future will bring changes in the scope of the grants office and how the office fits into the *total picture of resource development.*

I began experimenting with this resource development concept in 1988 while at the University of Rochester, School of Medicine, Department of Pediatrics. Dr. Robert Hoekelman, a proficient grant seeker and fund raiser, brought me to the University as the Director of Extramural Funding and Grants Management. I was responsible for pre- and post-grants activity and providing leadership in fund raising (with a special emphasis on a capital campaign to build a Ronald McDonald House). In other words, I was involved in both the research grants side of resource development ($20 million in pediatric research and demonstration grants and the "other"/fund raising resources side at $2 million).

Before you react negatively to the concept of *total* resource development, consider the larger picture. It does not mean that the grants administrator *must* become a fund raiser. It may mean that in the future everyone who works to support scholarly activity and the fulfillment of their institution's mission will need to be flexible and open to the best possible administrative environment in which to fulfill their potential and the institution's mission. It is only a small step from considering the role that each grant seeker plays in projecting a coherent and positive impression with a potential grantor, to considering the professor in a classroom as one of your institution's alumni ambassadors.

Approximately ten years after my first encounter with the *resource development* concept, the dean at UAB's School of Education and I brokered an arrangement with the Vice President for development to create a position jointly funded by grants and development to focus on resource development in the school of education. The position was funded partially by the Vice President for development's budget and partially by the indirect costs recovered from the school's grant seeking. I now had two bosses. The genesis for this new reporting structure resulted from my having to get permission from the Development Office every time I wanted to approach a corporation or foundation. This new job description resulted in a much clearer vision of foundation and corporate grant seeking. Private grant seeking began to be viewed as a vehicle for *resource development* rather than the bastion of development. My job description included development and grants responsibilities, and eventually included my becoming the Director for the Center for Educational Accountability as well as the Alumni Director.

Please share your insights and experiences (both positive and negative) on *total resource development* with Bauer Associates, and we will incorporate them into our Web site so fellow learners can profit from them. Our address and phone number are located in the ordering information at the end of the book.

3. *Technology*—While this book has sought to explore the challenges electronic proposal development, submittal, and grants management will create for the grants administrator, the future holds undreamed-of potential for positive and also some negative pressures on the grants office. There will always be grant seekers who do not follow the rules, but now some technology-savvy grant seekers will use the new opportunities presented by technology to bypass the grants office altogether and the grants office will learn of their grants only after they have already been awarded! While you seek to build user-friendly systems that encourage grants and contracts submission and acceptance, you must remain vigilant regarding the submission of proposals that place your institution at risk.

Keep the focus on the positive. In other words, your focus of support should be on only those proposals that reflect positively on your institution and move it toward its mission. After all, they are the reasons your grants office exists. No matter what technological innovations are brought to the grants marketplace, one constant by which you can measure their ultimate good is to determine how they will impact your institution and the meeting of its mission.

B. SEEKING TO DEFINE THE CHANGING ROLES OF THE GRANTS ADMINISTRATOR AND THE GRANTS OFFICE STAFF

The grants administrator plays a different role in each organization. While there are many similarities, the differences and added functions are a result of the past and present administrations and how they perceive and have perceived the relative importance of the functions outlined in the preceding chapters. A new President, Vice President, provost, or director may call for a reordering of the functions of the grants office to fit his or her idea of what the office's priorities should be and what the grants administrator's job description should include.

The objective of this book is not to impart the idea that there is a perfect structure for your grants office. The structure of the grants office, and where and how it fits into your administrative system, is based upon the functions that those individuals responsible for the administration decide the office should have. The grants administrator or other responsible official may decide that the inventories suggested at the end of each chapter should be periodically reviewed to ensure the health of the grants effort in the same way an individual undergoes a yearly physical examination.

You will strengthen your grants system by performing the analysis suggested by each chapter's inventory and survey questions. Individuals outside of the grants office may be assigned tasks that are revealed through the analysis and require attention. The inventory sheets suggest the resources that need to be provided along with the responsibilities and tasks that should be included in the job descriptions of these outside people as well as the the grants office personnel.

The role of the grants administrator will be determined by reviewing the responses to the survey questions at the end of each chapter and by compiling the grants office inventories at the end of each chapter. Place each of the duties or tasks that are to be the responsibility of the grants administrator on a project planner (see chapter 8). The sample project planner provided in exhibit 16.2 was developed from the analysis of a grants position that did not require an emphasis on the accounting functions sometimes found in a grants office. The job, entitled research coordinator, was designed to promote and expand the number of proposals developed and the amount of funds granted (pre-award activities).

The project planner should include the resources necessary to accomplish each task listed on the bottom of each inventory sheet. A job description should then be composed from the list of identified tasks. Recruiting an individual who has both the educational background and personality characteristics necessary can be problematic. A grants administrator with an accounting background, knowledge of federal grant rules, experience in budget preparation, skills in motivational techniques, and appreciation for preproposal contact with funders may be difficult to find.

PROJECT PLANNER

EXHIBIT 16.2

Sheet ____ of ____

PROJECT TITLE: Job Description - Research Coordinator (Pre-Award)

Proposal Developed for _____

PROJECT DIRECTOR: _____

Proposal starting date _____

Proposal Year _____

A. List Project objectives or outcomes A, B. B. List Methods to accomplish each objective as A-1, A-2, A-3 .... B-1, B-2 ...	MONTH BEGIN / END (C/D)	TIME (E)	PROJECT PERSONNEL (F)	PERSONNEL COSTS — SALARIES & WAGES (G)	PERSONNEL COSTS — FRINGE BENEFITS (H)	PERSONNEL COSTS — TOTAL (I)	CONSULTANTS - CONTRACT SERVICES — TIME (J)	CONSULTANTS - CONTRACT SERVICES — COST/WEEK (K)	CONSULTANTS - CONTRACT SERVICES — TOTAL (L)	NON-PERSONNEL RESOURCES NEEDED SUPPLIES • EQUIPMENT • MATERIALS — ITEM (M)	COST/ITEM (N)	QUANTITY (O)	TOT COST (P)	SUB-TOTAL COST FOR ACTIVITY — TOTAL I, L, P	TOTAL (Q)	MILESTONES PROGRESS INDICATORS — ITEM (R)	DATE (S)
A. Developing Staff Interest in Grants																	
A-1 Assist staff in developing profiles of their grants interests for research, demonstration projects, etc.	1/3		Research Coord. and Project Sec.							Subscription to data base provider (i.e. SPIN, IRIS)							
a) Work with new faculty at orientation on profiles																	
b) Work with department chairs to present Web site and information on how to enter profiles for searches and e-mail searching																	
b-1 Evaluate and improve Web site							5/wk	5,000	3,500								
c) Work with individual faculty members who request assistance in developing profiles																	
d) Work with consortias, institutes and centers to produce area profiles																	
A-2 Produce a "Department Research Review" to be disseminated monthly at faculty/staff meetings and to be posted on the office's Web site	3/12		Research Coord. and Project Sec.							Printing / Reproduction Expense		1,000					
a) Gather data for grants newsletter (Department Research Review)																	
b) Objectives of newsletter																	
b-1 To promote an increased awareness of the role																	

TOTAL DIRECT COSTS OR COSTS REQUESTED FROM FUNDER ▶

MATCHING FUNDS, IN-KIND CONTRIBUTIONS, OR DONATED COSTS ▶

TOTAL COSTS ▶

▼ % OF TOTAL

100%

© David G. Bauer Associates, Inc.
(800) 836-0732

PROJECT PLANNER JOB DESCRIPTION: RESEARCH COORDINATOR

EXHIBIT 16.2

EXHIBIT 16.2 Continued

PROJECT PLANNER™

PROJECT TITLE: Job Description - Research Coordinator (Pre-Award)

Proposal Developed for _____

PROJECT DIRECTOR: _____

Sheet ___ of ___

Proposal Year _____

Proposed starting date _____

A. List Project objectives or outcomes A, B. B. List Methods to accomplish each objective as A-1, A-2, A-3 . . . B-1, B-2 . . .	MONTH		TIME	PROJECT PERSONNEL	PERSONNEL COSTS				CONSULTANTS · CONTRACT SERVICES				NON-PERSONNEL RESOURCES NEEDED SUPPLIES · EQUIPMENT · MATERIALS				SUB-TOTAL COST FOR ACTIVITY		MILESTONES PROGRESS INDICATORS	
	BEGIN	END			SALARIES & WAGES	FRINGE BENEFITS	TOTAL		TIME	COST/WEEK	TOTAL		ITEM	COST/ITEM	QUANTITY	TOT COST	TOTAL I, L, P	ITEM	DATE
	C/D		E	F	G	H	I		J	K	L		M	N	O	P	Q	R	S
that sponsored programs play in the department																			
b-2 To promote an increased appreciation for the grant seekers who produce proposals																			
A-3 Develop a pre-proposal review procedure with Research Committee and develop ongoing review system	1/12			Research Coord. and Staff Members (Research Comm.)															
a) Review procedures of existing Research Committee. Examine ways to assist and improve process.																			
A-4 Develop research goals with staff and Research Committee.	1/12			Research Coord. and Staff Members															
a) Review the goals of the department. List areas of interests and needs to set-up goals for the Grants office. Include success rate, number of proposals by area, time allocated by area, and budget allocated by area. (1-year, 2-year, 3-year)																			
b) Develop a long range research plan for the department.																			
B. Contacting Funding Sources								Travel to funding sources - D.C.											
B-1 Identify government sources and contact by telephone, e-mail, letter and personal visit (six 3-day trips per year)	1/12			Research Coord.								Airfare	500	6	3000				
												Hotel 3 nights/trip	400	6	2400				
												Per Diem-meals	300	6	1900				
												Taxi, subway, etc.	150	6	900				

TOTAL DIRECT COSTS ON COSTS REQUESTED FROM FUNDER ▲

MATCHING FUNDS IN-KIND CONTRIBUTIONS OR DONATED COSTS ▲

TOTAL DIRECT COSTS ▲

% OF TOTAL ▼

100%

© David G. Bauer Associates, Inc.
(800) 836-0732

PROJECT PLANNER JOB DESCRIPTION: RESEARCH COORDINATOR

EXHIBIT 16.2 (*continued*)

PROJECT PLANNER

EXHIBIT 16.2 Continued

PROJECT TITLE: Job Description – Research Coordinator (Pre-Award)

Proposal Developed for:

PROJECT DIRECTOR:

Sheet ____ of ____

Proposal Year ____

Proposal starting date ____

A. List Project objectives or outcomes A, B. B. List Methods to accomplish each objective as A-1, A-2, A-3 ... B-1, B-2 ...	MONTH BEGIN C/O	MONTH END	PROJECT PERSONNEL	PERSONNEL COSTS SALARIES & WAGES (G)	FRINGE BENEFITS (H)	TOTAL (I)	CONSULTANTS · CONTRACT SERVICES TIME (J)	COST/WEEK (K)	TOTAL (L)	NON-PERSONNEL RESOURCES NEEDED SUPPLIES · EQUIPMENT · MATERIALS ITEM (M)	COST/ITEM (N)	QUANTITY (O)	TOT COST (P)	SUB-TOTAL COST FOR ACTIVITY TOTAL I, L, P	MILESTONES PROGRESS INDICATORS ITEM	DATE
a) Start b-1, develop linkage system on existing funding sources, start developing webbing and linkages with new funding sources. After identifying prospects, store contact information. Identify state and federal sources for projects. Gather information on each funding source (mailing lists, newsletters, annual reports, etc.)																
B-a. Identify foundation and corporate sources and contact by telephone, e-mail, letter and personal visit (four one-day trips per year). Integrate with Development office.	4/12		Research Coord.							Travel to funding sources Airfare	500	4	2000			
										Hotel/night/trip	100	4	400			
										Per Diem-meals	100	4	400			
										Taxi, subway, etc.	50	4	200			
a) See "a" under b-1																
C. Proposal Preparation and Submission																
C-1 Assist in providing researchers with samples of funded proposals and the backgrounds of reviewers. Coordinate quality circles/mock reviews. Provide researches with future interests of funding sources. Assist in proposal development (site of budgets, negotiations as needed, etc.) Provide editorial assistance.	1/12		Research Coord.													
C-2 Integrate proposals with existing grants system	9/12		Research Coord.													

TOTAL DIRECT COSTS OR COSTS REQUESTED FROM FUNDER ▶
MATCHING FUNDS, IN-KIND CONTRIBUTIONS, OR DONATED COSTS ▶
TOTAL COSTS ▶

% OF TOTAL ▶

100%

©David G. Bauer Associates, Inc.
(800) 836-0732

PROJECT PLANNER JOB DESCRIPTION: RESEARCH COORDINATOR

EXHIBIT 16.2 (continued)

PROJECT PLANNER

EXHIBIT 16.2 Continued

PROJECT TITLE: Job Description - Research Coordinator (Pre-Award)

Proposal Developed for _____

PROJECT DIRECTOR: _____

Proposal starting date _____   Proposal Year _____

Sheet _____ of _____

A. List Project objectives or outcomes A, B.
B. List Methods to accomplish each objective as A-1, A-2, A-3 ... B-1, B-2 ...

PROJECT PERSONNEL	MONTH BEGIN/END	TIME	PERSONNEL COSTS SALARIES & WAGES	FRINGE BENEFITS	TOTAL	CONSULTANTS · CONTRACT SERVICES TIME	COST/WEEK	TOTAL	NON-PERSONNEL RESOURCES NEEDED SUPPLIES · EQUIPMENT · MATERIALS ITEM	COST/ITEM	QUANTITY	TOT COST	SUB-TOTAL COST FOR ACTIVITY TOTAL I.L.P	MILESTONES PROGRESS INDICATORS ITEM	DATE

D. Politics of Grant Seeking

D-1 Develop and maintain a webbing and linkage system with corporate, foundation and government funding sources. — Research Coord., Project Sec., and Staff members — 1/12

D-2 Report to chairperson on political aspects of grant funding. Send e-mails, letters and telegrams and make phone calls to appropriate officials to educate them on how grants impact the college/university. — Research Coord. — 1/12

E. Conferences, meetings and trainings for research coordinator (for example, attend Society of Research Administrators' Conference.) — Research Coord. — 1/12 — Air fare, Hotel, Meals, Ground Transportation and Registration fees for conference/meeting

©David G. Bauer Associates, Inc.
(800) 836-0732

TOTAL DIRECT COSTS OR COSTS REQUESTED FROM FUNDER ▲
MATCHING FUNDS, IN-KIND CONTRIBUTIONS, OR DONATED COSTS ▲
TOTAL COSTS ▲

PROJECT PLANNER JOB DESCRIPTION: RESEARCH COORDINATOR

EXHIBIT 16.2 (continued)

The structure of the grants office should be developed based on the functions that are determined to be the office's priorities. The functions must make allowance for human factors such as finding a person who enjoys accomplishing them.

Individuals need to know the level of performance that is required for maintaining their positions. Most job advertisements do not state performance indicators, because most job descriptions do not. A review of the following job descriptions entitled "Director of Extramural Funding and Grants Management" (exhibit 16.3), "Proposal and Resource Development Specialist" (exhibit 16.4), and "Director of Contract and Grant Development" (exhibit 16.5) reveals differences in expectations although there are no stated measurement indicators for satisfactory levels of accomplishment. These job descriptions need to be accompanied by a project planner and an outline of the resources the successful candidate will command to reach the desired levels of performance.

Under the general direction of the department, the director of extramural funding and grants management will perform duties necessary to accomplish the following broad objectives:

- increasing the interest and broadening participation of faculty/staff in the development of proposals for the externally funded contracts and grants;

- providing assistance to faculty/staff in the conceptualization, preparation, and processing of proposals;

- establishing contacts with and collecting information from funding sources in both the public and private sectors;

- disseminating in a timely manner and making conveniently available to faculty/staff information on funding opportunities, program guidelines, application materials, and other relevant information;

- assisting in the formulation and implementation of a comprehensive plan for research and development that will help prioritize and enhance efforts to obtain external funding; and

- accomplishing various other tasks related to contract and grant development.

Minimum Qualifications

Education: Master's degree from accredited institution preferred. Professional experience that demonstrates that the applicant has acquired and successfully applied the knowledge and abilities shown below may be substituted in lieu of the desired education requirement.

Experience: At least 3 years of cumulative, successful experience in all, or most, of the following areas:

- writing grant proposals and competing for external funding;

- working with faculty and/or others to assist them on various aspects of contract and grant development;

JOB DESCRIPTION: DIRECTOR OF EXTRAMURAL FUNDING AND GRANTS MANAGEMENT

EXHIBIT 16.3

- developing contacts with federal, state, local and private funding agencies; and

- directing the development and operations of an office or program and supervising one or more staff persons.

Knowledge and Abilities: General knowledge of the following aspects of contract and grant development:

- sources of information on funding opportunities in both the public and private sectors;

- nature of externally funded research, training, and service programs in higher education institutions;

- federal, state, and institutional policies and regulations governing externally funded programs

- concepts and methods for preparing grant proposals and contracts; and

- principles and methods of office and personnel management.

Ability to assist faculty and staff in conceptualizing and developing grant proposals; ability to establish effective contacts with funding agencies; ability to supervise the work of both technical and clerical assistants; ability to develop good working relationships with faculty/staff; ability to creatively and independently plan, coordinate, and initiate actions necessary to implement administrative plans and decisions; and ability to communicate effectively both orally and in writing.

JOB DESCRIPTION: DIRECTOR OF EXTRAMURAL FUNDING AND GRANTS MANAGEMENT

EXHIBIT 16.3 (*continued*)

Information Assistance

For all practical purposes, proposals are developed by principal investigators with assistance possibly from their associates. However, proposals can be the result of information concerning prospective sources of funds for research in areas where the proposer has interests and capabilities. The present Information Systems Coordinator would assist the development specialist in this area.

Editorial Assistance

Such an individual would not necessarily be a professional writer but would provide editorial, photographic, graphical, data processing, and reproduction services when needed, as well as assistance in tailoring faculty ideas to fit the interests of different sponsors.

Interdisciplinary Research

Many faculty and organizational units do not have the orientation or flexibility to perform interdisciplinary research successfully. Faculty are normally discipline-oriented or

JOB DESCRIPTION: PROPOSAL AND RESOURCE DEVELOPMENT SPECIALIST

EXHIBIT 16.4

traditional in nature. Organizational units do not often provide the proper climate or organizational environment for interdisciplinary scholars. Individuals from different disciplines have little motivation to work together toward a common goal. The faculty director of an interdisciplinary project plays a critical role, but much of the load may be shared by the grants office through proper coordination by the development specialist. Leadership, administrative ability, and the power of persuasion can greatly assist the faculty director of a team project.

Government Relations

Greater attention must be paid to the development of our relationships with federal, state, and local government agencies. Knowledge of the people and the programs of each agency is critical. The interaction of the program monitor of an agency with a faculty member at _____is a key ingredient in any successful proposal effort. More than this, _____ as an entity needs to be aware of the growing edge of the present and future activities of all agencies. Concern must also be given to both the legislative and executive branches regarding science and technology. The development specialist would assist the grants office in coordination of efforts of the University in this area.

JOB DESCRIPTION: PROPOSAL AND RESOURCE DEVELOPMENT SPECIALIST

EXHIBIT 16.4 (*continued*)

Responsibilities and Duties

Under the general direction of the Dean of Graduate Studies and Research, the director will perform duties necessary to accomplish the following broad objectives: a) increasing the interest and broadening the participation of faculty/staff in the development of proposals for externally funded contracts and grants; b) providing assistance to faculty/staff in the conceptualization, preparation, and processing of proposals; c) establishing contacts with and collecting information from funding sources in both the public and private sectors; d) disseminating in a timely manner and making conveniently available to faculty/staff information on funding opportunities, program guidelines, application materials, and other relevant information; e) assisting in the formulation and implementation of a comprehensive plan for research and development that will help prioritize and enhance efforts to obtain external funding; and f) accomplishing various other tasks related to contract and grant development.

Minimum Qualifications

Education: Master's degree from accredited institution required. A doctorate or equivalent is desired. Professional experience that demonstrates that the applicant has acquired and successfully applied the knowledge and abilities shown below may be substituted in lieu of the desired education on a year-for-year basis.

JOB DESCRIPTION: DIRECTOR OF CONTRACT AND GRANT DEVELOPMENT

EXHIBIT 16.5

Experience: At least 3 years of cumulative successful experience in all, or most, of the following areas: a) writing grant proposals and competing for external funding; b) working with faculty and/or others to assist them on various aspects of contract and grant development; c) developing contacts with federal, state, local, and private funding agencies; and d) directing the development and operations of an office or program while supervising one or more staff persons.

Knowledge and Abilities: General knowledge of the following aspects of contract and grant development: a) sources of information on funding opportunities in both the public and private sectors; b) nature of externally funded research, training, and service programs in institutions of higher education; c) federal, state, and institutional policies and regulations governing externally funded programs; d) concepts and methods for preparing grant proposals and contracts; and e) principles and methods of office and personnel management. Ability to assist faculty, staff, and students in conceptualizing and developing grant proposals; ability to establish effective contacts with funding agencies; ability to supervise the work of both technical and clerical assistants; ability to develop good working relationships with faculty, staff, and students; ability to creatively and independently plan, coordinate, and initiate actions necessary to implement administrative plans and decisions; and ability to communicate effectively both orally and in writing.

JOB DESCRIPTION: DIRECTOR OF CONTRACT AND GRANT DEVELOPMENT

EXHIBIT 16.5 (*continued*)

Employing the techniques and strategies that culminate in this chapter will provide a grants system that serves your institution in a meaningful and measurable way. Your staff will develop realistic expectations of the grants office, and those employed in the grants system will understand what is expected of them. Morale will improve. Burnout and mistakes will be reduced and order will triumph over chaos. However, remember that just as this state is approached, a change will occur and adjustments will have to be made. Feedback will reveal that the system is not perfect, and the ever-changing nature of our work will constantly create new demands.

You may use the sample job descriptions provided in this chapter to help you develop your job descriptions and performance indicators. They should serve as points of departure as you analyze the tasks your grants system will provide. Remember, the job description and the prerequisite skills needed are a function of the tasks or services that are provided by your individually distinct grants office. One very large (and if you measure success by grants dollars awarded, successful) grants office once made it clear to me that the bottom line for its grants effort was how fast the office could turn around a proposal from its delivery to the university grants office to sign-off and submission, and how many proposals the office could handle. Obviously in a case like this, the grants administrator's job description would be based solely on ability to process the greatest number of proposals in the shortest amount of time possible. One would not look at success rate percentage or quality or the amount of funding awarded. In fact, those criteria would not be part of the evaluation of the staff or the grants administrator. It is interesting to note however, that when I asked why they were inquiring about my services, they remarked that they had dropped five places in a report listing the amount of funded research attracted by college and universities. This is particularly interesting when you consider that the office's evaluation was said to be based on speed of the submittal!

C. DEVELOPING A FIVE-YEAR GRANTS OFFICE PLAN

By evaluating what your office does now to encourage pre-award activities and post-award services, you will obtain an accurate description of where your office is currently functioning. I suggest you consider developing a grants office planning committee comprised of faculty, staff, and administration. This group consisting of your clients or users and representatives from your administration will provide valuable input on developing a five-year plan to improve your office's services. The committee should help you answer questions such as the following:

- Where do you think the grants office should be in five years?
- What will it look like (facilities, offices, etc.)?
- Where will it be located?
- What services will it provide?
- How will it be staffed?
- How will it be evaluated?

By compiling the answers to these questions, you will develop a vision for your office. You can better define the vision by addressing specific issues such as services, staff, budget for space, travel, equipment, etc. By placing the proposed services on a spreadsheet or project planner, the same tool you use to develop budget for grants, you can create a budget to support your office's five-year vision.

Work with your grants office planning committee to move backward from five years to one year. To foster the concept of accountability, build in measurement indicators to demonstrate your realization of success along the way. Your performance of *more* grant-related services will be monitored and evaluated, and the provision of the services themselves will result in

- more proposal ideas and interest,
- completion and submission of more proposals,
- a better image for your institution due to increased success rates and funding, and
- a stronger relationship between the mission and vision of your institution and that of the grants office.

By building these measurement indicators into each year's plan, your committee can see the value of the plan, as well as the projected costs. The costs of making this plan a reality can be clearly evaluated by the proposal outcomes. Funding for the incremental yearly increases in services and functions must be factored into your institution's budget under your administrative unit. Be careful about relying totally for the funding of this growth on increases in the recovery of indirect costs. If your plan calls for little or no support from the institution, this will surely influence your choice of potential grantees to receive your full attention. Those federal agencies that pay your full indirect-cost rates will be given priority over private and state grantors. Research and contracts with federal agencies will begin to take precedence over humanities and training grants that may only pay eight percent total direct costs or no administrative fees at all! If the mission of the institution is to create and foster a rich and diverse academic climate, then the grants office budget must reflect support for those areas that do not "hold their own" in terms of reimbursement for the grants services they use.

Because most colleges and universities already have a system for the allocation of indirect costs to Presidents, deans, department chairs, principal investigators, and project directors, the reinvestment of these funds in the system that generates this support seems logical. But when it comes to giving up some of these funds to improve the system that will generate more funds, logic may not prevail! In fact, many of the percent distributions of recovered indirect costs do not even allocate a percentage for the grants office. The assumption is that the unit that the grants office falls under administratively (i.e., V.P. for Academic Affairs, Provost for Research, etc.) will dedicate those funds to the grants office. Unfortunately, this is not a realistic assumption.

Your five-year plan must be compelling and must clearly relate to investment returns to succeed. Review the sample project planner in exhibit 16.2 that supports a position for a research coordinator.

This position as outlined is based upon pre-award services only, and could be a position in a centralized or decentralized setting. What you would need to adjust in the sample are the cost estimates for your area. (For instance, travel to D.C. from Maryland is a lot less costly than travel to D.C. from California.) Then you would need to place those estimates of change in the measurement indicators previously discussed. In fact, you may choose to provide expectations for this position over a two- or three-year period. For example, activity A-1 should have a measurement indicator that describes "how many faculty/staff profiles he or she creates and logs in your institution's database." If this will include placing a profile in supplemental systems such as a consortium-building system that matches profiles to other interested researchers, this should also be mentioned.

In seeking to quantify and qualify the tasks in this job description, it may be more useful to employ statistics or percentage of change that the research coordinator will be accountable for. For example, increasing the number or percentage of faculty in the School of Engineering who have a research profile on the Community of Science database from _____ to _____ .

By reviewing each function and seeking ways to measure the success or accomplishment of each task, you will have a job description and measurement indicators that assist both the supervisor and research coordinator by providing them with a clear set of expectations for the job. By surveying the faculty and staff for feedback and reviewing the measurement indicators, job success can be measured and job satisfaction and performance discussed in a more concrete manner. I have found that grants office staff prefer to have precise job descriptions and evaluations rather than vague ones that are based on subjective evaluations or are unfairly influenced by e-mails from a few disgruntled grant seekers who make unrealistic demands of staff people.

Use the survey questions in exhibit 16.6 to help you gather feedback from your staff on how well their existing job descriptions match with the actual duties they perform and if they are aware of what is expected of them and the level of performance that is required to maintain their positions. Completing the inventory in exhibit 16.7 will help you develop a plan that ensures the accuracy of your job descriptions and the existence of appropriate measurement indicators.

Share your project planner, job description, and job performance evaluation criteria with Bauer Associates and we will make them available for others to use.

For Grants Office Personnel

1. How adequate is your job description at depicting the actual duties you perform?
   _____Inadequate
   _____Adequate
   _____More than adequate

2. Could your job description be changed to better reflect your responsibilities and duties?   _____Yes   _____No

   a. If yes, how?

3. Does your job description provide the measurement indicators by which you are evaluated?   _____Yes   _____No

   b. If yes, do you feel they are fair? _____Yes   _____No
   c. If you do not feel they are fair, why not and how could they be improved?

4. If your job description does not provide measurement indicators, how are you made aware of what is expected of you and the level of performance you must achieve to maintain your position?

SURVEY QUESTIONS: THE GRANTS OFFICE PERSONNEL—PAST, PRESENT, AND FUTURE

EXHIBIT 16.6

For Each Activity/Item listed, Check Status

Activity/Item	Reviewed, Appropriate Part of Grants Office	Reviewed, Appropriate Part of Other Office (List)	Reviewed, Not Applicable	Reviewed, Inappropriate Needs Action	Non-existent, Needs Action
1. Grants Office Staff • review job descriptions • review performance measurements 2. Grants Administrator • review job description • review performance measurements 3. Review personnel budgets including travel, training, etc.					

Complete this Section for Each Activity/Item Needing Action

What Needs to be Accomplished?	By Whom? (Office/ Person)	By When? (Time Frame)	Resources Required— Personnel, Supplies, Equipment, Programming, etc.	Estimated Costs

GRANTS OFFICE INVENTORY: THE GRANTS OFFICE PERSONNEL—PAST, PRESENT, AND FUTURE

EXHIBIT 16.7

CHAPTER 17

Client Satisfaction Survey and Results

At this point you have reviewed each chapter and have begun to evaluate each of the functions that occur in grants offices at colleges and universities throughout the United States for the possibility of inclusion into your five-year plan to create a dynamic grants office. Each chapter contains suggested survey questions to obtain the feedback your plan requires to

- evaluate current functions;
- assess readiness, knowledge, and attitudes before changing or adding services; and
- improve services.

There are also two electronic surveys provided for your use on the CD-ROM accompanying this book. The surveys have been shared as a collegial contribution to further joint efforts to improve grant seeking in higher education. Special thanks are given to Eastern Michigan University (EMU) for sharing its survey, and its survey results and analysis for others to learn and extrapolate from. In the initial stages of survey development, Brian Anderson of Eastern Michigan University (EMU) decided to e-mail his faculty and staff and invite them to complete a client satisfaction survey. The e-mail invitation included a link to the survey. He decided that administering the survey electronically would not only be user-friendly (click-and-send format), but it would also provide an easy mechanism for tabulating and reviewing the results.

Programming of the EMU survey and data analysis of the results were provided by Rick Magyar from EMU's Research Office. After reviewing the survey, you may adapt it to fit your institution's and office's specific needs before you administer it. Check with your campus experts to determine what software they recommend to run and compile the data. In the original survey, the questions were placed on generic HTML available from any Web editor.

Boxes were then created and pre-coded. The HTML allowed any browser to get to the form and to type in data. When the respondents hit *submit*, there must be software on the server to accept the data. EMU used a program they already had in the research office entitled *NETCLOAK*. Rick used a Macintosh that ran off his server to process the forms. The software was used at its simplest level to gather the data from respondents. All they had to do was hit the submit command to place the data on a text file. You may use a variety of software applications, but Rick chose *FILE MAKER* to organize the data and research different elements.

You can easily change the wording of the questions and replace the EMU specific references with your own (i.e., name of your Web site, name of your grants office publications, the title of your grants office, etc.). You can even change the question totally, but it is a bit more difficult to change the responses. To change the responses, you must change the coding fields. You will find it easier to custom tailor the survey to your needs if you can arrange it so that your questions employ the same response choices as those on the original survey. (Please note that the same rules apply to the other sample survey (sample survey II), which also can be found on the accompanying CD-ROM and which includes both the pre- and post-award survey questions found at the end of each chapter.)

Rick has also included on the CD-ROM his pdf download to a pdf file, because the print version of the survey did not look like the Web version. The copy of the EMU survey presented in the print version in this book resulted from downloading to a pdf file. Because you will want to present the survey data to various groups and individuals (including your supervisor), the print version and the results are much more presentable when viewed in this manner.

Grouping Faculty and Staff

One of your initial decisions in surveying your faculty and staff involves determining the groupings you will use. You may decide to subdivide the client population into groupings that fit your specific purposes and maximize the usefulness of the results. In EMU's pre-award Client Satisfaction Survey a basic three-group format was used: Group A—active grant seekers, Group B—previously active grant seekers, and Group C—those who have never submitted a proposal.

Group A   Active Grant Seekers—This group included those who have submitted a proposal or have been funded in the past four years. There were some individual variations in this criteria, and you may want to develop subgroups within this group or make other distinctions that will make the survey more useful to you and your institution.

Group B   Previously Active Grant Seekers—This group included those faculty/staff who have submitted a proposal or have been funded, but not within the past four years. Like Group A (active grant seekers), this group could be further subdivided by separating out those who have submitted proposals but were never funded.

Please note that in determining criteria for both the active and previously active groups, there were discussions concerning whether EMU's survey should also include those faculty/staff who have successfully competed for and attracted *internal* grant funding. (Internal funding includes grant awards from the grants office, the vice president for research, academic affairs, deans and department funding, and other programs designed to stimulate grant seeking in college/university centers and institutes.) EMU's Client Satisfaction Survey considered *external* grant funding only; *internally* funded programs were excluded.

In other surveys that I have developed to evaluate grants offices, I have made special groupings or subgroups for those who had received internal funding so that I could compile data that might determine the effectiveness of internal awards and whether they could be related to future successful external grants/contracts funding. In addition, because most of the internal awards were administered through the post-award system of the grants office, I was interested in gathering feedback relative to the effect that the expenditure of these internal funds had on future grant seeking and the grant seeker's motivation to pursue other grant funding. The feedback I elicited demonstrated that the perceptions of the internally sponsored project directors had a dramatic effect on their seeking of more external resources. My evaluation showed that two-thirds to three-quarters of those funded internally went on to bring in at least the same amount in external funding that was initially invested by the institution. Many of the one-third to one-quarter who did not attempt to secure external funding were unhappy with their grants experience for reasons related to those already mentioned in chapter 1 and the study entitled "Satisfying and Stressful Experiences of First-time Federal Grantees," or they did not seek outside funds because they were able to complete their desired work and did not need or require more money.

Another piece of useful information that I was able to gather by surveying internally funded grantees was that the group required special attention from the pre-award staff. Because they had already been awarded a grant, they were treated the same as the other successful grantees; in reality they knew little about how to locate external funding and required greater assistance in getting their profiles in the office's grants database.

The point is that you may find it enlightening to survey a subgroup of these unique internally funded grantees to gather feedback about your institution's internal grant programs and its pre- and post-awards grants efforts related to this specific population.

Group C   Those Who Have Never Submitted a Proposal—Again, there are subgroups of this group that you may want to separate from the rest of the population. For example,
- those who have initiated pre-award activities but never applied, and
- those who have not submitted a proposal since they have been at your institution but have submitted a proposal(s) while at another college or university. (You could segment the population of those who submitted a proposal while at another institution further by looking at those who were funded versus those who were rejected.)

Group C could also be analyzed by program, college, and type of appointment (e.g., staff, tenured faculty, non-tenured faculty, contact position, etc.). Your survey results should provide you with feedback that you can utilize to improve services to this population of "yet to be successful" grant seekers.

When deciding on the groups and subgroups to survey, remember that the ultimate goal is to gather information that will help you improve your services and increase the likelihood that your client target populations will develop more external funding through grants/

contracts. What are their perceptions of the grants/contracts marketplace, its barriers and constraints, and the usefulness of the services you provide to overcome real or imagined obstacles to grants success? Each of the groups (and subgroups) represent your institution's grants potential.

Depending on your grants office plan, you may decide to restrict your services or expand your functions to those groups that hold the greatest potential for growth. One of my clients who is expanding the role of grant seeking within his institution is surveying only the active grant seekers (Group A) this year. His office's efforts will be directed toward gathering feedback from this target population to improve and increase the grants office's services to this group. After work with this group yields a greater recovery in indirect costs, the grants office will shift its focus to Group B—those who have have submitted a proposal or been funded, but not recently. After surveying this group for improvements and developing its potential, the grants office will finally, after three or four years, focus on Group C and develop the services and staff to move this larger group forward.

The print version of Eastern Michigan University's pre-award Client Satisfaction Survey and its analysis is presented in this chapter to help you develop and administer your own survey, analyze its results, and develop the steps necessary to respond to the needs highlighted by survey results. An invitation to complete a survey was e-mailed to all EMU faculty and staff who could be or have been involved in grant seeking. As previously mentioned, three groups were offered the opportunity to respond. The invitation to complete the survey was e-mailed to 790 clients. Invitations were sent mainly to faculty, but a small number of staff were also included.

In analyzing and discussing the results of this survey, it is important to take into consideration nonresponse bias. It is not valid to make generalizations or conclusions about the entire population when actually only those clients who returned the survey were represented in the data. While some researchers and statisticians would require a 70-percent response rate before making what they would consider valid and reliable conclusions, EMU's survey fell within the realm of action research, and therefore, much lower response rates are acceptable. In its action research, EMU's Office of Research Development was actually involved in an educational process aimed at teaching its clients about the office and its current or potential services while surveying them.

Of the 790 recipients of the survey invitation, approximately 150 fell into the Group A category—those who have submitted proposals or who have been funded in the past four years. Of this group, 48 percent or 72 clients completed the survey. While this is far less than a 70-percent return, it is a good response, especially when compared to the response rates of the other groups.

Group B—those who have submitted a proposal or have been funded, but not within the past four years, totaled approximately 50. Of this group, 36 percent, or 18 clients, responded.

Group C—those who have never submitted a proposal amounted to 590. Of this group, only 60 clients, or approximately 10 percent, completed the survey. Unfortunately, the 60 responses from 590 clients may not even be representative of this very large group. Therefore, we must be even more careful about generalizing beyond the respondents who completed the survey.

These responses occurred after the initial e-mail invitation to complete the survey and one reminder e-mail. The total response of 150 out of 790 places the response rate at just under 19 percent. This response rate is not that low when you consider the type of survey, the fact that this was the first time it was administered, and that the majority of the population that was invited/asked to complete it (approximately 75 percent) had never submitted a proposal (Group C).

If one considers the context in which the e-mail invitation and Web-based survey was received by the clients, the response rates are understandable. For example, clients in Group A were used to getting e-mail from the EMU Office of Research Development because they have been recently or are currently funded. Therefore, they were probably more likely than the other groups to read the e-mail request and click on to the survey.

Clients in Group B were probably less tuned in to the Office of Research Development because they have not recently submitted a proposal or been funded, and may have been slightly less likely to click on to and complete the survey.

Clients in Group C had not had any previous contact with the Office of Research Development and may have had a hidden prejudice against grant seeking. Whether deliberate or due to a lack of familiarity with the Office, clients in this group may have been predisposed to not even read the e-mail invitation. Considering this predisposition, a 10 percent response rate is low, but not that bad for a first attempt to reach this group.

In addition, it should be noted that in the midst of sending out the e-mail invitations to complete the survey, there was fire in the largest building at EMU that temporarily knocked out the e-mail service of many arts and science faculty members. Considering the context in which the e-mail invitation and Web-based survey was received by the clients, the close proximity to the end of the semester, and the disruption of e-mail service on campus, I consider the results encouraging!

Exhibit 17.1 provides a copy of EMU's survey. Before reviewing the survey, please note that the survey is based on pre-award functions only. The survey is divided into two sections. Section 1 is for those faculty and staff who have submitted proposals or who have been funded in the past four years (Group A) and those who have submitted a proposal or have been funded, but not within the past four years (Group B). Section II is for those who have never submitted a proposal (Group C). Questions 1 through 7 on both sections of the survey are identical. In other words, Groups A, B, and C were asked to answer these questions. Exhibit 17.2 tabulates the responses to the multiple-choice questions. Results from both surveys are combined for questions 1 through 7. Please note that some respondents did not answer all of the questions. However, all the individual calculations (percentages) for each question are based solely upon the number of people who responded to the question.

Question 1—Are you faculty or staff?

114 faculty and 32 staff accepted the e-mailed invitation to go the Office of Research Development's Web site and click on and respond to the Client Satisfaction Survey.

Question 2—Are you aware of Graduate Studies & Research STAR WATCH?

This questions refers to the publication that focuses on research at EMU (STAR WATCH). It is useful in recruiting, accreditation, and public relations, and in demonstrating how the role of sponsored projects and research is related to EMU's mission. Answers to

SECTION I

- Only for those who have submitted proposals or who have been funded in the past four years (Group A), and

- Those who have submitted a proposal or have been funded, not NOT within the past four years (Group B).

1. Are you: FACULTY STAFF ○ ○

2. Are you aware of Graduate Studies & Research STAR WATCH?   YES NO ○ ○
  a. If you are aware of it, have you read it?   ○ ○

If you have read it, please answer the following:

  b. Is it informative (does it provide useful information)?   ○ ○
  c. Is it interesting (do you enjoy reading it)?   ○ ○
  d. Do you think it encourages grant writing activity?   ○ ○
  e. Does it recognize faculty and staff efforts?   ○ ○

3. Are you aware of ORD's Web page?   YES NO ○ ○
  a. If you are aware of it, have you used it in the past year?   ○ ○

If you have used in the past year, please answer the following:

  b. Did it provide the information you were seeking?   ○ ○
  c. Could you easily find the information you need?   ○ ○
  d. Did it contain the information you expected?   ○ ○
  e. What additional information should be included?

CLIENT SATISFACTION SURVEY—EMU OFFICE OF RESEARCH DEVELOPMENT

EXHIBIT 17.1

4. Are you aware of the SPIN database?

YES   NO
○   ○

a. If you are aware of it, have you used it in the past year?

YES   NO
○   ○

b. If you are aware of it but have not used it, why not?

If you have used SPIN in the past year, please answer the following:

c. Was it easy to use?   ○ ○

d. Have you found potential funding opportunities by using it?   ○ ○

e. Have you written a proposal as a result of a SPIN search?   ○ ○

f. Were you funded from a grant opportunity found on SPIN?   ○ ○

5. Are you registered for SMARTS?

YES   NO   Don't Know
○   ○   ○

a. If "no," why have you not registered?

If "yes," please answer the following:

b. Did you receive assistance with selection of keywords?   ○ ○

c. Do you receive as many announcements as you would expect?   ○ ○

d. Are the announcements relevant to your interests?   ○ ○

e. Have you followed up on any announcements received?   ○ ○

f. Are you eligible for all the announcements you receive?   ○ ○

g. Have you updated your keywords in the last year?   ○ ○

h. Are you registered for any other funding database?   ○ ○

CLIENT SATISFACTION SURVEY—EMU OFFICE OF RESEARCH DEVELOPMENT

EXHIBIT 17.1 (*continued*)

6. Have you attended any ORD grant writing workshops? YES NO ○ ○

If "yes," please rate the value of workshops you attended.
If "no", or you don't remember, please leave blank:

		Little Value	Somewhat Helpful	Very Helpful
a.	Introduction to the World of Grants	○	○	○
b.	Identifying Funding Sources	○	○	○
c.	Proposal Development Strategies	○	○	○
d.	Professional Writing Tips	○	○	○
e.	Developing the Budget	○	○	○
f.	The Evaluation Component	○	○	○
g.	The Review Process	○	○	○
h.	EMU Research Support Programs	○	○	○

		YES	NO
i.	In general, were the presenters clear and concise?	○	○
j.	Did the workshops address your grant training needs?	○	○

k. What suggestions do you have for improving the workshops?

l. What suggestions do you have for additional workshops?

7. Are you aware that the Center for Research Support is available to provide assistance on any aspect of proposal development (design & evaluation)? YES NO

CLIENT SATISFACTION SURVEY—EMU OFFICE OF RESEARCH DEVELOPMENT

EXHIBIT 17.1 (*continued*)

8. Evaluation of ORD services (If services not used, please leave blank).

		Inadequate	Adequate	More than Adequate
a.	Assistance with concept development	○	○	○
b.	Assistance finding collaborators and partners	○	○	○
c.	Assistance securing external sources of funding	○	○	○
d.	Assistance obtaining matching funds	○	○	○
e.	Assistance securing/reviewing program guidelines	○	○	○
f.	Assistance establishing contact with grantors	○	○	○
g.	Proposal budget development / preparation	○	○	○
h.	Final proposal review	○	○	○
i.	Proposal editing	○	○	○
j.	Proposal assembly and submission	○	○	○
k.	Assistance in final award negotiation with agency	○	○	○
l.	Assistance with establishing a project account	○	○	○

m. What suggestions do you have for improving ORD services?

CLIENT SATISFACTION SURVEY—EMU OFFICE OF RESEARCH DEVELOPMENT

EXHIBIT 17.1 (*continued*)

9. Evaluation of your experiences with ORD project representatives

	Inadequate	Adequate	More than Adequate
a. Knowledge and expertise	○	○	○
b. Courtesy and professionalism	○	○	○
c. Attention to details	○	○	○
d. Promptness in addressing needs or requests	○	○	○

e. Please comment/amplify

---

10. What additional services could ORD provide to assist you with proposal development?

---

11. What additional services could ORD provide to promote sponsored project activity?

---

12. What barriers have you encountered since you were funded?

---

13. What would you describe as the most satisfying part of your grant experience?

CLIENT SATISFACTION SURVEY—EMU OFFICE OF RESEARCH DEVELOPMENT

EXHIBIT 17.1 (*continued*)

14. Does your unit head support your grant activity? ■ Not at All   Somewhat   Completely

15. Do your colleagues support your grant activity? ■ Not at All   Somewhat   Completely

SECTION II

- Only for those who have never submitted a proposal (Group C)

1. Are you: ■ FACULTY   STAFF   ◯   ◯

2. Are you aware of Graduate Studies & Research STAR WATCH?   ■ YES   NO   ◯   ◯
   a. If you are aware of it, have you read it?   ■ ◯   ◯

If you have read it, please answer the following:

   b. Is it informative (does it provide useful information)?   ■ ◯   ◯
   c. Is it interesting (do you enjoy reading it)?   ◯   ◯
   d. Do you think it encourages grant writing activity?   ◯   ◯
   e. Does it recognize faculty and staff efforts?   ◯   ◯

3. Are you aware of ORD's Web page?   ■ YES   NO   ◯   ◯
   a. If you are aware of it have you used it in the past year?   ■ ◯   ◯

If you have used in the past year, please answer the following:

   b. Did it provide the information you were seeking?   ■ ◯   ◯
   c. Could you easily find the information you need?   ◯   ◯
   d. Did it contain the information you expected?   ◯   ◯
   e. What additional information should be included?

CLIENT SATISFACTION SURVEY—EMU OFFICE OF RESEARCH DEVELOPMENT

EXHIBIT 17.1 (*continued*)

4. Are you aware of the SPIN database?

YES NO
O O

a. If you are aware of it, have you used it in the past year?

O O

b. If you are aware of it and not used it, why not?

If you have used SPIN in the past year, please answer the following:

c. Was it easy to use?

O O

d. Have you found potential funding opportunities by using it?

O O

e. Have you written a proposal as a result of a SPIN search?

O O

f. Were you funded from a grant opportunity found on SPIN?

O O

5. Are you registered for SMARTS?

YES NO Don't Know
O O O

a. If "no," why have you not registered?

If "yes," please answer the following:

b. Did you receive assistance with selection of keywords?

O O

c. Do you receive as many announcement as you would expect?

O O

d. Are the announcements relevant to your interests?

O O

e. Have you followed up on any announcements received?

O O

f. Are you eligible for all the announcements you receive?

O O

g. Have you updated your keywords in the last year?

O O

h. Are you registered for any other funding database?

CLIENT SATISFACTION SURVEY—EMU OFFICE OF RESEARCH DEVELOPMENT

EXHIBIT 17.1 (*continued*)

6. **Have you attended any ORD grant writing workshops?**　　YES　NO　○ ○

If "yes," please rate the value of workshops you attended.
If "no", or you don't remember, please leave blank:

Rating options for each: Little Value / Somewhat Helpful / Very Helpful ○ ○ ○

a. Introduction to the World of Grants

b. Identifying Funding Sources

c. Proposal Development Strategies

d. Professional Writing Tips

e. Developing the Budget

f. The Evaluation Component

g. The Review Process

h. EMU Research Support Programs

i. In general, were the presenters clear and concise?　YES NO ○ ○

j. Did the workshops address your grant training needs?　○ ○

k. What suggestions do you have for improving the workshops?

l. What suggestions do you have for additional workshops?

7. Are you aware that the Center for Research Support is available to provide assistance on any aspect of proposal development (design & evaluation)?　YES NO

EXHIBIT 17.1 (continued)

8. Do you believe that sponsored activity is important to EMU's mission? ▪ YES NO

9. Do you believe that sponsored activity is important to your unit's mission? ▪ YES NO

10. Although I have never applied for a grant, I have encouraged others to apply. ▪ YES NO

11. Would you consider writing a proposal in the future? ▪ YES NO Not Sure
○ ○ ○

If your answer is "no" or "not sure", please check all the following factors that apply:

a. Lack of knowledge about how to begin ▪ ☐
b. No likely sources of funding for my expertise/interest ☐
c. Bad experiences of colleagues ☐
d. Lack of formal recognition from department/unit ☐
e. Not relevant to my teaching/job responsibilities ☐
f. No interest ☐
g. No time due to existing workload ☐
h. Lack of monetary rewards ☐
i. Other:

12. Would you be more likely to participate in an externally funded project if you worked in collaboration with another individual? ▪ YES NO
○ ○

13. Would you be more likely to participate in an externally funded project if administrative support were provided by an EMU institute or center? ▪ YES NO
○ ○

14. How many years have you been employed by EMU: ▪ 1-3 4-10 11-20 21+
○ ○ ○ ○

CLIENT SATISFACTION SURVEY—EMU OFFICE OF RESEARCH DEVELOPMENT

EXHIBIT 17.1 (continued)

Question #	Responses	% Yes	% No
2 Are you aware of <u>Graduate Studies & Research STAR WATCH?</u>	146	86	14
2a If you are aware of it, have you read it?	133	81	19
2b Is it informative (does it provide useful information)?	111	89	11
2c Is it interesting (do you enjoy reading it)?	108	82	18
2d Do you think it encourages grant writing activity?	106	66	34
2e Does it recognize faculty and staff efforts?	107	95	5
3 Are you aware of ORD's Web page?	148	54	46
3a If you are aware of it have you used it in the past year?	107	36	64
3b Did it provide the information you were seeking?	38	81	19
3c Could you easily find the information you need?	36	80	20
3d Did it contain all the information you expected?	35	88	12
4 Are you aware of the SPIN database?	146	41	59
4a If you are aware of it, have you used it in the past year?	75	32	68
4c Was it easy to use?	8	50	50
4d Have you found potential funding opportunities by using it?	8	62	38
4e Have you written a proposal as a result of a SPIN search?	8	12	88
4f Were you funded from a grant opportunity found on SPIN?	8	0	100
5b Do you receive as many announcement as you would expect?	65	58	42
5c Are the announcements relevant to your interests?	63	82	18
5d Have you followed up on any announcements received?	62	67	33
5e Are you eligible for all the announcements you receive?	64	64	36
5f Have you updated your keywords in the last year?	63	22	78
5g Are you registered for any other funding database?	65	18	82
6 Have you attended any ORD grant writing workshops	148	33	67
6i i. In general, were the presenters clear and concise?	46	98	2
6j Did workshops address your grant training needs?	45	87	13
7 Are you aware that the Center for Research Support is available to provide assistance on any aspect of proposal development (design & evaluation)?	145	75	25
8-C Do you believe that sponsored activity is important to EMU's mission?	28	93	7
9-C Do you believe that sponsored activity is important to your unit's mission	27	63	37
10-C Although I have never applied for a grant, I have encouraged others to apply.	0	0	0
12-C Would you be more likely to participate in an externally funded project if you worked in collaboration with another individual?	30	80	20
13-C Would you be more likely to participate in an externally funded project if administrative support were provided by an EMU institute or center?	30	80	20

Question #	Responses	% Yes	% No	% Don't Know
5h Are you registered for any other funding database?	65	14	59	0
5 Are you registered for SMARTS?	148	43	30	27

(To see a sample of this survey in action visit: www.survey.sample.org)

TABULATION OF RESPONSES TO MULTIPLE CHOICE QUESTIONS

EXHIBIT 17.2

Question #	Responses	% Yes	% No	% Not Sure
11-C Would you consider writing a proposal in future?	29	51	11	38
14-B Would you consider writing another proposal?	4	50	1	1

Question #	Responses	% Not at All	% Somewhat	% Completely
14 Is your unit head supportive of your grant activity?	67	0	21	79
15 Your colleagues supportive of your grant activity?	67	4	47	49

Question #	Responses	% LittleValue	% Somewhat	% VryHelpful
6a Introduction to the World of Grants	29	3	51	46
6b Identifying Funding Strategies	31	16	46	38
6c Proposal Development Strategies	30	10	40	50
6d Professional Writing Tips	26	15	33	53
6e Developing the Budget	29	13	41	46
6f The Evaluation Component	24	8	42	50
6g The Review Process	23	4	48	48
6h EMU Research Support Programs	31	3	42	55

Question #	Responses	% Inadequate	% Adequate	% More Than
8a Assistance with concept development?	35	8	57	35
8b Assistance finding collaborators and partners	40	20	47	33
8c Assistance securing external sources of funding	47	28	44	28
8d Assistance obtaining matching funds	42	19	38	43
8e Assistance securing/reviewing program guidelines	46	11	43	46
8f Assistance establishing contact with grantors	40	15	58	27
8g Proposal budget development/preparation	59	7	44	49
8h Final proposal review	46	15	48	37
8i Proposal editing	43	14	51	35
8j Proposal assembly and submission	53	7	33	60
8k Assistance in the final award negotiation w/agency	38	8	55	37
8l Assistance with establishing a project account	46	15	45	40
9a Knowledge and expertise	81	11	36	53
9b Courtesy and professionalism	83	5	28	67
9c Attention to detail	80	12	36	52
9d Promptness in addressing needs or requests	82	18	30	52

Question #	Responses	% 1-3	% 4-10	% 11-20	% 21+
14-C How many years have you been employed by EMU?	30	23	33	23	21

TABULATION OF RESPONSES TO MULTIPLE CHOICE QUESTIONS

EXHIBIT 17.2 (continued)

the question show that over 80 percent of the respondents read it, believe it provides useful information, and that it is interesting. However, only 66 percent think it encourages grant-writing activity. This may be explained by the fact that many of the survey respondents include those who are actively involved in grant writing and hence, may be motivated by factors other than STAR WATCH. While this may be the case, 95 percent of the respondents still feel it is an appropriate way to recognize faculty and staff grants efforts. Based on the answers to question 2, it would seem beneficial to expand the dissemination of this publication and highlight its presence on campus. For example, the publication could be displayed on the desks or in the waiting areas of all administrators, in display cases on campus, etc.

Question 3—Are you aware of ORD's Web page?

This question refers to the Office of Research Development's Web site. There were 148 responses to this question and approximately 80 individuals or 54 percent of the respondents were aware of it. While there may be faculty and staff who are aware of the Web site, but did not complete the survey, only 80 out of a total invited population of 790, or a mere 10 percent, are likely to be aware of the Web site. Obviously, new and creative methods for increasing awareness need to be explored. Perhaps some appropriate techniques could be employed at new faculty orientations to increase awareness. In addition, ways to get faculty and staff to visit the Web site could be brainstormed.

While there were 80 individuals who said they were aware of the Web page, only 38 were aware of it and *used* it in the past year. Of the user group, over 80 percent thought it provided the information they were seeking, could easily find the information they needed, and contained all the information they expected.

Before a thorough critique of ORD's Web page can be made, more users should be surveyed. Especially, because 38 users out of a total invited population of 790 faculty and staff equates to less than 4 percent. This is one area where core user groups from each of the major client populations (Groups A, B, and C) should be elicited for more feedback on how the Web page could further the goals and objectives of the grants effort.

Exhibit 17.3 provides a sample of the responses to the open-ended question 3, part e concerning what additional information should be included on ORD's Web page.

Question 4—Are you aware of the SPIN database?

The SPIN database is the grants database used by EMU to search for potential funding sources. Of those responding to this question, 59 percent were *not* aware of this resource. Much more needs to be done to educate faculty and staff regarding access to this and other grants databases.

- Faculty and staff could be introduced to the availability of this resource during faculty orientation.
- Department chairs and deans could brainstorm ways to inform faculty and staff about SPIN.
- A demonstration of SPIN could be conducted at faculty meetings by grants office staff.

The 60 respondents who said they were aware of the database represented only 8 percent of the total 790 clients invited to respond to the survey. In addition, only 24 clients that were aware of the database said they used it in the past year. Of these 24, only 8 responded to

- Access to all university policies and procedures
- Rate and budget information (the current ORD rate sheet plus additional information like typical telephone charges per line, etc.)
- The most recent ORD annual report
- Lists of proposals currently submitted (You may not want to put some of this information out of for the whole world but I assume that there is a way to restrict access to particular parts of the Web page so that it can be accessed only by people with passwords or EMU faculty/staff computer IDs.)
- Applications online
- Information is fine, but formatting is not. Necessary information was double-encoded, therefore almost impossible to download. Someone had binhexed the information before putting it in pdf!
- I tried and tried to find indirect cost and mileage rates, which supposedly are there, but couldn't do it.
- Several of my *yes* answers could have been *maybe* if there was such a category.
- More information on RFPs that are available
- I wanted to use the search database feature to locate funding for a grant proposal. I had difficulty trying to figure out how to do the search. I think that I need to come to your office for help.
- Should post complete applications on the Web site. Seems as if important information must be picked up from the ORD office.

SAMPLE OF RESPONSES: QUESTION 3, PART E, SECTIONS I AND II—WHAT ADDITIONAL INFORMATION SHOULD BE INCLUDED IN ORD's WEB PAGE?

EXHIBIT 17.3

questions concerning how easy it was to use, if they found potential funding opportunities by using it, if they wrote a proposal as a result of their SPIN search, and if they were funded from a grant opportunity found on SPIN. Basically, 4 respondents thought it was easy to use, 5 respondents found potential opportunities by using it, 1 respondent wrote a proposal as a result of a SPIN search, and 0 got funding from a grant opportunity found on SPIN.

Before you go out to cancel your subscription to your office's grantor database, you should consider other factors. For instance, perhaps the faculty and staff at EMU are not largely involved in the use of SPIN or other grantor databases because grants office staff fulfill this task for them. Exhibit 17.4 provides a sampling of the responses to the open-ended question, "If you are aware of SPIN, and have not used it, why not?" (question 4, part b) and one respondent did reply that he/she didn't really have the need to find funding sources, because staff at the Office of Research Development (ORD) helped with that.

Question 5—Are you registered for SMARTS?

SMARTS is the custom searching and e-mail function of the SPIN grants database. (Other databases have similar components.) 148 individuals responded to this question. Of the respondents, 64 said they are registered, and more than half said they received as many

- I have not taken the initiative to consult it.
- Don't know much about it.
- No time! (This response or something very similar occurred six times.)
- Not used to using it.
- Haven't really had the need to find funding sources. Staff at ORD have helped with that.
- Too cumbersome and time consuming.
- Nothing has come up in my area of expertise.

SAMPLE OF RESPONSES: QUESTION 4, PART B, SECTIONS I AND II—IF YOU ARE AWARE OF THE SPIN DATABASE, AND HAVE NOT USED IT, WHY NOT?

EXHIBIT 17.4

announcements as they expected, found the announcements relative to their interests, followed up on the announcements they received, and were eligible for the announcements they received. From this data it is probably fair to conclude that more than half of those registered for SMARTS viewed the system favorably. This is interesting because no one said they were funded as a result of a lead from SPIN (question 4, part f). Question 5, part f may hold the key to understanding this phenomena. Only 14 people of those surveyed said they updated their search words (keywords) in the last year. With this in mind, the SPIN/ SMARTS database may not be locating appropriate, potential grantors for the majority of respondents. The Office of Research Development may need to brainstorm methods to encourage faculty and staff to evaluate and update their key search words on SPIN/ SMARTS and their interest profiles. Profiles cannot be done once and left for twenty years. An e-mail encouraging those who have a profile in the system to update it may be in order.

- Get information elsewhere. Other colleagues send me information from SMARTS.
- I'm already aware of many funding opportunities, and not searching for more.
- Don't know what this is. (This response or something very similar occurred seven times.)
- I need to register. I keep putting it off.
- Tried once, was unable to get in and just haven't done it. I need to.
- I am busy doing current projects. I will register this summer.
- I am not sure. But I will register in the future.
- I tried to register just two weeks ago and had a lot of trouble. I never was sure if I was registered after I answered the questions. I think that I need someone to help me.

SAMPLE OF RESPONSES: QUESTION 5, PART A, SECTIONS I AND II—IF YOU ARE NOT REGISTERED FOR SMARTS, WHY NOT?

EXHIBIT 17.5

Exhibit 17.5 provides a sample of the responses to question 5, part a—why individuals have not registered for SMARTS. It appears that "not getting around to it" and "not having enough time" are factors for many. Activities that encourage the investment of the time and effort of grant seekers need to be developed. Whether this takes the form of encouragement, time set aside at faculty meetings and orientations, or raffles and drawings, the object is to get faculty and staff registered for SMARTS and to have them maintain a current and updated profile.

Question 6—Have you attended any ORD (Office of Research and Development) grant writing workshops?

This question is aimed at evaluating ORD's educational efforts. Survey results suggest that these efforts are currently underutilized, with only 49 respondents claiming attendance at ORD grant-writing workshops. Of those that attended, the overwhelming majority felt that the presenters were clear and concise and that the workshops addressed their grant training needs. Based on this feedback, it is clear that these workshops need to be expanded and made more accessible to increase participation.

Parts a through h of question 6 list each of the seminars offered by ORD and ask the respondents to rate the value of the workshops they attended. The workshop on Identifying Funding Strategies seems to have been perceived as being the least helpful, although it was still rated fairly well (38 percent of the respondents found it very helpful, 26 percent found it somewhat helpful, and 16 percent found it of little value). This workshop may need to be evaluated and revised.

Exhibit 17.6 provides a sample of the respondents' suggestions for improving the workshops. Many of the suggestions are excellent and should be adopted. Suggestions relative to viewing funded proposals present a great avenue for developing and presenting quality circle

---

- The workshops I have been to have been very small. An overview packet followed by one-on-one meetings would have probably accomplished the goals more efficiently.
- Something specifically for new faculty
- I would have liked to have more examples of proposals to look at and compare for more or less successful presentation. This is true particularly for the budget material.
- Be more specific for the sciences versus the arts. A lot of the information is too vague.
- Introducing projects or grants being conducted by EMU faculty and staff
- To accommodate our teaching schedules, please arrange the same workshop at different times during any one semester.
- Broader spectrum of funding sources. More international opportunities for research
- None, they were helpful.

SAMPLE OF RESPONSES: QUESTION 6, PART K, SECTIONS I AND II—WHAT SUGGESTIONS DO YOU HAVE FOR IMPROVING ORD GRANT WRITING WORKSHOPS?

EXHIBIT 17.6

- Don't remember the workshop title, but I went to the whole-day one by an outside presenter and it was excellent.
- Target them to specific competitions; bring in partners (school/community).
- Managing funds and how to deal effectively with accounting
- Balancing concurrent teaching, research, and writing responsibilities so that all can be successful.
- Human Subjects Review Requirements at EMU
- None, they were helpful.
- Staffing and special pay arrangement processes for grant administration

SAMPLE OF RESPONSES: QUESTION 6, PART L, SECTIONS I AND II—WHAT SUGGESTIONS DO YOU HAVE FOR ADDITIONAL WORKSHOPS?

EXHIBIT 17.7

and mock review workshops. Exhibit 17.7 provides a sample of the respondent's suggestions for additional workshops.

Question 7—Are you aware that the Center for Research Support is available to provide assistance on any aspect of proposal development (design & evaluation)?

Answers to this question indicate that three-quarters of the respondents are aware of the grants assistance provided by the Center for Research Support. While this is very positive, it is still unclear as to whether the nonrespondents are aware of these services, and if they were aware, whether it would make a difference in their grants involvement.

Survey Section I—Groups A and B—Questions 8–15

Question 8—Evaluation of ORD services

Question 8 asks those who have used the pre-award services of the Office of Research Development (ORD) to evaluate them. Their responses are summarized on page two of exhibit 17.2. It appears that one of the strongest functions of the office is assistance with concept development. Ninety-two percent of the respondents rated this service as either adequate or more than adequate; 80 percent felt that assistance in finding collaborators and partners was also either adequate or more than adequate; and 20 percent felt it was inadequate. This area could possibly be improved by using EMU's existing grants database (SPIN) to locate potential collaborators as well as the Community of Science database or other databases that profile and advertise for co-investigators. In addition, this area could be addressed or addressed in more depth in one of ORD's educational workshops.

Of greater concern is the perception by the user population that the office is not proficient in assisting them in securing external sources of funding. (28 percent rated this service as inadequate.) One problem could be the interpretation of the question. Some may have thought it meant locating potential funding sources, while others may have thought it meant actually securing or getting funding. While this area needs some attention, 72 percent did rate this service as either adequate (44 percent) or more than adequate (28 percent).

The other listed areas of assistance held up well under the evaluation. One other area that may need attention is assistance in establishing contact with grantors. While 58 percent of the respondents rated this service as adequate, only 27 percent rated it as more than adequate, which was the lowest percentage of all in that category. Considering how important preproposal contact is in the development of a successful proposal, the Office of Research Development may want to consider offering an educational workshop in this area.

On a positive note, the highest rating went to proposal assembly and submission. Sixty percent of the respondents felt the ORD did a more than adequate job in this area and 33 percent felt it did an adequate job. ORD staff should receive positive feedback and recognition for this excellent rating. Please note that care should be taken not to react to the areas that got lower ratings by shifting focus and attention away from the areas that got excellent ratings.

Exhibit 17.8 provides a sample of the responses to open-ended question 8, part m—What suggestions do you have for improving ORD service? While this survey was of pre-award services only, several of the suggestions found in exhibit 17.8 relate to post-award services. Because research indicates that satisfaction with post-award services dramatically affects a

---

- Improve the discipline specific awareness of the Sciences representative.
- Great services. Just keep up what you are doing.
- Linking junior faculty with senior faculty with grant writing experience.
- The financial accounting for an outside grant is a nightmare. Not ORD's fault, of course, but any support ORD could give would be welcome including how to read those accounting printouts! ORD should also lobby for a Grants Secretary in each college to help with paperwork. (This response or something very similar occurred seven times).
- Help people look for nontraditional sources of funding, such as companies.
- Staff is too fragmented and over-tasked to be of timely assistance. I asked for help in writing a development proposal for a sponsored activity as opposed to a grant proposal and got copy editing—eventually went to Foundation for help.
- Staff training in order to meet faculty's needs in a timely manner
- Hire more individuals. This will allow those currently working more time to monitor and assist grantees.
- This is not a suggestion, but a comment. I know I would not have received funding if it had not been for ORD's help. Pre- and post-award. Thank you.
- I have made phone calls to ORD that were not returned and a request for information on funding sources that was never supplied.
- ORD needs at least two more grant officers who understand the business.
- More assistance with editing would be a great help.

SAMPLE OF RESPONSES: QUESTION 8, PART M, SECTION I—WHAT SUGGESTIONS DO YOU HAVE FOR IMPROVING ORD SERVICES?

EXHIBIT 17.8

faculty/staff member's desire to continue to be involved in grant seeking, these suggestions/comments are of considerable importance.

Question 9—Evaluation of your experiences with ORD project representatives

Knowledge and expertise of the ORD staff is perceived to be more than adequate by over one-half of the respondents. In fact, 89 percent rated knowledge and expertise as adequate or more than adequate. Sixty-seven percent of the respondents rated the courtesy and professionalism of the ORD project representatives as more than adequate, which was the highest score of all items listed under this question. Because this area is so important to continued grants involvement, the staff should be publicly acknowledged for their excellent service, but goals should be set to improve this area even more. Exhibit 17.9 provides a sample of the responses to open-ended question 9, part e in which survey respondents were asked to comment/amplify on their experiences with ORD project representatives. In general, the comments were very complimentary. Please note that comments which referred to ORD staff members by name were omitted from Exhibit 17.9. However, it is noteworthy to mention that survey respondents used this opportunity to comment very positively on several pre-award staff members with whom they had contact.

Question 10—What additional services could ORD provide to assist you with proposal development?

- Budgets are the area I believe faculty need the most help from ORD, and sometimes budgetary details seem to fall through the cracks.
- Some of the best and most professional people at EMU are found at ORD.
- Have contacted regarding opportunities but received no follow-up on occasion.
- Staff training in order to meet faculty's needs in a timely manner
- All staff have been extremely valuable in assisting in my grants.
- I could not have been funded without the support, knowledge, skill, and assistance of your staff.
- Staff do not communicate in a timely manner and frequently fail to return e-mail and telephone messages.
- Absolutely satisfied with ORD project representatives help!
- Your commitment and expertise is obvious.
- I always look forward to working with the staff at ORD. I think I have worked with all staff members.
- Improve your responsiveness to customer requests.
- The staff are excellent. The difficulty here is the mission of the university as a teaching institution and the tremendous level of effort required by our course loads.

SAMPLE OF RESPONSES: QUESTION 9, PART E, SECTION I—PLEASE COMMENT/AMPLIFY ON YOUR EXPERIENCES WITH ORD PROJECT REPRESENTATIVES.

EXHIBIT 17.9

- I will need lots of help for submitting via FASTLANE.
- Improved communication/speed with which human subject approval is granted.
- Be more imaginative about identifying funds that don't come from the traditional sources.
- Write the grant for me.
- Human subjects review guidelines and schedules. Manuscript editorial assistance for final reports
- Promptness in addressing needs and requests
- More assistance with editing
- I can't think of anything major.

SAMPLE OF RESPONSES: QUESTION 10, SECTION I—WHAT ADDITIONAL SERVICES COULD ORD PROVIDE TO ASSIST YOU WITH PROPOSAL DEVELOPMENT?

EXHIBIT 17.10

- More release time to develop proposals
- Have some workshops with institutes that fund primarily undergraduate research.
- Someone who works closely with the legislature and our congressperson to get increased funding
- Establish a grants accounting service. Help bring changes to the financial reporting statements. They are tremendously difficult!
- Seed money to develop data for proposals and release time to write proposals
- This may not be necessary in all cases, but possibly provide a workshop for department chairs and personnel committee chairs. Grants are often interpreted differently on this campus.
- I do not know if this would be practical from your standpoint, but possibly keeping track of researchers' interests and attempt to identify funding sources for them. I do not mean that you should do the researchers' jobs for them, but you could assist them with this task.
- Database of faculty whose research interests we can search by keywords. Coordination to encourage various campus research centers (e.g., Center for Corporate Training) to work together when submitting proposals, instead of potentially competing against one another.
- Lessons on how to put surveys on the Web like this one

SAMPLE OF RESPONSES: QUESTION 11, SECTION I—WHAT ADDITIONAL SERVICES COULD ORD PROVIDE TO BETTER PROMOTE SPONSORED PROJECT ACTIVITY?

EXHIBIT 17.11

Exhibit 17.10 provides a sample of the responses to this question. Unfortunately, some grant seekers still feel someone else could write their proposal for them, even though this simply does not work. Other comments are quite constructive.

Question 11—What additional services could ORD provide to promote sponsored project activity?

- Just time, balancing the heavy service and teaching load at EMU
- Human subjects approval
- Inconsistent reporting in the grant awards section of the STAR
- Getting paid for the work that I have done and being monitored too closely by the administration
- Accounting activities, payroll procedures, hiring procedures, and human resources. (This response or something very similar occurred six times.)
- Reinterpretations of approved contracts. Once the money is in, the rules change.
- Difficulty hiring faculty members to provide services because of rules
- Not barriers, but hurdles that need to be cleared. More related to who does what
- The business office must become able to provide timely budget feedback and to process purchasing, hiring, and grant/contract fund management more efficiently. This is the greatest barrier to conducting sponsored research on this campus. This is not a new problem and it is partially the result of insufficient staffing of the business office and excessive staff turnover within the office. Many faculty feel that there is a level of punishment implied whenever grant or contract funds are spent, as if these were EMU-state appropriate monies. Separate management of grant and contract funds would be highly advantageous.
- In general, grant administration is harder than it needs to be. For example, the information provided by grants accounting is not timely, and is of little use for projecting expenditures. We have to keep separate books to do that. Other administrative snafus (payroll, purchasing) take time to iron out, although purchasing has improved in recent years. It is sometimes difficult to get timely help from the physical plant. EMU is generally under-equipped, but that is a tough problem to solve. I think a start could be made if the institution would increase its overall budget for equipment. I suspect it compares very poorly with comparable institutions.
- The time demand to complete paperwork is a real barrier. Maybe it gets easier with experience, but I have found it to be daunting. I could spend my time more wisely. Also, the university does not really reward funding. In fact, some faculty are even punished.

SAMPLE OF RESPONSES: QUESTION 12, SECTION I—WHAT BARRIERS HAVE YOU ENCOUNTERED SINCE YOU WERE FUNDED?

EXHIBIT 17.12

Exhibit 17.11 provides a sample of the responses to this open-ended question. The comments are typical of a regional university such as EMU's, whose main interest is teaching and serving, not research. Some comments show a lack of understanding concerning grantor searching systems and several comments relate to problems on the post-award side.

Question 12—What barriers have you encountered since you were funded?

Exhibit 17.12 provides a sample of the responses to this question. The bulk of the comments deal with problems on the post-award side, and many of the barriers listed cannot be changed by ORD. However, there were some barriers mentioned that could be dealt with by the pre-award office. One example is the problem of locating other faculty to serve as collaborators and consortium partners.

Question 13—What would you describe as the most satisfying part of your grant experience?

The responses to this question are very similar to those uncovered in Jacobsen's and O'Brien's study, "Satisfying and Stressful Experiences of First-time Federal Grantees." Based on the responses, collaboration and working with a team is valued, as is the work itself. Working with subjects (i.e., beneficiaries) and having their own funds were also mentioned as satistying parts of their grants experience. See exhibit 17.13.

Question 14—Does your unit head support your grant activity?

Seventy-nine percent of the 67 respondents felt that their grant activity was completely supported by their unit head and 21 percent felt that they were somewhat supported. None felt that they had no support from their unit head for their grant activity.

Question 15—Do your colleagues support your grant activity?

Forty-nine percent of the 67 respondents felt their grant activity was completely supported by their colleagues. Forty-seven percent felt their grant activity was somewhat supported by their colleagues and 4 percent felt they had no support from their colleagues for their grant activity. More can be done to raise awareness of how grant seeking has benefitted the program, department, and/or college or university so that colleagues understand the positive influence it has had on the institution.

Survey Section II—Group C—Questions 8–14

The remainder of this analysis is related to section II of the client satisfaction survey, questions 8–15. This section was administered to Group C only—those who have never submitted a proposal. Obviously, this group was not asked to answer questions dealing with the evaluation of ORD's services because their exposure to ORD has either been nonexistent or limited. Instead, this section of the survey primarily explores the factors related to influencing the motivational levels of the 590 faculty/staff who have yet to submit a proposal. In EMU's case only 11 percent of the 790 invited to complete the survey have submitted a proposal. Therefore, section II of the survey is aimed at gathering feedback on why the remaining 89 percent have not.

Question 8—Do you believe that sponsored activity is important to EMU's mission?

Ninety-three percent of the respondents believe that sponsored activity (i.e., sponsored projects and research) is important to EMU's mission. However, keep in mind that this

- Interactions with collaborators at different institutions
- Having the resources to implement what I wanted to implement and to break through interdepartmental turf wars
- My collaboration with faculty from different departments
- Being able to initiate a research program
- I enjoyed every part except the administration.
- Helping junior faculty get experience
- Writing it up and getting funded
- Doing the research
- Publishing the results
- Having the surplus funding to support research on personal interests
- Getting the award
- Developing the methodology
- I was able to do the concept development for my role in this NSF grant with the faculty at another institution. ORD wrote the NSF paperwork and helped me develop a realistic budget, something that saved a lot of time and something that I had little experience with.
- Seeing the results for those individuals we have assisted through the funding opportunity
- Just the challenge of trying to get a grant with such a heavy teaching load and all of the other responsibilities that we have with community service, etc.
- ORD has been wonderful in its support.
- Developing the grant and conceptualizing the programs for which we are requesting funding. Working with other people across campus and the support they provide us
- Association with target beneficiaries of grant services
- Producing results predicted
- Ability to conduct research without general fund budget constraints. The wonderful way EMU recognizes research, large or small, and the celebration of each other on campus. The poster session this semester was a marvelous experience, and one not enjoyed by colleagues at any other state university.
- The expanded services now provided to assist us. The availability of involving our partner schools
- A personal sense of accomplishment in getting and disseminating good research results. Pride in seeing the students develop their capacity to work effectively on projects

SAMPLE OF RESPONSES: QUESTION 13, SECTION I—WHAT WOULD YOU DESCRIBE AS THE MOST SATISFYING PART OF YOUR GRANTS EXPERIENCE?

EXHIBIT 17.13

question only appeared in Section II of the survey (Group C) and only 28 individuals in total answered it.

Still, one wonders. If 93 percent believe it is important to EMU's mission, why aren't they involved in it and/or more supportive of others who are?

Question 9—Do you believe that sponsored activity is important to your unit's mission?

This question seeks to uncover information about how far down the administrative chain the message of mission and grant seeking goes and is reinforced. While 93 percent of 28 total respondents felt that sponsored activity was important to EMU's mission, only 63 percent of 27 respondents believed that sponsored activity was important to their unit's mission. Again, the number of respondents is very low. But even so, these results are typical of what would be found at most colleges and universities, and it suggests a problem at the department/program level. Why? The answer to this question has to do in part with the attitudes of the unit heads. To department chairs, grants activity can be synonymous with release time of faculty, and is therefore not held in high esteem with the department chair who has to locate adjunct professors to cover courses due to the absence of professors who have been released to work on grants. In addition, adjunct faculty do not take part in committee work, advising, or curriculum improvement, which creates even more problems for department chairs. Clearly, creative solutions need to be developed to address the problems grant seeking creates for department chairs. In addition, department chairs and deans need to be provided with techniques to help them get their faculty and staff to recognize how sponsored activity (i.e., grant seeking) is directly related to meeting their department's/program's goals.

Question 10—Although I have never applied for a grant, I have encouraged others to apply.

Question 10 tries to get at the grants atmosphere of fellow professionals (i.e., faculty and staff) and whether they encourage others to use the grants mechanism to explore interesting hypotheses, questions, problems, innovative ideas, etc. Survey results indicate that this may not be the case because no one answered the question. If this truly does indicate a lack of reinforcement by colleagues to bring in grants, then the ORD can deal with it through intensified public relations and department chair encouragement. Announcements at faculty meetings concerning who has submitted proposals and who has been successful would be helpful.

Question 11—Would you consider writing a proposal in the future?

Question 11 deals with the future interest of the respondent in using the grants mechanism. Fifty-one percent of the respondents reported that they would consider writing a proposal in the future; 38 percent were not sure, and 11 percent said no. The 51 percent that said they would consider writing a proposal in the future represents EMU's greatest potential for increasing the institution's grant effort.

For those that said "no" and "not sure," lack of time due to existing workload is an issue. EMU must deal with this if it wishes to get those in Group C to embrace grant seeking. Lack of knowledge about how to begin appears to be another significant factor or barrier. This can be dealt with through ORD's educational workshops. The next greatest barriers to grant involvement were lack of monetary awards and no likely funding sources. Both of these responses demonstrate a lack of sophistication regarding the grants process. The assumption of "no likely sources of funding" is probably based on very little research, and it is rare that a grant seeker cannot figure out a way to receive at least some monetary reward. The other responses deserve some attention. Lack of formal recognition from department/unit can usually be handled fairly easily and with little outlay of funds. This area should be explored with deans and department chairs. The "no interest" response is a function of the respondent's perception that the activity called grant seeking is not important and therefore, not rewarded. If grants activity was one of the factors considered in the awarding of merit raises at EMU, faculty and staff would be interested in it.

Question 12—Would you be more likely to participate in an externally funded project if you worked in collaboration with another individual?

Question 12 examines what factors might stimulate or foster grant activity and specifically asks if collaboration would be a positive force. Eighty percent of the respondents said working with others would be a positive force in encouraging their grant involvement. This factor is born out in the comments related to what grantees liked most about the grant experience. This response also relates to previous survey comments about getting assistance from the grants office in locating potential collaborators.

Question 13—Would you be more likely to participate in an externally funded project if administrative support were provided by an EMU institute or center?

Eighty percent of the 30 individuals responding to this question said yes.

Question 14—How many years have you been employed by EMU?

Of the 30 respondents, 23 percent had been employed by EMU for 1 to 3 years; 33 percent for 4 to 10 years; 23 percent for 11 to 20 years; and 21 percent for 21 years or more.

I hope that reviewing EMU's survey and my analysis of its results will help you in your surveying and evaluation efforts. All or some of the survey questions found at the end of each chapter in this book can be incorporated into EMU's survey for an even more comprehensive evaluation tool. To assist you in developing your survey and evaluation process, log on to www.survey.sample.org. At this Web site you will find an example of how the server works to process the survey into a database. This material demonstrates how the fields translate the text and how the survey responses are transferred to a database.

The feedback you gather by surveying your faculty and staff will help you develop a vital, worthwhile pre-award grants effort. The post-award questions found in the second survey included on the accompanying CD-ROM will help you determine the services that you need to improve and/or initiate in that area. In the same way, positive areas that stand out in the survey results should be acknowledged, possibly expanded, and replicated.

LIST OF RESOURCES

Government Grant Research Aids

GOVERNMENT PUBLICATIONS

Catalog of Federal Domestic Assistance (CFDA)

The *Catalog* is the government's most complete listing of federal domestic assistance programs, with details on eligibility, application procedures, and deadlines, including the location of state plans. It is published in June, with supplementary updates in December. Indexes are by agency program, function, popular name, applicant eligibility, and subject. It is available in print, CD-ROM, diskettes, and online.

> Price: Print $87.00 per year; CD-ROM $85.00 per year; diskettes $85.00
> Order from
> Superintendent of Documents
> P.O. Box 371954
> Pittsburgh, PA 15250-7954
> (202)512-1800, fax (202)512-2250
> Available online at http://www.cfda.gov/

Commerce Business Daily

> The government's contracts publication, published five times per week, the *Daily* announces every government Request for Pro-

posal (RFP) that exceeds $25,000, as well as upcoming sales of government surplus.
> Price: $275.00 to $324.00 per year, depending on type of postage
> Order from
> Superintendent of Documents
> P.O. Box 371954
> Pittsburgh, PA 15250-7954
> (202)512-1800, fax (202)512-2250
> Available online at http://cbdnet.access. gpo. gov

Congressional Record

> The *Congressional Record* covers the day-to-day proceedings of the Senate and House of Representatives.
> Price: $296.00 per year
> Order from
> Superintendent of Documents
> P.O. Box 371954
> Pittsburgh, PA 15250-7954
> (202)512-1800, fax (202)512-2250
> Available online at http://www.access.gpo. gov/su_docs/aces/aces150.html

Federal Register
Published five times per week (Monday through Friday), the *Federal Register* supplies up-to-date information on federal assistance and supplements the *Catalog of Federal Domestic Assistance (CFDA)*. The *Federal Register* includes public regulations and legal notices issued by all federal agencies and presidential proclamations. Of particular importance are the proposed rules, final rules, and program deadlines. You can also receive a monthly index for an additional $28.00
Price: $638.00 per year
Order from
Superintendent of Documents
P.O. Box 371954
Pittsburgh, PA 15250-7954
(202)512-1800, fax (202)512-2250
Available online at http://www.access.gpo.gov/su_docs/aces/aces140.html

National Science Foundation Bulletin
Provides news about NSF programs, deadline dates, publications, and meetings as well as sources for more information. The material in the electronic version of this publication is also available in a print-on-demand edition.
There is no cost for this service.
For information contact
National Science Foundation
Office of Legislative and Public Affairs
Arlington, VA 22230
(703)306-1070
http://www.nsf.gov

NIH Guide for Grants and Contracts
NIH Guide is published electronically each week and there is no subscription fee.
For information contact
National Institutes of Health
The Institutional Affairs Office
Building 1, Room 328
Bethesda, MD 20892
(301)496-5366
http://grants.nih.gov/grants/guide/index.htm/
To subscribe: http://grants.nih.gov/grants/guide/listserv.htm

The United States Government Manual
This paperback manual gives the names of key personnel, addresses, and telephone numbers for all agencies, departments, etc. that constitute the federal bureaucracy.
Price: $41.00 per year
Order from
Superintendent of Documents
P.O. Box 371954
Pittsburgh, PA 15250-7954
(202)512-1800, fax (202)512-2250
Available online at http://www.access.gpo.gov/nara/nara001.html

COMMERCIALLY PRODUCED PUBLICATIONS

Academic Research Information System, Inc. (ARIS)
ARIS provides timely information about grant and contract opportunities, including concise descriptions of guidelines and eligibility requirements, upcoming deadline dates, identification of program resource persons, and new program policies for both government and non-government funding sources. Reports are available online as well as in printed form and on diskette.
Prices: Prices vary depending on version and whether it is an institutional or individual subscription.
Biomedical Sciences Report, call for pricing information
Social and Natural Sciences Report, call for pricing information
Creative Arts and Humanities Report, call for pricing information
Order from
Academic Research Information System, Inc.
The Redstone Building
2940 16th Street, Suite 314
San Francisco, CA 94103
(415)558-8133, fax (415)558-8135
e-mail: info@grantsinfo.com
http://www.GrantsInfo.com

Education Grants Alert
This weekly publication provides quick access to federal and private funding opportunities available for education.

Price: $319.00 for 50 issues
Order from
Aspen Publishers, Inc.
7201 McKinney Circle
Frederick, MD 21704
(800)638-8437, fax (301)417-7650
http://www.grantscape.com/omaha/grants/
catalog/news.html

Federal Directory
The *Directory* includes names, addresses,
and phone numbers of federal government
agencies and key personnel.
Price: $325 per year; CD-ROM $800 per
year; online $800 per year
Order from
Carroll Publishing
4701 Sangamore Rd., Suite S155
Bethesda, MD 20816
(301)263-9800
http://www.carrollpub.com

Federal Grants and Contracts Weekly
This weekly contains information on the
latest Requests for Proposals (RFPs), contracting opportunities, and upcoming grants.
Each issue includes details on RFPs, closing
dates for grant programs, procurement-
related news, and newly issued regulations.
Price: $349.00 for 50 issues
Order from:
Aspen Publishers, Inc.
7201 McKinney Circle
Frederick, MD 21704
(800)638-8437, fax (301)417-7650
http://www.grantscape.com/omaha/grants/
catalog/news.html

Federal Yellow Book
This directory of the federal departments
and agencies is updated quarterly.
Price: $305.00 for annual subscription, each
additional subscription $214.00
Order from
Leadership Directories, Inc.
104 Fifth Avenue, 3rd Floor
New York, NY 10011
(212)627-4140, fax (212)645-0931
http://www.leadershipdirectories.com

Health Grants and Contracts Weekly
Price: $379.00 for 50 issues
Order from
Aspen Publishers, Inc.
7201 McKinney Circle
Frederick, MD 21704
(800)638-8437, fax (301)417-7650
http://www.grantscape.com/omaha/grants/
catalog/news.html

Washington Information Directory, 2000–2001
This directory is divided into three categories: agencies of the executive branch; Congress; and private or "non-governmental"
organizations. Each entry includes the name,
address, telephone number, and director of
the organization, along with a short description of its work.
Price: $119.00
Order from
CQ Press
Customer Service and Order Dept. WEB1
1414 22nd Street, NW
Washington, DC 20037
(800)638-1710; in metropolitan Washington, D.C. (202)822-1475; fax (202)887-
6706

FOUNDATION GRANT RESEARCH AIDS

Many of the following research aids can be found
through the Foundation Center Cooperating
Collections Network. If you wish to purchase
any of the following Foundation Center publications contact:

The Foundation Center
79 Fifth Avenue, Dept. FJ
New York, NY 10003-3076
(800)424-9836 or in New York state, (212)
807-3690
Fax: (212)808-3677
Internet: http://www.fdncenter.org

Corporate Foundation Profiles, 11th edition, February 2000, 778 pp.
A Foundation Center publication, this book
contains detailed analysis of 195 of the largest corporate foundations in the U.S. An

appendix lists financial data on hundreds of additional smaller grantmakers.
Price: $155.00
Order from
The Foundation Center

Directory of Operation Grants, 4th edition
Profiles on more than 800 foundations receptive to proposals for operating grants are provided.
Price $59.50
Order from
Research Grant Guides
P.O. Box 1214
Loxahatchee, FL 33470
Fax Orders to: (561)795-7794
Tel.: (561)795-6129, no credit card or telephone orders accepted

Foundation and Corporate Grants Alert
Price: $297 for 50 issues
Order from
Aspen Publishers, Inc.
7201 McKinney Circle
Frederick, MD 21704
(800)638-8437, fax (301)417-7650

The Foundation Directory, 2000 edition, 2,640 pp.
The most important single reference work available on grant-making foundations in the United States, this directory includes information on foundations having assets of more than $3 million or annual grants exceeding $200,000. Each entry includes a description of giving interests, along with address, telephone numbers, current financial data, names of donors, contact person, and IRS identification number. Six indexes are included: index to donors, officers, and trustees; geographic index; types of support index; subject index; foundations new to edition index; and foundation name index. The index to donors, officers, and trustees is very valuable in developing links to decision makers.
Price: $215.00 hardcover; $185.00 softcover; $595.00 CD-ROM; $19.95 monthly online subscription (single user); $195.00 annual online subscription (single user)
Order from
The Foundation Center

The Foundation Directory Part 2, March 2000, 1,200 pp.
This directory provides information on over 4,900 mid-sized foundations with grant programs between $25,000–$100,000. Published biennially.
Price: $185 *Part 2;* $485 hardcover *Directory, Supplement,* and *Part 2;* $455 softcover *Directory, Supplement,* and *Part 2*
Order from
The Foundation Center

The Foundation Directory Supplement, September 2000, 626 pp.
The *Supplement* updates the *Directory,* so that users will have the latest addresses, contacts, policy statements, application guidelines, and financial data.
Price: $125.00 *Supplement;* $300.00 hardcover *Directory* and *Supplement*
Order from
The Foundation Center

Foundation Giving Watch
News and the "how-to's" of foundation giving are provided in this monthly newsletter, along with a listing of recent grants.
Price: $149.00 for 12 issues
Order from
The Taft Group
PO Box 9187
Farmington Hills, MI 48333-9187
(800)877-8238, fax (800)414-5043
http://www.taftgroup.com/

The Foundation Grants Index, 2000 edition, 2,130 pp.
This is a cumulative listing of over 97,000 grants of $10,000 or more made by over 1,000 major foundations. A recipient name index, a subject index, a type of support/geographic index, a recipient category index, and an index to grants by foundation are included.
Price: $165.00
Order from
The Foundation Center

Foundation Grants to Individuals, 11th edition, 630 pp.
This directory provides a comprehensive listing of over 3,800 independent and cor-

porate foundations that provide financial assistance to individuals.
Price: $65.00
Order from
The Foundation Center

Foundation News and Commentary
Each bimonthly issue of the *News* covers the activities of private, company-sponsored, and community foundations, direct corporate giving, government agencies and their programs, and includes the kinds of grants being awarded, overall trends, legal matters, regulatory actions, and other areas of common concern.
Price: $48.00 for 6 issues
Order from
Council on Foundations
PO Box 96043
Washington, DC 20077-7188
(800)771-8187
http://www.cof.org/

The Foundation 1,000, 1999/2000 edition, 3,030 pp.
The 1,000 largest U.S. foundations are profiled by foundation name, subject field, type of support, and geographic location. There is also an index that allows you to target grantmakers with the names of officers, staff, and trustees.
Price: $295.00
Order from
The Foundation Center

Foundation Reporter 2000
This annual directory of the largest private charitable foundations in the U.S. supplies descriptions and statistical analyses.
Price: $425.00
Order from
The Taft Group
P.O. Box 9187
Farmington Hills, MI 48333-9187
(800)877-8238, fax (800)414-5043
http://www.taftgroup.com/

Grant Guides
There are a total of 35 *Grant Guides* available in a variety of areas such as higher education, children and youth, alcohol and drug abuse, mental health, addictions and crisis services, minorities, the homeless, public health and diseases, and social services. Each guide provides descriptions of hundreds of foundation grants of $10,000 or more recently awarded in its subject area. Sources of funding are indexed by type of organization, subject focus, and geographic funding area.
Price: $75.00 each
Order from
The Foundation Center

Guide to Funding for International and Foreign Programs, 5th edition, May 2000, 358 pp.
This guide includes over 800 funding sources that award grants to international nonprofit institutions and projects, as well as over 6,000 grant descriptions.
Price: $125.00
Order from
The Foundation Center

Guide to Grantseeking on the Web, February 2000, 408 pp.
Includes information on hundreds of grantmaker Web sites and a variety of related nonprofit sites of interest.
Price: Print $19.95, diskette $19.95
Order from
The Foundation Center

National Guide to Funding in Arts and Culture, 6th edition, May 2000, 1,138 pp.
This guide includes over 5,200 sources of funding for arts- and culture-related nonprofit organizations and projects, as well as over 12,000 grant descriptions.
Price: $155.00
Order from
The Foundation Center

National Guide to Funding in Health, 6th edition, June 1999, 2,032 pp.
This guide includes over 7,700 sources for health-related projects and institutions and over 16,900 grant descriptions.
Price: $150.00
Order from
The Foundation Center

National Guide to Funding in Higher Education, 5th edition, June 1998, 1,275 pp.

Over 3,900 sources of funding for higher education projects and institutions and over 15,000 grant descriptions are included in this source.
Price: $145.00
Order from
The Foundation Center

National Guides from the Foundation Center are also available in the following areas:
Aging, 1998, $95.00
AIDS, 1999, $75.00
Children, Youth, and Families, 1999, $150.00
Elementary and Secondary Education,1999, $140.00
Environment and Animal Welfare, 2000, $115.00
Information Technology, 1999, $115.00
Libraries and Information Services, 1999, $95.00
Religion, 1999, $140.00
Women and Girls, 1999, $115.00

Private Foundation IRS Tax Returns

The Internal Revenue Service requires private foundations to file income tax returns each year. Form 990-PF provides fiscal details on receipts and expenditures, compensation of officers, capital gains or losses, and other financial matters. Form 990-AR provides information on foundation managers, assets, and grants paid or committed for future payment.

The IRS makes this information available on aperture (microfiche) cards that may be viewed for free at the reference collections operated by the Foundation Center (New York; San Francisco; Washington, DC; Cleveland; and Atlanta) or at the Foundation Center's regional cooperating collections (see chapter 19, exhibit 19.4). You may also obtain this information by writing to the Ogden IRS Service Center, P.O. Box 9953, Mail Stop 6734, Ogden, Utah 84409 (fax 801-775-4839). Enclose as much information about the foundation as possible including its full name, street address with city, state and zip code, employer identification number (EIN, which appears in Foundation Center directories

and Infotax, a CD-ROM database), and the year or years for which returns are requested. It generally takes four to six weeks for the IRS to respond and it will bill you for all charges—$1.00 for the first page and $.15 per additional page or $1.00 for the first aperture card and $.18 for each additional card.

Try Web sites *www.irs.ustreas.gov*, *www. guidestar.org*, and *www.nonprofits.org* on the Internet to obtain information from 990s. For historical information on a private foundation, contact Indiana University/Purdue University Indianapolis University Library at (317)278-2329. It has 990-PFs dating from the late 1960s donated by the Foundation Center.

Directories of State and Local Grant Makers

Visit the Foundation Center cooperating collection (http://fdncenter.org/collections/index. html) closest to you to determine what directories are available for your state and surrounding region. The following state and regional guides are available through the Foundation Center:

*   *Guide to Greater Washington D.C. Grantmakers*, 3rd edition, August 1998, 233 pp., $60.00
*   *New York State Foundations*, 6th edition, June 1999, 1,095 pp., $180.00
*   *Directory of Missouri Grantmakers*, 3rd edition, June 1999, 159 pp., $75.00
*   *Southeastern Foundations II: A Profile of the Region's Grantmaking Community*, 2nd edition, November 1999, 152 pp., $19.95

Visit the Rural Information Center on the Internet at *www.nal.usda.gov/ric/ricpubs/ funding/funding 1.htm* for a comprehensive listing of available state directories. Please note that some directories are updated on a regular basis, but many are not.

CORPORATE GRANT RESEARCH AIDS

Corporate Contributions in 1997
This publication provides a comprehensive look at the state of corporate giving based on information from more than 200 companies.

Price: $45.00 for members; $180.00 for non-members
Order from
The Conference Board
845 Third Avenue
New York, NY 10022-6679
(212)759-0900, fax (212)980-7014

Corporate Giving Watch
This newsletter reports on corporate giving developments.
Price: $149.00 for 12 issues
Order from
The Taft Group
P.O. Box 9187
Farmington Hills, MI 48333-9187
(800)877-8238, fax (800)414-5043
http://www.taftgroup.com

Directory of Corporate Affiliations, 2000
This five-volume directory lists divisions, subsidiaries, and affiliates of thousands of companies with addresses, telephone numbers, key persons, employees, etc.
Price: $1,159, plus shipping and handling
Order from
Reed Elsevier New Providence
121 Chanlon Rd.
New Providence, NJ 07974
(800)323-6772
http://www.reedref.com/index.html

Dun and Bradstreet's Million Dollar Directory, 5 volumes
The five volumes list name, addresses, employees, sales volume, and other pertinent data for 140,000 of the largest businesses in the United States.
Call for pricing.
Order from
Dun and Bradstreet Information Services
3 Sylvan Way
Parsippany, NJ 07054
(800)526-0651
http://www.dnb.com/

The National Directory of Corporate Giving, 6th edition, October 1999, 1,092 pp.
Information on over 1,900 corporate foundations, plus an additional 1,000+ direct-giving programs, is provided in this directory. An extensive bibliography and seven indexes are included to help you target funding prospects.
Price: $195.00
Order from
The Foundation Center
79 Fifth Avenue, Dept. FJ
New York, NY 10003-3076
800-424-9836 or in New York State, (212)807-3690
Fax: (212)807-3677
http://www.fdncenter.org

Standard and Poor's Register of Corporations, Directors and Executives, three volumes
This annual register is made up of three volumes (volume 1, *Corporations*; volume 2, *Directors and Executives*; volume 3, *Indexes*). These volumes are available on a lease basis only. The volumes provide up-to-date rosters of over 500,000 executives of the 75,000 nationally known corporations they represent, along with their names, titles, and business affiliations. Available in both print and electronic versions.
Call for pricing.
Order from
Standard and Poor's Corporation
Attn: Sales
65 Broadway, 8th Floor
New York, NY 10006-2503
(212)770-4412

Taft Corporate Giving Directory, 2000
This directory provides detailed entries on 1,000 company-sponsored foundations and includes 14 indexes.
Price: $445.00 plus postage and handling
Order from
The Taft Group
P.O. Box 9187
Farmington Hills, MI 48333-9187
(800)877-8238, fax (800)414-5043
http://www.taftgroup.com/

Who's Who in America, 2000, 54th edition
Known for its life and career data on noteworthy individuals.
Price: $549.00
Order from
Reed Elsevier New Providence
121 Chanlon Rd.
New Providence, NJ 07974

(800)323-6772
http://www.reedref.com/index.html

GOVERNMENT, FOUNDATION, AND CORPORATE GRANT RESOURCES

Many of the following research aids can be purchased from Oryx Press, an imprint of Greenwood Publishing Group, Inc., 88 Post Road West, Westport, CT 06881-5007, 800-225-5800, http://www.oryxpress.com, e-mail: custserv@greenwood.com

Directory of Biomedical and Health Care Grants 2000, 14th edition
This directory provides information on biomedical and health care-related programs sponsored by the federal government, corporations, professional associations, special-interest groups, and state and local governments. Published annually.
Price: $84.50
Order from
Oryx Press

Directory of Building and Equipment Grants, 5th edition
Aimed at aiding in the search for building and equipment grants, this directory profiles more than 800 foundations.
Price: $59.50
Order from
Research Grant Guides
P.O. Box 1214
Loxahatchee, FL 33470
Fax orders to: (561)795-7794
Tel.: (561)795-6129, no credit card or phone orders accepted

Directory of Computer and High Technology Grants, 4th edition
This directory provides 500 foundation profiles to help organizations obtain software and computer and high-tech equipment.
Price: $59.50
Order from
Research Grant Guides
P.O. Box 1214
Loxahatchee, FL 33470
Fax orders to: (561)795-7794

Tel.: (561)795-6129, no credit card or phone orders accepted

Directory of Grants in the Humanities 2000/2001, 14th edition
Current data on funds available to individual artists and arts organizations from corporations, foundations, and professional associations as well as from the NEA, NEH, and state and local arts and humanities councils.
Price: $84.50
Order from
Oryx Press

Directory of Research Grants 2001
Information on government, corporate, organizational, and private funding sources supporting research programs in academic, scientific, and technology-related subjects is included. Published annually.
Price: $135.00
Order from
Oryx Press

The Effective Grant Office: Streamlining Grants Development and Management, 1998, 94 pp.
This book provides strategies to implement a well-organized grants development and management system.
Price: $64.00
Order from
Aspen Publishers, Inc.
7201 McKinney Circle
Frederick, MD 21704
(800)638-8437, fax (301)417-7650
http://www.grantscape.com/omaha/grants/catalog/news.html

Giving USA 2000
Annual report on philanthropy for the year 1999.
Price: $125.00 includes four quarterly newsletters
Order from
AAFRC Trust for Philanthropy
P.O. Box 1020
Sewickley, PA 15143
(888)544-8464
http://www.aafrc.org/

The *"How To" Grants Manual,* 4th edition, 1999, 266 pp.

>   Provides grantseeking techniques for obtaining public and private grants.
>   Price: $36.95
>   Order from
>   Oryx Press

COMPUTER RESEARCH SERVICES AND RESOURCES

Community of Science (COS) Funding Opportunities is a comprehensive source of funding information available on the Web.

>   Price: *COS Funding Opportunities* is included with fee-based membership in the Community of Scholars. Other institutions may purchase access to *COS Funding Opportunities* for a fixed annual subscription fee. Subscription pricing is determined by the amount of external research funding your institution manages. To receive more information about rates, subscriptions or free trials, contact Edwin Van Dusen, VP for Information Products at
>   1629 Thames Street, Suite 200
>   Baltimore, MD 21231
>   (410)563-5382 X225
>   Fax: (410)563-5389
>   E-mail: evd@cos.com

Computer Retrieval Information on Scientific Projects (CRISP)

>   CRISP is a biomedical database system containing information on research projects and programs supported by the Department of Health and Human Services. Among other things, the database provides valuable information on National Institute of Health (NII I) current and past grantees.
>   For more information contact
>   Dorrette Finch
>   finchd@od.nih.gov
>   (301)435-0656, fax (301)480-2845
>   Or visit
>   http://crisp.cit.nih.gov/

Congressional Information Service Index (CIS Index)

>   CIS covers congressional publications and legislation from 1970 to date. Hearings, committee prints, House and Senate reports and documents, special publications, Senate executive reports and documents, and public laws are indexed. *CIS Index* includes monthly abstracts and index volumes. Hard copies of grant-related materials are also available from *CIS,* including *CIS Federal Register Index,* which covers announcements from the *Federal Register* on a weekly basis.
>   Call for pricing information.
>   Order from
>   Congressional Information Services, Inc.
>   4520 East West Highway, Suite 800
>   Bethesda, MD 20814
>   800-638-8380
>   http://www.cispubs.com/

Dialog On Disc: Federal Register

>   This is a CD-ROM version of the *Federal Register.*
>   Price: The price for this service depends on whether your institution is currently a subscriber to other Dialog searching services.
>   For more information or to order contact
>   Dialog, Inc.
>   11000 Regency Parkway, Suite 10
>   Cary, NC 27511
>   (800)334-2564, fax (919)468-9890

Dialog On Disc Grants Database

>   *Dialog On Disc Grants Database* lists approximately 10,000 grants offered by federal, state, and local governments; commercial organizations; professional associations; and private and community foundations. Each entry includes a description, qualifications, money available,and renewability. Full name, address, and telephone number for each sponsoring organization are included as available.
>   Call for pricing information.
>   Order from
>   Dialog Inc.
>   11000 Regency Parkway, Suite 10
>   Cary, NC 27511
>   (800)334-2564, fax (919)468-9890
>   http://www.dialog.com

For more information contact:
Oryx Press
4041 North Central Avenue, Suite 700
Phoenix, AZ 85012-3397
(800)279-6799, fax (800)279-4663
http://www.oryxpress.com/grants.htm

FC Search

This is the Foundation Center's database on CD-ROM. It includes more than 52,000 U.S. grantmakers, over 200 associated grants, more than 200,000 names of trustees, officers, and donors, and links to more than 1,000 grantmaker Web sites. The 4.0 version also includes hundreds of grantmaking public charities and in-depth program descriptions and application guidelines for the nation's largest funders. Price includes two disks and one User Manual.
Price: $1,195.00 stand-alone (single user) version; local area network (2-8 users in one building) $1,895.00; additional copies of User Manual $19.95 each
Order from
The Foundation Center
79 Fifth Avenue, Dept. FJ
New York, NY 10003-3076
(800)424-9836 or in New York State, (212)807-3690
Fax: (212)808-3677
http://www.fdncenter.org

Federal Assistance Program Retrieval System (FAPRS)

The *FAPRS* provides access to federal domestic assistance program information. All states have *FAPRS* services available through state, county, and local agencies as well as through federal extension services. For further information, call (202)708-5126 or *FAPRS* toll-free answering service at (800)669-8331, or write to your congressperson's office; he or she can request a search for you, in some cases at no charge.
For more information contact
Federal Domestic Assistance Catalog Staff (MVS)
General Services Administration
300 Seventh Street, SW

Reporters Building, Room 101
Washington, DC 20407

FEDIX

FEDIX or the Federal Info Exchange is a free online database of federal grant and research opportunities for the education and research communities. Participating federal agencies use *FEDIX* as an outreach tool to enhance communications with colleges, universities, and other educational and research organizations.
Order from
RAMS/FIE
(800)875-2562
http://www.fie.com

GrantScape

This is an electronic fundraising database that highlights nearly 15,000 private, corporate and community foundations and corporate direct giving programs.
Price: $595.00
Order from
Aspen Publishers, Inc.
7201 McKinney Circle
Frederick, MD 21704
(800)638-8437, fax (301)417-7650
http://www.grantscape.com/omaha/grants/catalog/news/html

GrantSelect

This database is available on the World Wide Web, and provides information on more than 9,500 funding programs available from over 3,600 nonprofit organizations, foundations, private sources, and federal, state, and local agencies in the U.S. and Canada. Grantseekers can subscribe to the full database or to any one of five special segments offered: children and youth, health care and biomedical, arts and humanities, K-12 schools and adult basic education, and community development. An e-mail alert service that notifies grantseekers of any new funding opportunities within their area of interest is also available.
Price: Yearly subscription full database $1,000; e-mail alert service only $1,000; full database plus e-mail alert service $1,500; single database segment $350; single seg-

ment e-mail alert service only $350; single segment plus e-mail alert service $500; prices are for one campus/institution only; add 25% for each additional campus; a 25% discount is available for 2-year subscriptions; consortia pricing available on request.
Order from
Oryx Press, an imprint of Greenwood
    Publishing Group, Inc.
88 Post Road West
Westport, CT 06881-5007
800-225-5800
http://www.grantselect.com

Illinois Researcher Information Service (IRIS)
The *IRIS* database of funding opportunities contains records on over 7,700 federal and non-federal funding opportunities in the sciences, social sciences, arts, and humanities. It is updated daily and is available in WWW and Telnet versions.

Price: *IRIS* is a subscription service. It is available to colleges and universities for an annual subscription fee.
For more information on the subscription policy and/or an *IRIS* trial period contact:
Illinois Researcher Information Service (IRIS)
University of Illinois at Urbana-Champaign
128 Observatory
901 South Mathews Avenue
Urbana, Illinois 61801
(217)333-0284, fax (217)333-7011
http://www.library.uiuc.edu/iris/

The Sponsored Programs Information Network (SPIN)
This is a database of federal and private funding sources.
Price: Ranges from $1,000 to $6,000 depending on the institution's level of research and development expenditures.
For more information or to order contact:
InfoEd
2301 Western Avenue
Guilderland, NY 12084
(800)727-6427, fax (518)464-0695
http://www.infoed.org/products.stm

ORDERING INFORMATION

ORDER THE FOLLOWING MATERIALS FROM ORYX PRESS

The Oryx Press, an imprint of Greenwood
Publishing Group, Inc.
Attn: Customer Service
88 Post Road West
Westport, CT 06881-5007

Call toll free (800) 225-5800
http://www.oryxpress.com

The "How To" Grants Manual, 4th Edition—266 pages of text, forms, and worksheets to improve grantseeking skills. $36.95.

ORDER THE FOLLOWING MATERIALS FROM
DAVID G. BAUER ASSOCIATES, INC.

1217 Jones Ranch Rd.
Gardnerville, NV 89410
Call toll free 800-836-0732

Grantseeking Materials

The Teacher's Guide to Winning Grants—A systematic guide to grantseeking skills that work for classroom leaders. $24.95.

The Principal's Guide to Winning Grants—Strategies principals can apply to support grantseeking at their schools. $24.95.

Successful Grants Program Management—Practical tools for the superintendent or central office administrator to assist in developing a district wide grants support system. $29.95.

Creating Foundations for American Schools—Provides information on how to set up and use a school foundation. Price to be announced.

Technology Funding for Schools—Explains the grant-seeking and fund raising process that will help you generate dollars for your school's technology related goals. Includes a disk containing many of the book's worksheets and letters. $29.95.

Proposal Organizing Workbook—Set of 30 Swiss cheese tabs. $9.95 per set; 10 or more sets, $8.95 each.

Project Planner—Pad of 25 worksheets for developing workplans and budget narratives. $8.95 per pad; 10 or more pads $7.95 each.

Grants Time Line—Pad of 25 worksheets for developing time lines and cash forecasts. $3.95 per pad; 10 or more pads, $2.95 each.

Fund Raising Materials

The Fund Raising Primer—112 pages that provide basic information on various fund raising strategies. $24.95.

Fund Raising Organizer—Pad of 25 spreadsheets for planning and analyzing fund raising events. $8.95 per pad; 10 or more pads, $7.95 each.

Donor Pyramid—3-fold visual depicting various levels of donor activities and volunteer involvement. $9.95 each; 10 or more $8.95 each.

Fund Raising Organizer Activity Cards—Pack of 25 cards that summarize resource allocation, costs and net funds. $3.95 per pack; 10 or more packs, $2.95 each.

Video Tape Programs

For more information, or to order call 800-228-4630.

Winning Grants 2—Proven grant winning system on 5 video cassettes. Produced by the University of Nebraska Great Plains Network. $495.00.

How to Teach Grantseeking to Others—Two-hour video providing the essential know-how to instruct others in the strategies and techniques of successful grantseeking. Comes with a companion text and computer disk that provide detailed support and supply all necessary forms and checklists. $189.00.

Strategic Fund Raising—Five 60-minute video cassettes designed to help non-profit organizations increase board and staff involvement and understanding of basic fund raising principles and the development of a funding plan. $495.00.

Software Programs

For more information, or to order call 800-836-0732, 9–5 Monday through Friday, 9:00–5:00 Pacific time.

Grant Winner—For IBM-PC or compatible. Organizes grantseeking techniques and includes the worksheets found in *The How To Grants Manual*. $189.00.

Winning Links—IBM-PC or compatible software package that records the contacts of your board members, staff and volunteers, and allows you to retrieve by funding source, individuals' names, etc. $139.00

Seminars/Consulting

Use David Bauer on-site at your institution or organization to increase your staff and/or board members' skills and interest in the following areas: federal grantseeking, foundation and corporate grantseeking, fund raising, evaluating your grants and/or fund raising system, and motivation/ productivity. For more information on these services call 800-836-0732.

INDEX

by Monica Smersh